TEENAGE KILLERS

Barbara k, Tiffany, Heather, an eimann. "If we get cau re going to blame Jeff.

When B esponsibilities to her teenage gang, Marriam Oliver couldn't hear every word. "I knew I was supposed to stab him with a knife," she said, "but I wasn't sure about the others' responsibilities because the cartoons on television drowned out Opel's voice."

According to Grote, until the last minute, he debated whether he would get involved. But when Heimann walked through the door, Grote smacked him in the nape with a full swing of the bat. Heimann dropped to the ground, Grote said. Each time Heimann tried to struggle to his feet, Grote or one of the "Marysville boys" pummeled him back to the floor.

Kyle Boston punched Heimann in the face, and Michael Smathers whacked him once with a miniature bat before the two of them got scared and ran away while Heimann was still alive. They returned, however, for Heimann's car keys.

Acting as a one-woman cheering section, Barbara Opel allegedly shouted encouragement from the basement during the attack. Marriam Oliver, however, didn't share Mrs. Opel's enthusiasm. As Jerry Heimann yelled for help, she put the knife on the kitchen counter and ran downstairs, where she had spent most of the spring break week. She packed up her stuff—a curling iron, a lunch box full of coloring pens, and some gym clothes—and jumped out a basement window.

"Come back here right now," screamed Barbara Opel. "What kind of best friend are you? Are you going to run away when Heather is killing someone?"

MOM
SAID
KILL

BURL BARER

PINNACLE BOOKS
Kensington Publishing Corp.
http://www.kensingtonbooks.com

Some names have been changed to protect the privacy of individuals connected to this story.

PINNACLE BOOKS are published by

Kensington Publishing Corp.
850 Third Avenue
New York, NY 10022

Copyright © 2008 by Burl Barer

All Kensington Titles, Imprints, and Distributed Lines are available at special quantity discounts for bulk purchases for sales promotions, premiums, fund-raising, and educational or institutional use. Special book excerpts or customized printings can also be created to fit specific needs. For details, write or phone the office of the Kensington special sales manager: Kensington Publishing Corp., 850 Third Avenue, New York, NY 10022, attn: Special Sales Department, Phone: 1-800-221-2647.

Pinnacle and the P logo Reg. U.S. Pat. & TM Off.

ISBN-13: 978-0-7860-1909-0
ISBN-10: 0-7860-1909-3

First Printing: October 2008

10 9 8 7 6 5 4 3 2 1

Printed in the United States of America

The mother is the primary influence on the child.
If the mother is wise, the child will be guided to wisdom.
If the mother is compassionate, the child will manifest compassion.
If the mother is just and fair, the child will likewise honor justice and equity.
If the mother is ignorant, selfish and cruel, the child will be influenced accordingly.

'Abdu'l Bahá (adapted)

This is the most unusual and mind-boggling case we've ever been involved in.

Chris Dickinson, Snohomish County deputy prosecutor

PROLOGUE

On Saturday, April 7, 2001, Jeffrey Grote received the type of flattering invitation millions of seventeen-year-old boys hope to get every year. A pretty thirteen-year-old blonde sent her best friend across the roller-skating rink to tell Grote, "My friend Heather thinks you're cute." Grote introduced himself, the two skated together a few times, she gave him her phone number, and he promised to call.

The next day, true to his word, Jeff invited Heather to go bowling. She accepted the invitation. A few hours later, Heather Opel and Jeff Grote had sex in her younger brother's bedroom.

When the sweat-drenched and sexually satiated teens emerged from the bedroom, they found Heather's mother, Barbara Opel, waiting for them. Heather asked whether Jeff could spend the night and sleep with her in the same bed. Mrs. Opel had no objection. Grote lingered on past the second day, ingratiating himself to the mother.

As would any concerned parent, Mrs. Opel wanted to "have words" with her daughter's suitor. Barbara Opel sat Jeff down for a serious chat. The topic wasn't safe sex. It was murder.

Barbara Opel, a live-in caregiver for eighty-nine-year-old Alzheimer's-afflicted and wheelchair-bound Evelyn Heimann, asked Jeffrey Grote to help kill her employer Evelyn's son, Jerry Heimann. Heather was already committed to the project, she explained.

According to Mrs. Opel, the crime's justification was that Jerry Heimann was cruel to Heather. That was a lie. In truth, Jerry was exceptionally kind and generous to Barbara and her three children, Heather, thirteen, Derek, eleven, and Tiffany, seven.

"Barbara Opel nagged me to find someone to kill her boss," said Grote. "That's all she talked about—hiring people to kill Jerry Heimann. At first, I refused, but changed my mind when she promised to buy me a car and give my friends some cash. She said if we got rid of Jerry Heimann, we could get our hands on forty thousand dollars he had in his bank account."

As for young Heather, her rationalization for killing Mr. Heimann was in perfect consonance with her emotional maturity. "I want a new bike," said Heather. "Mom says that if I help kill Jerry, I can have one."

Less than one week after Jeff Grote met Heather Opel, on the night of Friday, April 13, Jerry Heimann was savagely attacked in his own Washington State home by a ragtag gang of teens and children, some as young as eleven. Seven-year-old Tiffany helped clean up the blood and dutifully put pieces of the victim's shattered skull in the trash.

Adorable, intelligent, charming, and affable, Heather Opel was a brilliant student and an accomplished sports star at Evergreen Middle School. She was the kind of girl you could hold up as a role model. And yet, this same intelligent, energetic girl murdered an innocent and defenseless man, stabbing him repeatedly with a butcher knife, while her best friend, Marriam Oliver, also a bright and promising youngster, bashed his head in with a baseball bat.

"Heimann was not only beaten with baseball bats and fists," recalled Sergeant Boyd Bryant, of the Everett Police Department (EPD), "but also repeatedly stabbed and slashed with kitchen knives."

"This wasn't the first plot Barbara Opel hatched to kill her boss," explained Snohomish County deputy prosecutor Chris Dickinson, "it was just the first one that resulted in one death and several destroyed lives—not the least of which is that of her own daughter, the gifted and talented Heather Opel."

Heather Opel was born to Bill and Barbara Opel on September 22, 1987. Within a year, neighbors in a Mill Creek apartment complained Barbara Opel was screaming at her baby. One anonymous caller said "the level of violent screaming is escalating, and recently one of the neighbors has heard slaps to the baby." Child Protective Services (CPS) workers visiting the apartment reported the baby was clean, and no evidence of abuse found.

The complaints continued, and neighbors reported the children were left unsupervised. Even Opel's landlord called CPS, stating, "The mother has been yelling at Heather since the child was three months old."

"Heather's environment was nonstop violence, both in language and behavior," commented a local social worker. "That little girl has been in counseling, on and off, since she was five or six years old."

Barbara was married for seven years to the father of Heather and Derek. She claimed that husband Bill Opel was physically abusive. He accused her of the same. According to statements given by Barbara Opel, her husband forced Heather to drink Tabasco sauce for not going to the bathroom when told, hit the child with a pan, and locked the kids in a room as punishment.

Barbara obtained a series of restraining orders against William Opel, before and after their 1991 divorce. When eleven-year-old Derek Opel was interviewed by a psychologist, the boy couldn't remember his father's name. He did recall, however, that the man broke his nose when Derek was five.

Barbara's alleged behavior toward her offspring is equally distressing. Court records show the children were left alone for hours at a time as toddlers. A CPS report tells of an instance where little Derek tried running away from his mother. "She caught him and hit him and dragged him by the hair. It was reported that Derek was yelling, 'Don't hit me, Mommy!'"

There's no indication that CPS tried to remove the children from their mother's custody, but every indication that CPS continually offered parenting classes and stress management training to the Opel family—offers that Barbara Opel always refused.

Barbara Opel herself may have suffered abuse in her early life, and her mother, according to court documents, "has mental health issues of her own," and was investigated on allegations that she abused Barbara's children.

Allegations of mistreatment and abuse were rampant. The bitter divorce between Barbara and Bill Opel was described by a consulting psychologist as "an active battleground, and Barbara Opel's subsequent relationship was yet another minefield."

Explosive anger and top-volume tirades taught little Heather the importance of sidestepping anything that triggered her mother's volatile emotions. Blessed with high intelligence, the child adapted to her scream-filled and chaotic environment. Heather quickly learned and internalized her life's number one rule: always mind your mother.

"Heather is such a good kid," said a former school teammate, "but her mom always had, like, this big control over her. I mean, you're supposed to do what your mom says, but when your mom tells you to murder somebody, maybe it's time to not be so obedient, you know?"

"Heather's allegiance to her mother was her downfall," said her father. "If her mom says do it, Heather does it. Heather does not question Mom." Everyone, however, questioned Barbara Opel's constant screaming at her children—screaming that reduced Heather to tears.

"I couldn't believe it," said Lane Erickson, a Verizon computer network engineer who coached for a Boys and Girls Club ball team in Everett. "Heather was the only girl on the boys' team, and she was the best player by far. The only problem was that the mom would yell and scream at her, and Heather would start crying."

"Barbara Opel was so overbearing and out of control," confirmed William Tri, the coach of Heather's baseball team, "that I made her one of my assistant coaches so I could control her from the dugout."

Known as "the screaming bitch from hell," Barbara Opel's foul mouth was well-known in three neighborhoods. People who lived near her described Barbara Opel as a woman who constantly screamed at her children. According to her ex-husband, she grew up in Bothell and moved frequently. Court records show she was evicted at least three times for not paying rent.

"She was a lady I would never forget in my entire life," said Chris Perry, twenty-five, who lived across the street from her for a couple of years. Barbara Opel had previously lived next door to Perry's best friend, Megan Slaker.

"I was dismayed when the woman moved into her

neighborhood. She was just so mean," Perry said, "screaming at her kids all the time, all hours of the night. You would never hear her lovingly talking to her children."

"I wanted them to feel some love," said Slaker. "Opel's kids were often locked out of the house, so I would let them help me do yard work. She just didn't want them in the house, I guess," she said. "You feel compassion for children who you don't think are getting the love and attention they need."

During an eviction process, Opel and her brood suddenly vanished from Perry's and Slaker's neighborhood in the middle of the night. Candy Ochs, whose son was a classmate of Heather Opel's at Everett's View Ridge Elementary, said that Barbara Opel used to say mean, derogatory things to her children.

Barbara Opel denied Heather any contact with her father—a father who, despite any admitted character defects, promptly and regularly paid child support.

"In the seven years I've gone without seeing my thirteen-year-old daughter and eleven-year-old son, I've never stopped thinking about them," said Bill Opel. "But I gave up on their mother years ago."

Barbara Opel refused to stick to the custody agreement after she and Bill Opel divorced in 1991. She kept the children from him for years. According to court records, prosecutors charged her with custodial interference in 1997 for not letting her ex-husband see the children. As an analysis of the case indicated low probability of conviction, prosecutors dropped the charges.

"Finally," Bill Opel said, "I stopped trying and moved to Wenatchee with my current wife and children. I've just been writing my child support checks and hoping they go to a good cause. I guess they didn't."

"Barbara Opel wanted [Heimann's] money," said Prosecutor Dickinson. "She solicited near strangers to carry out her plan and, in the end, swayed a group of teens from broken homes to do her bidding. She took them in," he said, "partied with them, gave them a place to hang out. By meeting Grote, Barbara hit the jackpot because he was willing to actually follow through and commit murder. Altogether, we have uncovered four distinct plots by Barbara Opel to murder Jerry Heimann."

Wednesday, April 18, 2001, 2:30 P.M.

"This is a matter of life or death."

Mary Kay Standish, intake worker at Child Protective Services, urged the woman on the phone to stay calm.

"Barbara Opel is trying to murder [someone] by poisoning him," insisted the caller.

"How do you know this?" asked Standish.

"She told my husband."

"When?"

"When she asked my husband to kill him."

"Call the Everett Police Department immediately," Standish said after securing the alleged victim's address, "and tell them everything."

"I'll tell them everything except my name," said the woman. "I'm scared that if Opel finds out, she'll kill me too."

The woman, as directed, called the Everett Police Department and spoke to Sergeant Peter Grassi. Consistent with her previous call to Standish, the woman refused to reveal her name. That wasn't necessary. The Everett Police Department has caller ID. Grassi directed Detectives Callaghan and Phillips to determine the origin of the anonymous call and then interview the caller in depth.

"I found the name of the person for whom the telephone number is issued," recalled Detective Jimmy Phillips. "A computer records check revealed the number belonged to Johan Folden, of Stanwood, Washington. We drove to the Folden residence, where we met Mrs. Folden and her daughter, Terrica Goudeau. It was Goudeau who admitted that she called Sergeant Grassi."

"I called," Mrs. Goudeau explained, "because of information that I heard from my husband, Henry. He's been visiting his ex-girlfriend Barbara Opel, who works as a live-in caretaker for a man's sickly and elderly mother. About two weeks ago, Henry spent the night at Barbara's. He said it was because he'd had a couple beers and didn't want to drive home after drinking. While he was there, she asked Henry to kill the guy she works for, and she promised him five thousand dollars before and five thousand more afterwards if Henry would kill the guy."

When Mrs. Goudeau first revealed the nefarious plot to Sergeant Peter Grassi, of the Everett Police Department, Mary Kay Standish had already reported the call to her supervisor, James Mead. He, in turn, called Gary Bright, an Adult Protective Services (APS) investigative social worker assigned to Home and Community Service for the State of Washington, Department of Social and Health Services.

"Adult Protective Services is a branch of home community services," explained Bright, "and our agency investigates allegations or concerns of or neglect of vulnerable adults. With the exception of issues around picking up children or having an ability to take somebody into custody, we don't have those custodial rights to incarcerate somebody or put them in a facility without their will or against their will. We get reports on a daily basis from the community, from mandated reporters, regarding concerns of abuse and neglect of the elderly, or people over the age of eighteen, who are classified as developmentally delayed in some way, and we respond to those reports. Of course, we have policies and procedures regarding how we handle complaints of abuse and neglect. We have a tip line that people can call in with concerns about people who are being neglected or abused. It's called 1-800-END-HARM. Some people identify themselves when they call—other tips are anonymous. Both types of tips, identified people and anonymous tips, are investigated by our agency, and that is exactly what transpired when that call came in about Mr. Heimann. Mead asked me to call 911," confirmed Bright, "and requested a welfare check on an alleged poisoning of a man in North Everett. I made the initial call, and then called to tell them that I was on my way to the residence to personally investigate, and they could call me on my cell phone."

Bright found the home dark and quiet. On the front porch was a bundle of blankets held down with a brick. When his repeated knocks received no answer, he requested information from a friendly neighbor woman. "After I went to the front door to see if anybody would answer, and nobody answered," Bright explained, "I went to a neighbor, who was next door, asked them if they knew anything about the people living in that home. The neighbor told me that somebody had moved out and had taken a U-Haul filled with belongings, and there were some children involved. And the person, the older gentleman who was living there, drove a maroon sports car."

Bright looked for the maroon sports car behind the house, but found no vehicles. He was knocking on the front door one more time when his cell phone rang. "It was the Everett Police Department," said Bright. "They told me that there wouldn't be a police officer dispatched because they can't force their way into someone's home simply because of a phone call. I decided to come back the next day."

Gary Bright drove away. It was several hours before anyone found the demented old woman in the blood-stained wheelchair.

PART I

CHAPTER 1

For Gregory and Teresa Heimann, the nightmare began when their TWA flight from Atkins, Arkansas, arrived at Seattle-Tacoma International Airport. The couple quickly collected their carry-on items from the overhead bin, followed their fellow travelers up the narrow airplane aisle, and stepped out into the bustling passenger arrival area, where they anticipated a warm welcome from Greg's father, Jerry Heimann, whom they hadn't seen in five years.

Eager to share special time with his son and daughter-in-law, Jerry Heimann personally made the flight reservations and wired money into his son's bank account to pay for the tickets. This was more than a long-awaited get-together. Mr. Heimann, sixty-four, a retired Boeing employee, was recently diagnosed with terminal cancer.

Greg and Teresa scanned the crowd, seeking the happy wave summoning them to a heartfelt reunion. Sadly, Greg's father wasn't awaiting them at baggage claim, nor was his car idling in the loading and unloading zone. Assuming he was on his way, they retrieved their luggage from the

TWA baggage carousel and moved it to the passenger pickup area.

Standing outside, suitcase in hand, a disappointed Gregory Heimann watched strangers embrace their loved ones, while he and Teresa comforted themselves with excuses and explanations—traffic delays and/or car trouble.

After an hour, anticipation became concern; after three, intense anxiety. Greg repeatedly telephoned the Everett, Washington, residence shared by Jerry Heimann and his eighty-nine-year-old Alzheimer's-afflicted mother, Evelyn "Eva" Heimann. Caregiver Barbara Opel, thirty-eight, and her children lived with the Heimanns full-time, yet the telephone calls yielded only incessant ringing. The nagging question of his father's whereabouts remained unanswered.

Perplexed and dismayed, the couple called Greg's mother, Marylou Cannon. Earlier that week, Cannon delivered some blankets to her former husband's home and was surprised that no one answered the door. She left the blankets on the front porch and returned home. Contacted by Greg and Teresa, Marylou agreed to meet them at Jerry's residence.

"We got a shuttle, and it took us directly to Jerry's house in Everett," recalled Teresa. "Once we arrived, we waited outside for Marylou to show up, and we spoke to some of Jerry's neighbors. One of them told us that the caregiver, Barbara Opel, had packed up a U-Haul, took her kids, and moved out at about noon.

"We knew that Jerry was having trouble with Opel," acknowledged Teresa. "In fact, Greg and I wanted to bring our kids with us to see their granddad, and Jerry was going to buy them tickets too, but he couldn't afford it because Barbara Opel had written checks on the bank account he shared with his mother."

"He told us that she forged Grandma's signature on the checks," confirmed Greg, "and that Everett Police investigated her for allegedly filling out a check for eighteen hundred dollars and attempting to cash it at a local check-cashing place. These stolen checks caused his account to get overdrawn, and he was having a lot of trouble getting the stores to believe that it wasn't his fault, and that he didn't have anything to do with it. Dad told me that he had to close his checking account because of all this, but he said that he kind of felt that since she'd taken such good care of Grandma in other ways, that he would overlook it. I strongly disagreed. I told him, 'That isn't something you overlook, Dad.'"

"I assumed Jerry planned on getting Mrs. Opel and her kids out of there after the check incident," said Teresa, "so I thought maybe he told her to move out before we flew in."

Greg's mother and her boyfriend, Stan, arrived, and they went all around the house, checking the doors and windows. The backyard Jacuzzi hot tub was running and half full, but the house itself was lifeless behind drawn shades. Greg found one window slightly ajar, pushed it open, crawled inside, and opened the front door.

The first thing they noticed was the significant absence of furniture. "The place looked like it had been stripped," said Teresa. "Almost anything of value in the house was missing."

"There were no couches in the living room," added Greg. "There was just outside patio furniture, such as plastic chairs. It was pretty dirty, like someone moved out hastily, except for the kitchen floor, which was pretty dang clean compared to the rest of the house. Normally, Dad keeps a clean house, and the place looked fairly bad. My father was very meticulous about his furniture and that sort of thing. He enjoyed entertaining, and he always kept a very clean, well-ordered, and tidy home. There were no couches, chairs, TV sets, or anything that my father would normally have in his living room."

The second thing they noticed was Greg's wheelchair-bound grandmother sitting in soiled diapers and eating torn pieces of paper.

"Grandma can't reach very far," Greg said, "and there was no water on the table. There were some graham crackers in the middle of the table, but she couldn't reach them. She'd been chewing on a piece of paper from the cable-TV guide. She had paper in her mouth, and we took it out when we got there."

"She was so dehydrated that her lips were all cracked and broken," Teresa said. "It was horrible. I had to clean her up because she had soiled herself." Marylou and Teresa immediately tended to Greg's grandmother, removed her soiled clothing, and gave her food and water, dressed her, and put her to bed. "She had very little light pants on, light little top, little zip-up jacket, and a little pair of booties that were almost off her feet. Her diapers and undergarments were soiled, had been soiled for quite a while. They were saturated, almost falling apart they had been on her so long. She was raw and red. It was quite painful for her, even in her state. It hurt her for us to clean her up because her urine and her feces was eating at her skin."

Teresa Heimann, a certified nurse's assistant, had worked in medical wards, and was familiar with this type of situation. "When people sit a lot in wheelchairs," she explained, "you need to make sure that they are clean and dry at all times."

"One thing we needed to find out right away was details about what medications Grandma was taking, or what medications she should be taking," added Greg. "I figured perhaps my sister, or my former stepmom who also lives in Everett, and who is still close with Jerry and the family, would know. When I went to call them, that's when we discovered what was going on with the telephones."

What they found gave more cause for concern. "The answering machine was unplugged from the telephone," said Teresa. "The battery was removed from the caller ID unit, the downstairs phone was unplugged from the wall, and the phone in Jerry's bedroom was missing."

"We needed that phone working," said Greg emphatically. "When we finally got it all plugged back in, we called my sister and talked to her, and we called several others about Grandma and her medications."

"Greg also called the Snohomish County Sheriff's Office, Washington State Patrol, Sedro-Woolley hospital, because Jerry has property in Skagit County, and even the Lynnwood police," said Teresa.

"We called everywhere trying to find my father," confirmed Greg, who also spoke with an attorney relative who advised Greg to contact Adult Protective Services in the morning.

As a matter of course, Greg opened the refrigerator. "It was full of meat, and a turkey, and other nice things that he bought for our visit," said Greg sadly. "He bought buffalo meat for me especially, and he also had some fancy ribs, and some seafood. We planned on having a nice big picnic with the whole extended family and friends."

For Jerry Heimann, extended family included three of his four ex-wives: Marylou Cannon, Shirley Hots, and Ruby Adams. Marylou was the mother of his children, Shirley was his second wife and best friend, and Ruby was wife number four, who possibly was on the cusp of renewed nuptials with the romantic Mr. Heimann.

Everyone who knew Jerry Heimann described him in much the same manner. "Jerry was simply the most likeable guy," observed a longtime acquaintance. Jerry Heimann loved women, and women loved him. It was easy for Jerry to get married, but not so easy to *be* married. It's a true testimony to his unique character and personality that three of his ex-wives were his best pals, and his most ardent well-wishers. He wasn't perfect, no one is. But in a world where selfishness is all too common, Jerry Heimann was remarkably selfless. He saw the best in people, whether they saw it or not, and he overlooked their faults. When he looked at casual acquaintances, he saw close personal friends. Here was a man who had pain—physical pain from cancer, emotional pain from the death of one of his children, and financial pain from the projected costs of his mother's care. He was hungry for happiness, and if there was a man on earth who deserved it, it was definitely Jerry Heimann.

Teresa Heimann was hungry for food after the long trip, so Greg, Stan, and Marylou went to the store for pizza and soda pop, while Teresa looked after the elderly Mrs. Heimann. Shortly after the trio left the house, the phone rang. Teresa about jumped out of her skin in eagerness to answer it.

The call was from Shirley Hots, one of Greg's former stepmothers, checking to see if the couple made it in safely. She had no idea Jerry was missing, and now she, too, was concerned.

When the late-night shoppers returned to the house, Teresa ate pizza, but Greg couldn't eat, too preoccupied with worry. "The more I looked around the house, the more upset I became. For example, Dad regularly padlocked his bedroom door from the outside when he left the house. The bedroom door was broken open, the padlock and the part connected to the door frame were on the floor, and all his personal files—bank statements, insurance policies—were scattered all over the place. Dad wasn't so far gone that he would leave his paperwork out. There was private numbers in there that he wouldn't want other people to have. There was some insurance paperwork there he wouldn't want other people to see. If he left the house, which he had, then he would have [picked] that stuff up. He doesn't leave stuff out. He keeps a nice and tidy house and puts stuff away."

Marylou and Stan went home distressed; the exhausted and confused couple went to an upstairs bedroom and attempted to rest. Tossing and turning, a troubled Greg Heimann got back up at 3:00 A.M. From the moment he and his wife had arrived in Seattle, everything was unsettling, inexplicable, and unnerving. Greg checked every part of the house for some clue as to his father's whereabouts.

"I even looked in the crawl spaces under the house, and then I sat down and made a list of everyone I would contact in the morning. And while I was sitting at the kitchen table drinking coffee, I was looking at Grandma's chair, just spacing out a little bit, thinking what I had to do, making a list of who I needed to call in the morning, and I noticed there was some blood on the back of the chair. And I looked closer, and there were quite a few spots of blood on the back of the chair. There was some blood on the walls in the kitchen, there was blood on the trash can. It was either paint or blood, it looked more like blood to me than paint that had run down the back of the trash can."

Greg Heimann made his list. First, call the police. Second, call Adult Protective Services. "About seven in the morning," said Greg, "I was just about to call the police when my mom called and asked me to wait to call the police until after she got there. She wanted to be there when the police arrived."

Greg opened up all the blinds and window shades to let some sunshine in, and he looked out the front window. "It was about eight in the morning, and I saw a guy sitting outside in a car. He was just sitting there, looking at the house as if something was the matter. I was just about to go outside and see what he was up to when the phone rang."

The caller was Greg's former stepmother Shirley, calling to see if Jerry had shown up. Told that Jerry was still missing, Shirley promised to come over and help find him.

"Then there was a knock on the door. I opened it up, and there was this little guy standing there. He looks at me like he is really relieved to see me, and says that he's glad to see that I'm okay."

"If you're looking for my dad, Jerry Heimann," said Greg, "so am I. I'm his son Greg. My father is missing."

"Well, that's why I'm here," said the gentleman. "My name is Gary Bright. I'm from Adult Protective Services."

"I was relieved that he showed up," said Greg, "I had it on my list to call Adult Protective Services, and there he was. Next he showed me the report about an anonymous caller saying Barbara Opel was poisoning my dad, and that something needed to be done immediately. Naturally, I wasn't too thrilled to hear about that."

Bright came inside, Greg introduced him to Teresa, and together they brought Bright up to speed on the trauma of their anticipated reunion with Jerry Heimann. Bright flipped open his cell phone and punched in three numbers.

"I called 911 for an officer to respond on the allegations of abandonment of Evelyn Heimann," said Bright. "When Officer Wardlaw arrived at about eight-fifteen, I met her outside and briefed her on the abandonment issues, and also told her that Evelyn Heimann's son, Jerry, was missing."

"As I entered the house," reported Wardlaw, "I noticed that most of the furniture had been removed from the living room. Evelyn lay in her bed in the only main-floor bedroom, awake but unresponsive. Greg told me that his grandmother had not spoken in quite some time and suffers from dementia. I then called for Aid to check on Evelyn."

"Officer Wardlaw and Mr. Bright asked us what we knew about Barbara Opel," said Greg. "To tell the truth, we didn't know much about her beyond what Dad told us. We only knew that, at first, Dad was thrilled to have her take care of Grandma, plus Dad was crazy about her three kids, who were, I believe, thirteen, eleven, and seven."

Jerry Heimann first met Barbara Opel in November 2000 at either the Albertsons supermarket or the Dairy Queen restaurant, depending upon whom you ask. Opel was struggling for cash and living in a string of Snohomish County motels; he was looking for someone to help take care of his mother. A few weeks later, Heimann asked Opel and her three children to move into his home. He sold that residence to generate available cash, and then rented a larger house from Huber Development agent Jesse Eline.

"The residents in the house," explained Eline, "were Evelyn Heimann, her son, Jerry Heimann, Barbara Opel, and her three children. A few days prior to Greg Heimann's arrival, I had a phone call from Barbara Opel telling me that they needed to break the lease and move out in a matter of days. I told her that the law allowed that for an additional month's rent, and Opel quickly agreed. She mentioned something about Jerry moving to Arkansas to be with his son. When I told her that I needed to go to the house and place a rental sign in the front yard, and that a move-out inspection would have to be done, she seemed to get anxious and upset."

Opel had good reason to get anxious. She'd recently murdered Jerry Heimann and, in the opinion of some, was about to leave his mother to die of dehydration and starvation. The last thing she needed was a "move-out" inspection.

"Here we have," commented crime writer Jeff Reynolds, "obvious indications that Barbara Opel has all the refined thought processes of a toddler—a psychotic toddler, but a toddler nonetheless. There are, admittedly, things Barbara Opel did well. Like most psychopaths, she can cry on cue, elicit sympathy, and misrepresent herself to get what she wants."

Shirley Hots's memories of Opel validate Reynolds's assessment. "Opel sobbed as she told Jerry that she was down on her luck. She told Jerry that she had experience taking care of the elderly, and he offered her a job. He invited Opel and her children to live in his basement," said Hots. "Jerry let Opel use his car and even bought a Christmas tree and gifts for her children. She said she took care of people, and he needed someone. He was such a good man. He trusted anyone."

"My father gave generously to Barbara Opel and her

children," said Gregory Heimann. "He gave them a roof over their heads. He extended to them his trust and his affection. He gave them all Christmas presents."

Barbara Opel represented herself as an experienced caregiver, but her personal résumé includes no glowing letters of recommendation from the Department of Social and Health Services (DSHS). "Mrs. Opel was not hired with state funding, or overseen by state social workers," said Kathy Spears, DSHS spokeswoman.

"One of the sad facts in this case," commented Chris Dickinson, Snohomish County deputy prosecutor, "is that Barbara Opel's wants and Jerry Heimann's needs converged at the end of the year 2000. Barbara wanted a better place to live, a better living situation. Jerry Heimann wanted a caretaker, a live-in caretaker for his elderly mother, and their paths crossed. And that's the beginning of the tragedy in this case. This was a guy, Jerry Heimann, who was dying of cancer, who chose to treat it his way, not to take chemotherapy or any other type of invasive therapies, was basically drinking the last days of his life away. He was also trying to care for his invalid mother. He could have taken the easy way out, he could have gotten her in a nursing home, some sort of convalescence center, but he chose to stay and keep her in his own home and care for her and hire caregivers for her and be with her. But he made one fatal mistake, and that fatal mistake was Barbara Opel."

Gary Bright, of Adult Protective Services, stayed at the residence until well after Greg's grandmother was transported to the hospital. "I made sure Greg and Teresa knew full details of what programs and services were available to assist in the elderly woman's care and well-being."

Marylou and Shirley arrived at the house within minutes of each other. There was no rancor between them whatsoever, and they offered full and unfettered assistance to Officer Wardlaw as she took a closer look around the house.

"I noticed that there was a dark brown substance that appeared to be blood on the side of the kitchen garbage can," recalled Wardlaw. "It was a drip that ran down the side of the can as it dried."

"The first blood I saw," recalled Teresa, "was on the kitchen wall, and on the dining-room wall. Then Greg noticed some on the back of the wheelchair wheels."

Wardlaw summoned detectives from the Everett Police Department, and after speaking with them, she returned to impound the wheelchair and garbage can. "I then noticed that there were three small spots of blood on the living-room wall near the bathroom. I also noticed several small dark spots that might have been blood on the carpet."

The closer detectives looked, the more startling was the scene. "We found copious quantities of bloodstains. Not only were there bloodstains on the wheelchair, in the carpet, and on the walls, but also on the chandelier."

It was becoming obvious to the police that the Heimann residence was a crime scene. One of the most important aspects of securing a crime scene is to preserve the scene with minimal contamination and disturbance of physical evidence. Unfamiliar with crime scene protocol, Teresa Heimann began to tidy up the residence.

"Teresa had cleaned off the kitchen table," said Greg. "It was messy with paper torn up on it and stuff like that. We had pulled the table out and we were going to start cleaning the house. We hadn't started yet when Officer Wardlaw said, 'You probably better not clean the house.'"

"What happened next," remarked Detective Joe Neussendorfer, "was so perfectly timed, it was either divine intervention or amazing coincidence." The telephone rang; Greg answered it.

"I think this must be for you," said Greg, and handed the phone to Officer Wardlaw.

"I picked up the phone," she later recalled, "and Officer

Sessions introduced himself and told me that he was working on an accident involving a U-Haul truck registered to
Jerry Heimann. Driving the truck was a teenage boy
named Jeff Grote. Inside the truck were two items of significant interest—a load of furniture and Barbara Opel."

"I moved out of the house because Jerry kicked me out,"
Opel insisted to Wardlaw over the phone. "All the furniture
in this truck belongs to me and my children."

"Why did you leave Evelyn alone without food or water?"

"Well, I thought Jerry would be right back. I don't know
where he is. He always goes out drinking—he was very
abusive."

Wardlaw asked Opel about the stolen checks.

"I didn't take any of the checks," insisted Opel. "I only
used the checks when Jerry told me to. Yes, I signed his
name, but I only wrote one check without his permission because I lost the check that he had signed for me."

"Who rented the U-Haul?"

"Jerry rented it for me."

"Why would he rent you a truck," asked Wardlaw, "if he
was mad at you and throwing you out?"

"I don't know," said Opel, "but he agreed to rent the truck
on his credit card. He went there and paid for it himself."

No sooner did that phone conversation end than a new one
began. The U-Haul rental agency, on Evergreen Way, noti-
fied of the accident by Everett Police, called the Heimann
residence.

"When U-Haul called, Teresa, Shirley, and I immediately went down there and took a picture of my father with
us. We asked for a copy of the rental agreement and the
credit card form he'd signed. Barbara Opel said my dad
paid for it himself. Well, when we got there, I showed the
lady my dad's picture and she said that he was not the one

[who] rented the truck, and I can tell you for certain that the signature on the forms was not my dad's."

"Barbara apparently rented two trucks," Teresa said. "But she kept one for only two hours, put ten miles on it, and then brought it back. She said that they couldn't drive a stick shift, even though they were driving a stick shift vehicle at the time. They replaced it with a seventeen-foot truck."

Barbara Opel had called U-Haul on April 16, saying that they needed to reserve a truck for Jerry Heimann, and she needed to use his credit card. "I said that was fine," said Dianna Burgermaster, manager of the U-Haul location on Evergreen Way. "She said she was calling for him because he was indisposed. So I took the reservation for the following day for a large truck with his credit card."

"Barbara came over," said a neighbor of Jerry Heimann's, "and talked my boyfriend into driving a U-Haul truck for her because the company would not rent the truck to anyone under eighteen or to anyone without a valid license. My boyfriend picked the truck up for her, but she didn't like it because it was too big for her, so they took it back and got a different one." Barbara, having a suspended license, couldn't rent the truck on her own.

Ms. Burgermaster wasn't present when Opel picked up the first truck, but took the phone call requesting a different vehicle. "I got a phone call," she said. "They said that the truck was too big, it was a twenty-six-foot [one], and they didn't need one that large, and they wanted to bring it back the following morning and exchange it for a seventeen-foot automatic because they had trouble driving a stick."

They picked up a large truck on April 17 and, according to Burgermaster, "they brought the truck back on April eighteenth, and I rented them the seventeen-foot one that morning. But it was to a young gal and a gentleman. They brought the big truck back and exchanged it for a smaller truck. So we closed one contract and re-rented them another truck. This was also on Jerry Heimann's account."

The day before Greg and Teresa arrived, Heather Opel asked the next-door neighbor's boyfriend if he would now do the driving for them. He begged off. The next morning, Barbara Opel showed up with a U-Haul van and moved furniture out of the house. "She asked me to mow the lawn for her," said the neighbor. "She said she wanted it to look nice when Mr. Heimann came back from Las Vegas."

Despite this obvious indicator of foul play, Greg, Shirley, and Teresa visited the various places where the outgoing and friendly Jerry Heimann often socialized, such as the Cozy Tavern, Casbah's, Boomer's, Port Gardner, the Turn a Round, the Flame on Evergreen, the Homeport, the Casino Tavern, and Kodiak Ron's.

Bob Whalen, employed at Kodiak Ron's, knew Jerry Heimann for almost fifteen years. "I remember a few weeks ago," Whalen told them, "Jerry came into the bar and complained about how Barbara Opel scared him. In fact, he said that he was afraid that he would wake up with his throat cut."

CHAPTER 2

Greg, Teresa, and Shirley didn't really expect to find Jerry relaxing at one of these local watering holes, but they held out hope of finding clues to his whereabouts. "I wanted to find Ruby Adams," said Shirley. "She and Jerry had talked about getting back together—maybe even getting remarried. There was a chance, although a slim one, that Ruby was with him, or knew where he was. The problem was that we were having a hard time finding her."

While Gregory Heimann sought out his father's friends and lovers, police were checking up on so-called caregiver Barbara Opel. "That woman has one hell of a temper," said one of Jerry's neighbors. "She moved in a while before the new year, and I could hear her screaming and yelling and cussing at her kids inside the house a lot of the time."

Wardlaw wondered if perhaps Jerry Heimann flew off to Las Vegas to remarry Ruby Adams. "Not likely," said Marylou. "First of all, Jerry was so excited that Greg and Teresa were coming to see him. This was a big deal to him, and he was really looking forward to the visit. Plus, if he and Ruby were going to go off and get married, he would have asked me to pick up Greg and Teresa at the airport. Jerry and I talked on April sixth. He told me he was picking up Greg and Teresa at the airport, and he asked me to bring over some blankets because he didn't have enough bedding at the house. I brought it over earlier in the week, but there was no answer at the door. I left the blankets on the porch."

"Jerry asked me to move back in with him," revealed Ruby Adams, Heimann's most recent wife. "We got married six years ago, and stayed married for three and a half years. Recently we seriously discussed getting remarried or at least moving back in together. He made the offer, and it was up to me. The target date was the weekend of April sixteenth. That's when I was going to move in with him. I was supposed to call him by April eleventh and let him know for sure, one way or the other, if I was going to move in."

Ruby accepted Jerry's offer, and called numerous times to share her joyous decision. "Every time I called Jerry's house, Barbara told me he wasn't there. Finally she told me that Diane Jensen had shown up on Tuesday, April tenth, and they had been together ever since. I couldn't make sense of that," said Ruby. "I know Diane Jensen, and I knew she wasn't with Jerry. I had just seen Diane."

Diane Jensen was Evelyn's former caregiver. "I had known Jerry for about four years," said Diane. "I was the live-in caregiver for his mother. Well, Jerry and I started to get involved. Things didn't work out for us, so I moved out."

When Jerry asked Barbara Opel to fill the caregiver position, Diane Jensen actually helped Barb and the kids move to Jerry's new house.

"Diane and I did almost everything," confirmed Barbara Opel. "My job was to pack everything downstairs and to help with the kitchen and the living room. Diane did the kitchen, living room, and all of Jerry's stuff and Evelyn's things."

Opel's responsibilities within the Heimann household

included cooking, cleaning, and caring for the elderly Mrs. Heimann. "After I took the children to school," explained Opel, "I would come back, give her medicine, fix her breakfast, feed her breakfast, and then I would do the dishes, fix her lunch, feed her, and then she would come in for a while to watch some TV, and fix her dinner, do the dishes, things like that. I also did the cleaning and cooking and laundry for everyone in the household."

When the Yuletide season arrived, Jerry Heimann and the Opels moved into the new home. "They had about one week until Christmas," recalled Jensen. "Jerry was so sweet to them. He gave Barb about three hundred dollars to go buy the kids presents for Christmas, I went out and got the tree for them."

"It was Diane's job to go and pick out a Christmas tree," confirmed Opel. "The children and I were in charge of picking up decorations and getting the decorations, decorating the house and decorating the tree. It was when we attempted putting up the tree that Jerry insulted us for the first time."

According to Opel, she isn't good at putting up a live Christmas tree. "I've always had flocked trees because that's what my kids always wanted. We've never had a real tree. Well, this was a real tree. We went back over to the old house, we picked up the Christmas stand that was there, and Heather and I were trying to saw off the bottom branches so we could get it to fit into the stand properly. We worked on it probably a couple hours, and we were not having any luck at all. And so we decided we're going to give up and we would try in the morning. And I told Jerry, I said, 'We can't do it, and we're getting tired.' I said, 'We'll work on it tomorrow.' I said, 'I don't think the tree is the problem, I think it's the stand.' Because the stand was quite old and had been left outside and rusted. And Jerry started saying that Heather and

I were incompetent bitches, and we didn't know what we were doing, and we were pretty sad if we couldn't even put up a Christmas tree.

"My children and I had Christmas together with Grandma. Jerry spent Christmas Day with Diane," said Opel, "and that was fine with me and the kids."

The holidays were happy for all concerned, and the children especially loved Jerry Heimann's elderly mother. "The kids loved being around her," said Barbara Opel. "They were always close to their grandma, and she wasn't around at the time, and so they just bonded with her real well."

While the new house provided more ample living space, it also put a heavier workload on Barbara Opel. "It's a lot more work because it is a bigger house," she said, "plus the added responsibilities at that time. Besides more to clean up, at that time I became responsible for getting Evelyn up in the morning—getting Grandma up—taking her to the bathroom, changing her clothes, and I became responsible for putting her to bed at night also."

Cleaning Mrs. Heimann in a bath required the combined efforts of both Barbara and Heather. "That was something that Heather and I did every Saturday morning. It took two people to give her a shower."

An examination of Barbara Opel's daily schedule shows the imperative nature of time management and strategic planning—elements lacking in her alleged murder plot.

"Sometimes there are three different schedules for the kids, depending on if Heather had band or not that morning," explained Opel. "If she didn't, her and Derek could be to school, and since I couldn't be making that many trips with the car, I had to get Tiffany up usually and take her with me also. So we usually left the house at approximately about seven in the morning."

Barbara Opel would arrive back home a little past nine,

and start doing the housework. "I would put in some laundry, and then it would be close to time to get Grandma up. Then I would take her, put her [in her] wheelchair, wheel her into the bathroom, put her on the potty, change her clothes, give her a sponge bath, clean her up, and put her back in her wheelchair. And then I would take her to the dining-room table, and there, first thing, she was awake enough, I would give her her pills, and then if there was still—if she was pretty awake at that time, I would give her a large breakfast. If she wasn't quite awake, I would just give her a snack to hold her over until lunchtime before doing the rest of the housework—vacuuming, dusting, and as there wasn't a dishwasher, I did a lot of dishes and every-one's laundry."

Time passed quickly, and soon it was time to pick up the kids from school. "Each child had their own pickup time, so that made things a bit complex. Jerry, of course, gave me permission to use his vehicles to get the kids."

As for Jerry Heimann, once they moved into the new house, he didn't come downstairs as early in the morning, because he had his own refrigerator and microwave upstairs. "Jerry would have a couple cups of coffee," explained Barbara, "then he would take off for the day to do all his errands and then see his friends at the bar. He would come home about six that evening. We all sort of mingled together on the main level, and got along okay, except for a few insulting remarks Jerry would make from time to time."

Asked for an example, Opel cited the evening that Heather and her friend Marriam were getting ready to go to the New Year's Eve skate at the Skate Deck. "Marriam was putting on makeup, doing her hair, getting their clothes ready, and she was also doing Heather's hair and makeup. And when they came out, Jerry asked Marriam how come she looked like a whore.

"'You're too young to be wearing all the makeup. You look like a slut,' he said. 'Are you going to put makeup on Heather and Tiffany so that they look like sluts like you too?'"

Barbara Opel recalled that she and the youngsters dealt with Jerry's comments in a conciliatory and diplomatic fashion. "We told him he was an asshole," said Barbara, characterizing the essential nature of their interaction with Jerry Heimann as "getting along okay."

Despite Barbara's assurances, within three months, Diane Jensen saw disquieting signals that there was more on Barbara Opel's mind than homemaking and mothering.

"He was so good to them," said Jensen. "If the kids wanted to go roller-skating, he would give them money. He would let them use his car. He did a lot for them. He had a heart of gold. I would occasionally go over there simply to spend time with Jerry," Jensen said. "I remember Barb asking me if, when Jerry sold his house, if she would get some of the money. That was an odd question, and I told her that I had no idea. That struck me as a bit out of line, really. But I really got concerned around March twentieth when I talked to Jerry on the telephone."

"Listen to this," said Jerry. "I was just sitting here at the table, when out of the blue, for no reason, Heather's friend Marriam ran up and hit me with a baseball bat!"

"She what?"

"You heard me. She hauled off and whacked me with a baseball bat. I have no idea why the hell she did that."

"For God's sake, Jerry," said Jensen, "she could have killed you. Did you call 911?"

"No, you know me. That's not my style. I'm not a cop caller."

"What did you do?" asked Jensen. "Did you do anything at all?"

"Yeah, I told the little bitch to get the hell out of my

house and never come back. I yelled for Barbara, told her never to let that kid back in my home."

"After I hit him with a baseball bat," recalled thirteen-year-old Marriam Oliver, "he got mad and said that Heather couldn't have visitors anymore. He was very restrictive and wouldn't let her have any fun. I mean, Heather was only thirteen, and she should be allowed to have friends over and have fun, right? This wasn't the time I killed him with a baseball bat," added Oliver for clarification, "this was another time, earlier."

Prosecutor Chris Dickinson shook his head in dismay at the mention of this incident. "Did he throw out this family after the first time he was attacked with a bat in that incident with Marriam? He didn't do that. He allowed them to keep living there with him. He didn't even call the police. He gave them all a chance to stay with him. He banned the Opels from having visitors, particularly young people over, after he was attacked that first time with the bat. Is that an unreasonable thing to do? I mean, this family allows some kids in, and he, Jerry, gets hit in the head with a bat as a result. It's nothing unreasonable in what Jerry chose to do about that situation, nothing unreasonable at all."

On April 16, after serious consideration, Ruby Adams decided that it was perfectly reasonable to move in with Jerry Heimann. "I was going to put my things in storage, move in with Jerry, and he was going to kick Barbara Opel out of the house," said Ruby Adams. "I waited at his house for about four hours on the sixteenth, but he never showed up. His car wasn't in the driveway, and his truck was down at the corner. I went upstairs to his bedroom to see if I could find some cigarettes. When I got there, I noticed that his bedsheets were missing. I told Barbara that Jerry will need those sheets when he returns, and she told me that the sheets were in the laundry.

"Jerry was such a good person," said Adams, fighting back tears. "Did you know that when Barbara Opel tried to cash a stolen eighteen-hundred-dollar check belonging to Jerry, he didn't even get mad at her? He even let her drive his Firebird. He was so kind to Barbara and the kids. He was always kind to little Tiffany, Derek, and Heather."

"You know, if Jerry wasn't such a hell of a nice guy, he probably would have drop-kicked Barbara Opel and her kids back to the Dairy Queen long before it got that far. If he sensed how dangerous these people were, he refused to believe it," crime writer Jeff Reynolds remarked.

Jerry Heimann not only sensed it, but believed it. He talked about it to his second cousin Kenny Heimann. "Jerry told me several things on several different occasions," confirmed Ken Heimann. "About two months before his death, Jerry called me up and told me that he was having trouble with Barbara Opel. He told me that she had tried to kill him twice, and that she wanted his money."

Detective Gary Fortin, speaking to Ken via telephone from Florida, pressed him for details. "Ken told me," recalled Fortin, "that Jerry confided in him that he thought Barbara was trying to poison him, and that he had been getting sick. Jerry told Ken that he'd been to the library to look up his symptoms in an effort to determine what she was giving him."

Ken urged Jerry to get rid of Opel or contact the police. "Jerry told me that he'd thought about it," said Ken, "but had his reasons for not doing it. Jerry never wanted to go to the police. He always said that 'wasn't his style.'"

Perhaps Jerry Heimann believed that his kindness could influence Opel for the better. "He couldn't turn her around," said Jeff Reynolds. "Instead, they turned on him, and damned if they didn't do it just as he was about to have some honest-to-God happiness."

CHAPTER 3

Thursday, April 19, 2001, 1:59 P.M.

Twenty-four hours after Greg and Teresa's TWA flight touched down at Sea-Tac, Everett Police Department detectives sat down together to map out their investigative strategy. Sergeant Peter Grassi assigned Detective Callaghan and Detective Phillips to locate and interview Henry Goudeau, and designated Detective Fortin as lead investigator in the case.

"When Officer Sessions encountered Barbara Opel and Jeffrey Grote earlier that morning following the U-Haul mishap," recalled Fortin, "they indicated that they were staying at the Rodeway Inn on Everett Mall Way. We contacted the motel, and the clerk told us that Mrs. Opel had recently returned in a U-Haul."

Two officers were immediately dispatched to the Rodeway Inn. Officer Williams, the first to arrive, ascertained that Opel and Grote were staying in room 126. Officers knocked on the door; Barbara Opel answered.

"I recognized her as Barbara Opel, because I arrested her on prior occasion for 'driving while license suspended/revoked third degree,'" said one of the officers. "I observed additional people inside the room as Opel held the door open—I saw a younger male, later identified as Jeff Grote, and two other children, one male and one female. I explained to Opel that I was knocking on her door only in an attempt to verify that she was there. I informed Opel that detectives from the Everett Police Department wanted to speak with her. I did not specify as to what detectives wanted to speak with her about."

Officer Williams made casual conversation, politely asking Barbara Opel about her kids. "She pointed to the oldest teenager, Jeff Grote, and explained that he's her daughter's boyfriend. Grote and another boy were playing video games, so I chatted with them about the game," said Williams. The primary purpose of the officers' visit was simply to find out if Opel and Grote were at the motel and to keep an eye on them until Detectives Fortin and Neussendorfer arrived.

April 19, 2001, 2:35 P.M.

"Detective Fortin and I arrived at the Rodeway Inn," said Detective Neussendorfer, "and went directly to room 126, where Officer Sessions was standing by with Barbara Opel, Jeffrey Grote, and Opel's two younger children—her eleven-year-old son, Derek, and seven-year-old daughter, Tiffany. Opel told us that her other daughter, thirteen-year-old Heather, was at track practice and wouldn't be home until approximately four P.M."

Neussendorfer asked Opel and Grote for permission to search the back of their U-Haul van and their motel room. "When we searched the back of the moving van," recalled Fortin, "we found a box spring and mattress, a couch and dresser, boxes of toys, clothes, shoes, and stuffed animals.

During the search of the moving van, I discovered a wood souvenir bat, which was blue in color. I examined the bat for any noticeable bloodstains, but did not find any. I left the bat in the back of the van."

A thorough search of the U-Haul confirmed an important fact: the furniture inside did not belong to Jerry Heimann. Every item was the rightful property of Barbara Opel's family.

Fortin explained to Opel that the detectives were investigating the apparent abandonment of Evelyn Heimann. "We would like to interview you regarding your care of her," said Fortin, and he asked Barbara Opel if she would be willing to come down to the Everett Police Department to give an official statement.

"The main reason I asked her that," explained Fortin, "was because the environment there in the motel room at the time was poor for getting somebody to sit down and concentrate on what they were doing. The kids were jumping up and down and yelling and just having a good time, like kids usually do, and there really isn't a desk or a private area to really sit down and just get done what needs to get done. I told her that we needed a statement about what she knew about Jerry and when the last time she saw him, that sort of thing."

Mrs. Opel agreed, and asked Jeffrey Grote to watch her children, and pick up Heather from track practice. "Prior to leaving the scene, Detective Fortin and I made arrangements to drive Barbara Opel to the Everett Police Department for her interview," said Detective Joe Neussendorfer. "I spoke with Sergeant Grassi by Nextel radio. He informed me that he wanted us to impound the moving van until the investigation was completed. As we were leaving, I spoke to Officer Sessions. He told me that Grote admitted having sexual intercourse with thirteen-year-old Heather. Being that Grote is sixteen, but she isn't, he could face charges of child rape."

With the U-Haul impounded, Grote was incapable for picking up Heather from track practice. Police requested school resource officer Somerville pick up Heather and bring her to the Everett Police Department. Detective Jonathon Jensen, of the Special Assault Unit, interviewed her while Detective Neussendorfer spoke to her mother.

Chatting with Barbara Opel, detectives got the breakdown on the names, ages, and parentage of Opel's three offspring. "Heather is thirteen," said Barbara, "and Derek is eleven. Their father is Bill Opel. They don't see their father very often, because he lives in Wenatchee. Tiffany is seven years old. Her last name isn't Opel. She's Tiffany Goudeau," she explained. "Her father's name is Henry."

"Do you know where Henry lives?" asked Neussendorfer.

"He lives in room number 103 at the City Center Motel in Marysville," Opel replied. Neussendorfer politely excused himself and immediately contacted Detectives Callaghan and Phillips, and informed them of Henry Goudeau's location at the City Center Motel.

"I don't see Henry on a regular basis," elaborated Barbara Opel. "I saw him last maybe about a month ago. Henry Goudeau married someone else, which has limited my contact with him. I last talked to him on the phone more than a month ago. After that phone conversation, his current wife threatened to harm me if I continued calling Henry. Actually, Henry Goudeau came over and saw Tiffany and me near the end of March, but he didn't meet Jerry, because Jerry wasn't home at the time."

The investigation moved at whirlwind speed. Henry's wife called on April 18; Greg and Teresa arrived that same day. Within twenty-four hours Barbara Opel and her kids were being interviewed at police headquarters, and two detectives were on their way to find Henry Goudeau. Meanwhile, neither the family nor the police knew what happened to Jerry Heimann. It was 3:15 P.M. when Barbara Opel went up to a third-floor interview room with Detective Fortin; by 4:00 P.M., she was answering questions, and two detectives were scooting up to Marysville for a little chat with Henry Goudeau.

"First we attempted to find him at his workplace," recalled Detective Callaghan. "He worked at a construction-type field, I believe in painting, and he worked at numerous places. We looked around Monroe for him, where he had been working. Not locating him, we went back to their residence later in the evening."

"I don't know anything about anything," said Henry.

"Obviously, Mr. Goudeau wasn't eager to talk with us," recalled Detective Callaghan.

"I've known Barbara for about five years," said Henry. "We have a seven-year-old daughter together."

"Well, if your daughter is seven, you must have known Barbara for more than five years," said the detective. Goudeau contemplated the mathematical underpinnings of Callaghan's statement.

"Yeah," agreed Henry Goudeau, "you have a point there. Maybe it's been more than five years."

Henry Goudeau met Barbara Opel in June 1993 after he placed a classified ad in the *Everett Daily Herald* newspaper. Opel responded to the romantic invitation and soon the two were an item. Their relationship lasted six years and produced one child, Tiffany Goudeau, born May 24, 1993.

Their relationship ended because, according to Barbara Opel, "we were getting evicted for the—I don't know how many times—because Henry being unable to hold a job, so at that time our choice was to move in at my mom's house, which I chose to take my children to my mom's house and live there until I could get some stability, and Henry took off and left us."

"I'm originally from Los Angeles," Henry explained to the detectives. "I used to live with Barbara in Lake Stevens, Washington. I accidentally ran into her at the Laundromat in Marysville, and I visited her a couple times. You know," added Henry, "she still has some of my things—some furniture and tools at People's Storage in Everett."

"Did Barbara Opel ask you to kill someone?"

"Yeah," said Henry, "Barbara told me that she wanted to kill the guy she worked for and she asked me to get rid of the body afterwards. In fact, she said she would give me five thousand dollars. Well, I'm not into murder. It's not right."

The detectives agreed, and Henry continued. "Barbara said that if I refused, she could get a couple kids to kill the guy with a baseball bat. Barbara told me that she wanted this guy gone for his money. He had something like thirty thousand dollars."

Henry said he visited Barbara at her house in Everett two times. The first time he was over there for five or six hours. "The last time was on a Sunday night, when I went over there around noon and stayed until six A.M. the next morning. At that time I was in most parts of the house. The man's bedroom was on the second floor, and the older lady that she was supposed to take care of lived in the bedroom on the first floor, to the right as you come in the front door.

"The bottom line, I guess," said Henry, "is that Barbara asked me to kill her employer because she didn't think the weed killer that she was using was doing the job."

"Weed killer?"

"Yeah, Roundup. She was putting it in his food, using it

as seasoning on his pizza, stuff like that. She asked me if I knew anything stronger, and I said that I didn't."

"Did she bring up the idea of you killing her boss, more than once?"

"Oh sure," said Henry. "The last time she asked me if I had made a decision about it, I told her that I was thinking it over, and I would get back to her. Hell, I never went back, I never spoke to her again. I told my wife, she told you, and now here we are."

"Mind if we search your van?"

"Hey, go for it," said Henry. "I didn't use my van to carry any bodies anywhere."

"We saw no signs of a body being in the van," recalled Detective Callaghan. "They were keeping a cat out in the van, so there was a cat, a cat box, and a few tools. Nowhere in this old white '78 Chevy van did we see any obvious signs of blood."

"Do you have any idea what happened to Jerry Heimann, Henry?"

"No. The person you should be asking is Barbara," he suggested, and they concurred completely.

Ask Barbara Opel about the Roundup incident, and you won't hear a story of attempted murder. "I had already made dinner," explained Barbara Opel, "and Heather was putting some vegetables in the salad, and I walked upstairs from probably doing something with the laundry and caught Heather spraying some stuff on the salad. I told her that she couldn't be going around doing that kind of thing and threw the salad out. I never actually gave that salad to Jerry."

Not that salad, no; another weed-killer-laced meal, yes. Approximately a night or two later, while the "evil" Jerry Heimann was helping little Tiffany with her homework, he asked Tiffany to get up and get him a beer out of the refrigerator and a pack of cigarettes from the cupboard.

"I became angry," admitted Barbara, "and I told him [to] get off his own lazy ass and do it himself, that Tiffany wasn't his maid. It led to another big argument for about twenty minutes. He was yelling at me, I was yelling at him. I was really angry. So the next night I did exactly the same thing that Heather did before—I put Roundup weed killer in his food, covered it up, and put it in the fridge."

Jerry Heimann came home, took his dinner out of the refrigerator, went upstairs, and heated it in his personal microwave. "My goal," said Barbara, "was to make him very sick. The next day I called an 800 number on the back of the Roundup bottle, and I called and talked to somebody that was on that line—told them the bottle I had, gave them the date on it. And they told me it was the . . . like the least strongest type of Roundup that they have, and that it had been out of date for two or three years, so the most it would do to somebody would be to make them sick."

"Tell me, Barbara," asked Detective Fortin, "do you have any idea where Jerry Heimann could be?"

"No, I don't," said Barbara. "The last time I saw Jerry was at eleven-thirty in the morning on Wednesday the eighteenth. He didn't say where he was going. He just said, 'See you later.' He knew that I was moving out, because it had been planned for some time. Jerry left that day in his maroon Camaro. He was by himself and he left the residence at approximately eleven-thirty. We finished packing the U-Haul and left at approximately eleven forty-five."

"I was concerned about Evelyn Heimann," she added, "but Jerry reassured me that he would be back shortly. Actually, I considered leaving the residence earlier, but was concerned about the welfare of Evelyn Heimann. One of Jerry's girlfriends, Diane Jensen, told me that I should leave and not be concerned about Evelyn because Jerry would take care of her.

"Evelyn Heimann was not doing that good before I took over," said Barbara Opel. "As for Jerry, he and I got along well, but we did not discuss personal things, and we didn't have any kind of dating relationship. I first met Jerry Heimann in November of 2000," Barbara explained. "It started out where my kids were going over to his place after school, on the weekends, and watching his mother while he ran his errands. They were making thirty dollars a day. And then we got to where we needed a place to live, and he said that we could move in at that time.

"I initially lived with Jerry and his mother, Evelyn, at a house located near Mariner High School. We lived there only three weeks before Jerry sold the house and moved to a rental house in mid-December of 2000. My role in the Heimann residence expanded to cooking, cleaning, and shopping, in addition to caring for Evelyn Heimann. I paid Jerry Heimann the reduced rent of three hundred and fifty dollars a month, as well as two hundred dollars for our portion of the food bill."

Jerry Heimann would frequent local bars, Barbara said, and he would often bring girlfriends home. "He went to bars for a few hours to socialize every day, but his drinking was never a problem, and it didn't interfere with his ability to function in any way. He would always come home in time to have dinner."

When asked about Heimann's disposition, she said he was usually happy, but one time he did yell at Heather. "He could get mean and he threatened to throw us out from time to time. We planned on moving out of the house, which was located inconveniently away from my children's schools in South Everett."

According to Barbara Opel, Heimann told her in mid-March that he'd "had it with the kids" and wanted them out.

Opel asked him to wait until the first of April when she had more money to pay for a move.

"Opel was aware that Heimann had a lot of money," Fortin said later. "She acknowledged that she often used Heimann's vehicles to conduct household business. She described the vehicles as a black Dodge pickup and a silver Firebird. She said that Heimann drove a maroon Camaro as his primary personal vehicle."

"Do you know where these vehicles are right now, Barbara?" Fortin asked Barbara.

Rather than remain silent, which was her right, she fabricated another blatantly false answer. "Well, the truck broke down on Monday, April sixteenth, a couple of blocks from the house," she replied. "I last used the silver Firebird over the weekend, possibly on Saturday, to drive my kids to the Everett Skate Deck. The Firebird was parked at the house when we moved out."

Detectives knew otherwise. Research showed that Jerry Heimann's silver Firebird was towed to an impound lot from the Everett Mall shopping center the day before, April 17, after a security guard at the Everett Mall erroneously thought that three boys were attempting to break into a random vehicle. The boys were Brandon Carcas, Justin Vessey, and Kyle Boston.

"I was at home," recalled Justin Vessey, "when Kyle Boston drove up in a silver Firebird and asked me if I wanted to go with him to the Everett Mall. I had never seen him in that car before. We didn't go directly to the mall. First we stopped and picked up Brandon Carcas, and then we stopped at the Smathers home, where Kyle walked into the backyard by himself, then returned with a gun and put it in the trunk of the car. Kyle told us the gun was 'just in case.' He didn't say in case of what."

"Before we got to the mall," added Brandon Carcas,

"we went to McDonald's. Kyle ordered fries and a drink. The reason we were going to the mall was to buy shoes for Kyle's girlfriend. I heard Kyle say that he had one hundred dollars—sixty dollars were for the shoes, and forty to buy an earring. That was a lot of money for Kyle."

"After we got to the mall," Vessey said, "Kyle removed the gun from the trunk of the car and placed in into the console in the passenger compartment. When we went inside, a female employee told us that they were closing and we had to leave, so we did."

"We had trouble getting into the car for some reason," said Carcas. "Maybe there was something wrong with the locks, but whatever it was, we had to force our way back into the car."

An Everett Mall security guard noticed this suspicious-looking activity, and asked the three juveniles for some identification. Kyle Boston gave a wrong date of birth.

"When one of the security guards said that the police would be called," said Carcas, "Kyle took off running. Justin and me stayed there and told the officer what we knew, because we knew we didn't do anything wrong. Then we just waited for our folks to come and get us."

Brandon and Justin didn't know to whom the car belonged. All they knew was what Kyle Boston had told them. "Kyle told me that it belonged to a friend named Jeff," said Carcas.

"I had never seen the car before," added Vessey. "Kyle told me that he got the car from Jeff Grote because Grote owed him money."

Vessey and Carcas weren't the only two youths who encountered Kyle Boston behind the wheel of Jerry Heimann's Firebird. "I was walking from the Skate Deck to the bowling alley with my cousin Bud Fraser," recalled Anthony "Tony" Martinez, of Marysville, Washington, "when Kyle Boston and Mike Smathers drove up in a silver Firebird and offered us a ride. Boston bragged about beating up someone and killing him in Everett, but I didn't believe him. Then Kyle and Mike showed us some blood on Kyle's shoes."

"Detective Fortin and I knew that Barbara Opel was lying about the Firebird," recalled Neussendorfer. "And police officers were out rounding up Kyle Boston and Mike Smathers." Barbara Opel's veracity and integrity, proven questionable, prepared detectives for further false-hoods, lies, and omissions.

"We began asking Opel questions about the U-Haul truck she rented and used to move from the residence," said Neussendorfer. "We were aware that the U-Haul truck was rented with Jerry Heimann's credit card and picked up by a neighbor who had a valid driver's license. We were also aware that Opel had apparently told this neighbor that Jerry Heimann had left for Las Vegas to marry one of his girlfriends."

"I didn't actually have Jerry's credit card when I rented the U-Haul," said Barbara. "I just read the credit card number over the phone to the employee at the U-Haul location."

Returning to the subject of the missing Mr. Heimann, Barbara Opel insisted that she couldn't imagine where he could be. "It surprises me that he's gone so long. I knew his relatives were coming to visit—I think his son was coming. I know they debated whether Jerry was going to visit them, or if they were coming to see him here.

"I had a conversation with Ruby Adams, Jerry's ex-wife," Barbara continued. "She told me that I should go on vacation when Jerry's kids came to visit him, because they would probably get really drunk and obnoxious."

Asked if it was suspicious for Jerry Heimann not to be home when his son came to visit, she began telling a story about Jerry Heimann failing to stay home when another relative visited from Spokane. "She attempted to offer this story," said Neussendorfer, "as a means of showing that Heimann's behavior was not entirely out of character."

"As I already told you," Barbara Opel insisted, "I have no idea where Jerry is. I didn't see Jerry pack any bags or anything. I last saw him on Wednesday the eighteenth. He was in a good mood."

On Wednesday the eighteenth, Jerry Heimann was five days dead, and Barbara Opel had already forged his signature on a $6,000 check given to Laurie Pohren as a deposit on the apartment on McDougal Road.

CHAPTER 4

"I can remember the ad we put in the *Herald* newspaper," said Mrs. Pohren. "Three-bedroom, one-bath, had a large yard, the building itself was like a house probably years ago, so it was on like a hill slanted, so the top part actually from McDougal Road just looked like a house. So it was an upstairs and a downstairs unit, and the upstairs is the one that was available. Basically, it was one big house that had been divided into two. I think either unit was probably eleven hundred square feet."

Barbara Opel contacted Pohren on April 17 and requested a tour of the unit. "They liked it," recalled Mrs. Pohren, "they looked around and they liked it. And they commented on this room, it had like the Disney border, and the teenage daughter said this would be good for, and she mentioned a child's name, and I don't recall the name, and she said this would be good because so and so likes Disney, and this is good and has a nice big yard. And they talked about that they liked it and would like to rent it."

Opel and Pohren reached an agreement on renting the unit. "Barbara Opel mentioned that she needed a place right away, and we were just fixing it up and pretty much getting to the point where we could be done, and so we said, 'Well, okay, since [you] need it right away, we [will] forego all the credit checks and stuff.' She had mentioned that she would like to pay in advance. It was something with her daughter playing baseball or softball, one of the two, and they would probably be gone a lot during the summer, so she wanted to make sure the rent was there on time, so she was just going to pay in advance."

Barbara wrote Mrs. Pohren a check covering "a good six to eight months in advance. It's kind of strange when a renter wants to pay that much in advance, but some people have done it in the past too. So it's not totally unheard of. But, you know, you kind of wonder where the money comes from, you know—all of a sudden, a big check."

Mrs. Pohren was naturally pleased with the advance payment, especially considering the recent remodeling costs. "We had repairs we had just done, so it would cover that and everything. She wrote us a check for six thousand dollars. The name on the check, however, was Jerry and Evelyn Heimann. And the signature on the check was supposedly by a Jerry Heimann."

Barbara Opel explained that Evelyn Heimann was her mother, that she had received a large cash settlement, and that she was helping Barbara out financially. All of this made sense to Pohren, as Barbara had written down her mother's name as "Evelyn" on her credit application.

As a precautionary measure, Mrs. Pohren took the check to Bank of America the next day. "I told Bank of America that I didn't want this check to come back on me, and I asked them to check it out first, and they did. So they cashed the check, and I deposited the money into a separate rental account that we use to pay for repairs and this and that. So it was in there. We thought everything was fine."

With the unit prepared and the keys ready, Laurie

Pohren was surprised that Barbara Opel and her kids didn't show up to move in. "I left the keys for her to move in, but she didn't," said Laurie. "I didn't hear from her, so I tried to track her down. We called the various phone numbers we had for her, because I wanted to make sure she knew she could move in and the check cleared, all that kind of stuff."

When news of Barbara Opel's arrest on suspicion of murdering Jerry Heimann reached the Pohrens, they contacted the Everett police.

"My husband, Kent, and I thought it was suspicious that she gave us a check in the names of Mrs. Evelyn Heimann and Jerry Heimann, when her name was neither of those," Laurie told detectives. Laurie and Kent had no qualms about sharing this information with the police. They also kept the $6,000.

Thursday, April 19, 2001, 4:30 P.M.

Everett's detectives interviewed eleven-year-old Derek Opel, knowing full well that questioning a child is a risky proposition. "I don't like interviewing kids when I don't have to," said Brent Turvey, expert criminal profiler and forensic scientist. "It's a very tricky proposal and one I'm not comfortable with, because the susceptibility of children to suggestion while being questioned, in addition to difficulty in reconstructing long-term memories, can be dangerous."

The problem with interviewing a young child is that children are easily influenced, and vulnerable to suggestions from the interrogator and other external sources, such as other people and the media.

"Children also are very eager to please," said Turvey, "and could pick up on the types of answers an interviewer is seeking—and then shape responses to the examiner's liking.

Even regular people going into a lineup are susceptible to the subtle approval given by law enforcement when you pick the right person."

In Turvey's opinion, the person who interviews the child should know nothing about the case. "They shouldn't be someone who can accidentally slip something in and inadvertently reward them for going down a certain path."

The challenge facing anyone who interviews children is learning how to separate out what the child knows on his or her own and what he or she has learned from other sources. "Without independent corroboration," insisted Turvey, "it is virtually impossible to distinguish a memory that is a result of true experience from one that is a result of suggestion, confabulation, imagination, or some other process."

According to Turvey, the first or second statements given to police are the most reliable. "As time goes on, things get blurred, things get forgotten, and new memories rise up to take their places."

Luckily, Everett detectives were questioning Derek and Tiffany Opel regarding a recent event, one that was possibly traumatic. "Prior to those two interviews with the children," according to Neussendorfer, "there was kind of a meeting of the detectives involved and a discussion or debate as to whether or not we had enough information to establish that a criminal event had occurred. There was not enough information to push it over the edge into strictly a criminal investigation."

"I don't know anything about what happened to Jerry," Derek told the friendly detective. "We got kicked out of the house on Wednesday the eighteenth."

Detective Neussendorfer allowed a moment of distracted silence to frame his next question. "When exactly did you last see Jerry?"

"I last saw him on Tuesday, about two o'clock, when we

moved out," said Derek, contradicting the statement he made only moments previous. "He was going upstairs to take a shower because he lived on the top floor. Grandma lived on the main floor, and we lived in the basement until we moved out."

Derek Opel said that Jeffrey Grote helped them move from the residence, but Grote and Heimann never met. As for the Firebird, Derek told Neussendorfer that Jerry often let Barbara Opel drive the Firebird, and that Jeff Grote had also driven it because Barbara Opel's license was suspended.

"If you don't know what happened to Jerry," asked Neussendorfer, "do you at least know what happened to the Firebird?"

"No," said Derek. "I don't know what happened to it. It was there when we moved out, but it's not there now."

"How do you know that it's not there now?"

Derek thought for a moment, then came up with an answer.

"Well, we went back to the house on Wednesday because I forgot something when we moved out. When we got there, I noticed the Firebird was missing."

Having read the report regarding the impounding of the Firebird at the Everett Mall, the detective knew that local teenager Kyle Boston had been driving the vehicle.

"Do you know Kyle Boston?"

"Sure," said Derek. "He's one of Jeff's friends. He came by the house a couple times to say hi to Jeff, but Kyle never drove the Firebird."

"Immediately after completing my interview with Derek Opel," said Neussendorfer, "I went back to the hallway where she and Derek were previously sitting, and I asked Tiffany in the same manner if she would be willing to speak with me. I interviewed seven-year-old Tiffany Goudeau in the office of child interview specialist Kelly Bradley—

a small office away from the main hallway of the third floor. It is designed to put children at ease, and is filled with toys and teddy bears. It has wallpaper that has more of a children's-type theme to it. It also has kid-size furniture."

"I live in a house with my brother, sister, and mother," said the little girl. When asked if anyone else lived in the house, she replied by asking, "Did Derek say someone else lived there?"

"I told her that I wouldn't be telling her what Derek told me, just as I would not tell Derek what she told me," said Neussendorfer.

"Tiffany," he asked, "do you know anyone named Jerry?"

"Yes," she answered, "he's some guy, and my mom takes care of his mother. We all call her 'Grandma.'"

"Tell me, Tiffany," the detective kindly requested, "did something happen to Jerry?"

"Yeah."

"What exactly happened to Jerry?"

"He died," said Tiffany.

"Tiffany described for me how Jerry died," Neussendorfer recalled. "She said he was beaten to death with a baseball bat. It was obvious to me and the rest of the detectives that we were now dealing with a homicide."

When little Tiffany made the first pronouncement that Jerry Heimann was dead, detectives finally had the wedge they needed to pry some truth from her siblings and Jeff Grote. "We went back and chatted further with her eleven-year-old brother. I told Derek that we knew Jerry had been injured and that he was dead," recalled Neussendorfer.

"He could have got drunk," said Derek, "and fell downstairs."

"We know that isn't what happened," replied Neussendorfer, "we need the truth. Tell me, Derek, what happened to Jerry?"

"He got beat up."

"How bad did he get beat up?"

"Pretty bad."

"Is he all right?"

"No."

"How is he?"

"Well, uh . . . mmmm."

Not finding that answer of sufficient precision, detectives pressed for added clarity.

"Is Jerry alive?"

"No. He's dead."

Derek confirmed that it was Friday the thirteenth when Heimann met his demise, and that he didn't meet Kyle Boston or Michael until the night of the murder.

"My mom opened the door and then Jeff said, 'These are my best friends, Kyle and Michael.' Then Mom closed the door and they came inside and hung out in Grandma's room until Jerry came home, then they beat him. Kyle and Michael used bats. You know, those little Mariner bats. They used that and Jeff used his fists."

Derek's lower lip and chin quivered, and he fidgeted in his chair as he told detectives his version of events. "Me and Mom and Tiffany were in the basement, but I heard a lot of banging and pounding. When we came up, the first thing I saw was blood," said Derek. "Then I saw Jerry on the floor by the kitchen. We all helped clean up the mess. There was blood on the floors, wall, and on the carpet in the dining room. On the hard floor we used, um, a mop, and my mom rented a Rug Doctor from Safeway. Tiffany was trying to be helpful too. She helped Mom with vacuuming and with the Rug Doctor. We wrapped up Jerry in a sheet, and then we all took Jerry's body out in the woods on the reservation. Mom told me that we were putting Jerry's body in the woods until she could afford to buy him a real grave at the cemetery."

Detectives asked little Derek if he knew how his mother paid for the U-Haul. "She paid for that with the credit card she got out of Jerry's wallet. After she took out the credit card, we threw the wallet in the dump."

Derek said he thought he could locate the place on the reservation where Jerry's body had been dumped. "But I can find it better in the daytime," he said.

While Neussendorfer built rapport with Derek Opel, Detective Steve Kiser and Detective Jensen sat down with Derek's big sister, Heather. As with other Everett detectives, Jensen was well trained in the art of interviewing youngsters.

"I've had at least three different classes I've gone to about interviewing children," said Detective Jonathon Jensen. "And just being in the unit, you have to have an ability to talk properly with children, you know, get along with children, because they're not going to talk to you if you don't relate to them in a pleasant manner. You know, if you're a rude police officer, you get less information than if you're pleasant and polite to people. There's a measure of gentleness that goes along with speaking with thirteen-year-olds, but I had to be firm with Heather Opel at times. But it was a polite firmness, and a normal tone."

Jensen began by asking where she lived.

"I live on Forty-eighth Street," she lied.

"Heather, you don't live on Forty-eighth Street, you live on Twenty-second, don't you?"

"Umm . . . yes. Forty-eighth is where my softball coach lives, and it's my family's mailing address, and I sort of live there at times. In fact, my softball coach's daughter said to me, 'Heather, you almost live here.'"

Asked with whom she actually lived, Heather listed off her mother, brother, sister, and "an old lady who lives in the rest of the house."

"Isn't there a guy there named Jerry?" asked Detective Jensen.

"Umm . . . no."

"Didn't a guy named Jerry live there or come by?"

"Well," said Heather, "a guy named Jim or Jerry came by, but I don't remember when that was."

"It was painfully obvious that the girl was just making things up as she went along," recalled the detective. "It was sad."

"We moved out of the house on Wednesday, but I didn't know we were moving until I came home from school on Tuesday and saw the U-Haul at the house. Mom had been talking about it, and then she just said, 'I think we should move.'"

Before leaving the room and consulting with other detectives, Jensen asked her a few more questions: "Did you ever hear any arguments or disturbances coming from the upstairs part of the house?"

"No," replied Heather. "There was no yelling, no arguments, no disturbances."

Jensen then steered the conversation around to Heather and Jeff's sex life. It wasn't prurient interest motivating Jensen's questions. He was part of the Special Assault Unit. "We handle sexual offenses against adults and children, and physical abuse of children," he explained. All detectives in this unit receive specialized training, and Jensen was assigned to the Special Assault Unit in spring 2001.

"The reason I was brought into the investigation," Jensen said, "was because there was information that one of the girls in the case, Heather, had been having a sexual relationship with a boy named Jeff, and because of the age differences involved, she was thirteen and he was seventeen, it constituted a crime under our state laws."

Heather admitted having "regular sex" with Jeff Grote.

"He's the first boy I've ever had sex with," said Heather. "We did it three times altogether," she clarified, "not three times in a row. He didn't wear a condom, and I don't know if he ejaculated or not, but I can't get pregnant because I haven't had any periods yet."

Jensen took a deep breath, then mentioned something that made Heather quite nervous. "We found blood in the house—"

"Grandma cut her arm," blurted out Heather, speaking rapidly. "We had to put a bandage on it and treat it with Neosporin. I bet the blood came from that."

Jensen left the room and had a chat with fellow detectives Fortin and Neussendorfer. "We knew she was lying about just about everything. Her lies didn't even match the initial false statements of the others involved."

"Do you own any baseball bats, Heather?"

"Sure," she replied, "I own two aluminum softball bats and lots of other softball stuff."

It was time for detectives to play hardball with the cute little sports star. "Jerry is dead, Heather. We know that he was murdered with a baseball bat."

"I suspected that Jerry was dead," replied Heather, as if this information confirmed her own suspicions. "The last time I saw Jerry was when I went to take a shower. He was sitting at the kitchen table in his pajamas. When I came back from my shower, my mother and Jeff said that Jerry had passed away."

Pressed for further details, Heather gave a succinct, if completely inaccurate, reply. "I came upstairs from the basement," said Heather, "and I saw Jerry lying on the floor and not moving. Next to him was one of my baseball bats. I asked what happened and Jeff told me that Jerry was dead. My mom was sitting on the couch, and she said, 'Yeah, he probably is dead.'"

Perhaps realizing the blatant absurdity of her story, Heather revised it, adding a bit more color, yet omitting basic facts.

"My mom and Tiffany were upstairs. Me and Derek were downstairs. Derek was playing Nintendo 64 and I was in the room listening to music, and all of a sudden, I heard a thumping noise. I ran upstairs and I heard Jerry cussing at Jeff, Kyle, and Michael. Then I seen Jerry lying on the ground on the kitchen floor with blood all around him. Jeffrey had taken a baseball bat to Jerry. The baseball bat was beside it. Jeff was beside the baseball bat. I really didn't see anyone hit Jerry," claimed Heather, "but I did help clean up. I used a sponge and Clorox bleach, and I had to stand on a table and cleaned up the blood.

"Jeff helped my mom and Derek load the body into the back of the truck and they drove up to Tulalip Indian Reservation and threw the body on the side of the road."

Heather initially said that she'd only gone along when the body was dumped and had not helped dump the body, and then she said, "Well, I don't want to lie, I climbed into the back of the truck and threw the bat into the woods."

"What kind of bat was it, Heather?"

"It was a Louisville Slugger with black tape on the handle. It was green and yellow on the barrel and approximately thirty-two inches long."

Asked about the sponges, Heather said that there were two blue and one yellow. "They were thrown away in the house garbage. There was blood all over the walls and on the ceiling, so I cleaned off all the walls and ceilings with a blue sponge and Clorox bleach and used a scrubbing brush." Heather's revised version portrayed her as an efficient cleaning girl whose primary concern was not life or death, but simply keeping a tidy residence.

"Here you have a thirteen-year-old girl," commented

investigator Fred Wolfson, "alone in a room with two adult detectives—not just one interview, but several—and they never actually tell her that they are investigating the disappearance of Jerry Heimann, never advise her of her rights, and don't get her parent's permission or anything. This has to be a most fearful and intimidating experience for a kid. Hell, put anybody that young in a room with two cops doing interrogation and they will wind up saying pretty much whatever you want."

The cops wanted to know how to find Jerry Heimann's body. Derek Opel agreed to show Detective Kiser where the body was dumped. "In the morning we drove him to the reservation," reported Detective Steve Kiser, "and Derek Opel led me directly to the location of the victim's body."

CHAPTER 5

Friday, April 20, 2001, 8:00 A.M.

"I was told that Detective Steve Kiser was going to take Derek Opel, the young song of Barbara Opel, and drive out to the Tulalip Reservation and attempt to locate the area where Jerry Heimann's body had been supposedly dumped," recalled Detective Brouwer. "I was told to ride with Lieutenant Hegge, who was going to follow Detective Kiser. We drove about 8.5 miles from I-5 westbound on Marine Drive. Kiser pulled over, and he and I, with flashlights, checked the south side of the roadway."

"There were wild grasses, weeds, short and sparse trees," recalled Detective Callaghan, who also went on the excursion. "It was very weeded, untended. There isn't any real walking path in that area, it wasn't an area generally where people would walk, fairly open. Some of the weeds and grasses might be three feet tall, others were lower, some places it was a little higher."

Brouwer observed a dark-colored object approximately forty feet down the slope from the edge of the roadway. "I walked down the slope," he said, "and when I got to within ten or twelve feet from the object, I saw a pair of dark-colored boots, with the toes pointing up. The object was covered by a dark-colored blanket or tarp." The "object" was the body of Jerry Heimann.

"Unless you were looking closely," Detective Callaghan recalled, "you might not notice the body because of the brush and the trees area. It was wrapped in, as we found later getting closer, a comforter or quilt. From the road you could see some dark black blanket-looking object of some kind. What first we saw was the black side of a comforter that had a gray-and-white check on the other side. Underneath this there were two sheets, they were multicolored, I think pink and gray, and they were wrapped closer to the body.

"The body was dressed in a gray pullover sweater that zipped partially down, maybe a quarter of the way," reported Detective Callaghan. "He had black jeans, these were fairly new. The brand was Rustler, Legendary Gold. He was wearing black cowboy boots. These jeans were black also. The gray pullover sweater had a little pouch in front, and he wasn't wearing a hat, but he appeared to have dark brown hair, and he possibly had a hairpiece, a dark toupee. There was a watch on his left wrist."

The Snohomish County chief medical examiner, Dr. Norman John Thiersch, arrived about 9:00 A.M. and took a closer look. Thiersch is a doctor of anatomic and forensic pathology. "My job," explained Thiersch, "involves determining the cause and manner of death for any unexplained, unexpected, or violent death that occurs in Snohomish County."

Well qualified for the position, Thiersch completed four years of medical school at the University of Washington, following that with four years of residency training in anatomic and clinical pathology at the University of Washington. "Following that, I completed two years of forensic pathology fellowship at the King County Medical Examiner's Office, within the state of Washington. I spent a year in Tucson, Arizona, at Pima County, as forensic pathologist, and returned to King County in 1994. I assumed the role of chief medical examiner for Snohomish County in 1998."

Part of his duties is to go to scenes where there have been homicides and deal with the body of the deceased. "It's the practice of the office," explained Thiersch, "that if there's suspicious death or homicide, that the pathologist on call responds to the scene, does a brief examination of the body at the scene, notes the setting, and takes a body core temperature at that time as well. Once I've conducted a brief examination, the body is then placed in a body bag, sealed, and then transported to the office for the autopsy and a more complete examination."

An autopsy is a detailed examination of a human body after the person has died. This involves looking at the external surfaces for signs of injury and identifying marks. "In case of homicide," said Thiersch, "there is the detailed collection of important evidence or findings that are there. Then, once the external exam has been done, the bodies are incised, cuts are made, and the organs are examined— heart, lungs, those sorts of things. And the internal examination is performed."

Responding to the death of Jerry Heimann, Thiersch showed up to perform his duties as chief medical examiner. "I recall standing in the road, viewing the body, walking down a steep hillside to examine the body. It was covered with a comforter and a few sheets. We took those off, photographing the scene and the body, and then did a brief examination of the body, including a body core temperature."

Body core temperature is typically done on bodies at death scenes to get an idea about the time of death, how long it's been since the person died. Within the first twenty-four hours, that gives a fairly rough estimate of when death occurred. The body core temperature of Jerry Heimann was, according to Thiersch, within a degree or two of the ambient temperature. "That indicated to me that the body had been there for at least twenty-four hours if not longer."

Jerry Heimann's body was transported to the medical examiner's office, where Thiersch conducted the autopsy that same morning. Always eager to educate and inform, Dr. Thiersch readily explained the steps involved in his autopsy of Jerry Heimann.

"First we took extensive photographs of the external surfaces of the body. We also try and clean up the body so that we can see the injuries if there's blood or dirt. Sometimes we might shave the hair off certain parts of the body to get a better look at the underlying injuries just so that we can document them better. We examine the body for evidence of trace evidence that might be retained underneath the nails, on the hands, on various aspects of the body. Also during this process we undress the body and preserve the clothing for law enforcement to examine after we're through with it."

Once that had been done, Dr. Thiersch took X-rays of the head, chest, and abdomen, looking for evidence of projectiles, bullets, or other foreign objects in the body.

"We then, of course, did a complete internal examination of Mr. Heimann's body," said Dr. Thiersch, "and the total number of listed injuries in my report is forty-seven, but that is probably less than the actual number of injuries. Some of the injuries were grouped together by type, so some of those represent actually more than one single injury."

There were a number of different types of injuries to Mr. Heimann's body. "There were blunt-force injuries such as contusions or bruises, abrasions, which are scrapes and scratches," said Dr. Thiersch, "and also lacerations, which is a tearing of the tissue of the skin. Those are all caused by blunt objects, either being hit by a blunt object or falling onto some blunt surface. There were also injuries caused by sharp objects, such as a knife, machete, or something of that sort. The injuries were distributed over his body in a number of different areas. There were a number of blunt-force injuries to Mr. Heimann's head. I also found incisions to both sides of Mr. Heimann's neck, and also an incision to the back side of his neck."

The autopsy also documented a stab wound that went into the left chest at the level of the second rib, but missed any vital organs. Jerry Heimann was stabbed seven times in the lower left abdomen. Four of those stab wounds went into the abdominal cavity but didn't hit any vital organs.

There were another two stab-type wounds a little bit higher up on the left lower abdomen that went into the soft tissues, but did not go into the abdominal cavity and just stopped.

"In the process of doing an autopsy," the doctor explained, "the skin of the scalp is cut, then the scalp is peeled back or reflected, and then the skull is examined. Mr. Heimann's skull had multiple, multiple fractures associated with the blunt force, the injury to his head, and the lacerations to the back of his head. It would be something akin to a crushed eggshell. If you took an eggshell and smashed it on the ground, it was similar in appearance.

"Mr. Heimann," he further explained, "died due to lacerations of his brain due to the blunt impact to his head. The lacerations are evidence of the sort of impact injury that occurred to his head, and then the underlying cuts and injury to his brain is why he died."

A number of detectives searched the area for possible evidence. "There was a full-size baseball bat found," said Callaghan, "but it was another forty feet west of the body.

This was a metal bat, it was a greenish black dark color, indicate, I believe, yellow Louisville Slugger. It had a black rubber grip around the metal bat. I didn't measure the length of it exactly, but it was a full-size metal baseball bat."

Detectives also discovered a white plastic bottle labeled *Muriatic Acid*. Muriatic, or hydrochloric, acid causes severe irritation or burns to skin and eyes. If the acid had been poured on Heimann's face, that would explain what Callaghan described as "abnormal facial coloring—almost an ashen white, giving it a masklike appearance."

Detective Brouwer had found the body when Detective Jensen showed up. "The major crimes detectives were there already, along with the crime scene van and some of the other technicians. They had already searched the scene and were pointing out items that were evident. I helped with measuring the crime scene and collecting the Rug Doctor Anti-Foam, the baseball bat, and other items."

Brouwer was assigned to photograph the scene. In addition to photographing the victim, he took photos of the area, the roadway, a baseball bat, and other items of evidence collected by Jensen.

"When the cops were recovering the body," recalled Tony Stevens, news director for Everett radio station KRKO, "we had already received a press release from the Everett Police Department announcing that they arrested Barbara Opel, Heather Opel, Jeff Grote, and some unnamed juveniles. Grote was held on two-million-dollar bail. Barbara Opel was booked for investigation of first-degree murder and ordered held without bail in the Snohomish County Jail, pending a formal charging hearing. Her daughter and the other teens were placed in the juvenile center on cash-only bond of one hundred thousand dollars each."

In addition to Mrs. Opel and a 17 year old boy, read the Everett Police Department press release, *three other juveniles, two boys and a girl between the ages of 12 and 17, were arrested. Police believe that all were involved in the homicide.*

Police did not disclose any details of Heimann's homicide, how the juveniles were involved, where and how the body was discovered, if the young suspects had been formally booked, or in which of the twenty-one Washington State detention facilities the juveniles were held.

"Washington State law mandates that counties develop and implement detention intake standards to determine whether detention is warranted," explained Stevens, "as well as the type of detention facility in which a juvenile should be placed. Here in Snohomish County, youth may be held after arrest for allegedly committing an offense or on a warrant."

There are other reasons for placing juveniles in detention, such as giving them protection from threatening conditions or protecting the community from threatening behavior.

"When these youths were arrested on April nineteenth," said Sergeant Boyd Bryant, "we knew they were well enough acquainted with each other to participate in something like this together. As they were juveniles, their names were not released to the press."

"Reporters want to report," stated Tony Stevens, "that's what we do. But in this case, there wasn't much to report. Detectives were still pulling together details and additional information. Basic facts of the arrests were all they could really provide us at the time."

Providing copious quantities of damning details was an honor reserved for Opel's two youngest children, Derek and Tiffany. In a series of overlapping subsequent interviews, the cherub-faced children confessed their presence when their beloved mother, Barbara Opel, convinced, coerced, and bribed a cadre of kids into killing her generous employer.

According to her children's statements, on the night of Friday the thirteenth, Barbara Opel armed a fourteen-year-old Marysville boy, Kyle Boston, and his year-younger cousin, Mike, with little Mariner souvenir bats and told them to hide in two stairwells. She gave Grote a full-size aluminum bat and told him to hide in a bedroom.

Barbara Opel went downstairs with Derek, Tiffany, Heather, and Marriam Oliver to wait for Heimann. "If we get caught," Barbara told the children, "we're going to blame Jeff."

When Barbara Opel was assigning roles and responsibilities to her teenage gang, Marriam Oliver couldn't hear every word. "I knew I was supposed to stab him with a knife," she said, "but I wasn't sure about the others' responsibilities because the cartoons on television drowned out Opel's voice."

According to Grote, until the last minute, he debated whether he would get involved. But when Heimann walked through the door, Grote smacked him in the nape with a full swing of the bat. Heimann dropped to the ground, Grote said. Each time Heimann tried to struggle to his feet, Grote or one of the "Marysville boys" pummeled him back to the floor.

Kyle Boston punched Heimann in the face, and Michael Smathers whacked him once with a miniature bat before the two of them got scared and ran away while Heimann was still alive. They returned, however, for Heimann's car keys.

Acting as a one-woman cheering section, Barbara Opel allegedly shouted encouragement from the basement during the attack. Marriam Oliver, however, didn't share Mrs. Opel's enthusiasm. As Jerry Heimann yelled for help, she put the knife on the kitchen counter and ran downstairs, where she had spent most of the spring break week. She packed up her stuff—a curling iron, a lunch box full of coloring pens, and some gym clothes—and jumped out a basement window.

"Come back here right now," screamed Barbara Opel. "What kind of best friend are you? Are you going to run away when Heather is killing someone?"

Accusing Oliver of being a terrible best friend to thirteen-year-old Heather, Mrs. Opel pointed out that Heather was upstairs murdering Mr. Heimann, and Oliver should do her part. Returning to the attack, Oliver saw that Heimann was gasping for air and "there was a lot of blood," she recalled.

Heather Opel and her boyfriend, Jeffrey Grote, told Marriam Oliver to stab Heimann. "But I just couldn't," she said. Heather Opel stabbed Heimann in the side several times. Jeff Grote tried to cut his neck. When there was still disagreement among the youths over whether Heimann was still alive, Marriam Oliver made sure he was dead by delivering a deliberate, life-ending blow.

"I picked up a softball bat and hit Jerry Heimann in the head three times," said Oliver. The medical examiner described Heimann's damaged skull as "something akin to a crushed eggshell."

Barbara Opel put a decidedly different spin on events. "I seen Jerry's car pull up in front of the house, so everybody went to their places. Tiffany was screaming, so I was with her downstairs. Mostly, I just heard the 'ping' of the bats, and Jeff yelling at everybody and telling them what to do. You know, he was saying, 'Get a knife. You guys need to do this. Somebody get over here and help me. Marriam, you need to get over here and do something.'

"I was getting scared," said Opel. "I went up there because Heather and Derek were up there crying. Marriam had come downstairs and was crying. I said, 'Just forget it, Marriam,' but she says, 'No, Mom'—she's my daughter's best friend, so she calls me 'Mom'—I said, "Just forget it,

Marriam,' and she said that she was Heather's best friend and she ran back upstairs.

"When I got upstairs and saw Jerry's body, I told Marriam, 'I think he's dead,' and she said, 'Yeah, watch this,' and she took the bat and hit him on the back of the head and shit splattered all over everything. It was gross."

Kyle Boston and his cousin Michael quickly left the scene in Heimann's Firebird, picked up a pregnant fifteen-year-old Everett girl, Misty Moore, at her house, and took her with them to a bowling alley, where they later met up with Barbara Opel, Heather Opel, Jeff Grote, and Marriam Oliver. Boston said he was paid about $220 for his involvement, giving $110 to his cousin Mike, who used it to buy a baby blue sweat suit. While at the bowling alley, the youngster brazenly displayed his bloodstained shoes.

Following the brutal murder of Jerry Heimann, and the complicated process of moving the body and finally dumping in on the Tulalip Reservation, "Mother Opel" rewarded her macabre charges with a hearty breakfast at Denny's.

"Everybody was scared and tired," Barbara Opel told detectives, "but nobody wanted to go home. Nobody wanted to go back there. Nobody wanted to go to sleep, so we went to Denny's. And then Misty went with us, it was everybody."

"Barbara wanted food that we were no longer serving and made a scene until she got what she wanted," recalled Leslie Kaestner, their waitress. "She and her daughter ordered lots of food, but the two boys with them didn't eat anything. Barbara told me that she had been working for her employer but now was looking for work. Her daughter laughed very loudly at this. In fact, Barbara and Heather were so loud and obnoxious that several guests got up and left."

Kaestner noticed dried blood on and around Derek's right ear. "I asked the kid if he hurt himself, and Barbara said that he recently had his ears pierced, and that the ears must be infected."

They paid for their meal with a credit card, according to Kaestner, and then left the restaurant. "Then she was calling in orders for, like, four or five days after that," Kaestner recalled. "Coming in and complaining about everything. I do believe all those orders were paid for with credit cards. She parked that U-Haul right across the street. Opel said that she couldn't get it into [the] parking lot."

Kaestner admitted a twinge of regret for not double-checking the ID on the credit card Opel presented for payment. "Three days later, I was watching television and they showed the suspects on TV. I called my boss, Todd Bailey, and I said to him, 'I took a stolen credit card.'"

"How would you know that?" asked Bailey.

"Todd," replied Kaestner, "I'm watching the news, it's seven in the morning. Those people who were just arrested for murder, I served them that night!"

Kaestner's skin crawled as she recalled Barbara Opel's remarks over her Denny's Grand Slam breakfast. "She said that all of a sudden she became unemployed, and they all started to laugh. Not all of them. I'm not trying to protect the little one and Jeff, but they were just staying out of it. Barbara Opel and her daughter were the real loud ones, real obnoxious. Rude," said Kaestner, "extremely rude."

Since Opel and the kids often ate at Denny's, Kaestner's memory of events, and their sequencing, is problematic. Barbara Opel rented the U-Haul several days after the murder, and no charges to Heimann's credit card were made for meals at Denny's following the U-Haul rental. This is not a character defect for Kaestner, rather simply validation of the old police adage that eyewitness accounts, especially after the passage of time, are always subject to revision.

Various versions of the attack, and the chaotic aftermath,

differ slightly, one from the other, but the essential elements remain unchanged: emotionally immature and easily manipulated children, under the influence of a demanding and deceptive adult, killed Jerry Heimann.

"Hiring children, particularly a group of children, to commit a crime is extremely rare, and unwise," said Pete Smerick, a former FBI profiler and now a member of the Academy Group, which does behavioral and forensic consulting.

"Normally, you don't find somebody recruiting a whole slew of people, particularly young people. That becomes very risky," Smerick commented. "And it's the old story— the more people who know, the more likely you are to get caught. What motivated the young defendants in this case may never be known. It could have been kicks or cash," he said. "Kids under the influence of alcohol or drugs might do something they might not ordinarily do. You've got to look at what kind of a background does the kid have who's going to consider doing something like this."

"If you wanted to hire teenagers to murder someone," asked Chris Dickinson rhetorically, "where would you look? You wouldn't go to the ranks of the Eagle Scouts. You wouldn't track down the honor students to commit a crime like this. You would go and find the very people that Barbara Opel employed in this case—kids with no significant adult influences in their lives, who are just drifting and hanging out."

None of these youths were from remarkably stable backgrounds, and each was singularly ripe for exploitation. Barbara Opel's persuasive abilities relied less on reasonable arguments than on lies, coercion, and intimidation.

"This murder, its aftermath, and the attempts by those involved to cover it up," said newsman Stevens, "is so incredibly bizarre, so twisted in both its conception and execution, that I don't think we have ever witnessed a more tragic destruction of human life—not only by homicide, but by the manipulation of vulnerable youngsters. This story isn't a 'whodunit,'" Stevens rightly noted, "it is a 'how the hell did this ever happen in the first place?'"

The very mention of the Heimann homicide stirs emotions. Anger, disbelief, and outrage often becloud the overarching issues. Jerry Heimann was murdered at either the direct command or indirect encouragement of a greedy, sick, manipulative woman who did nothing to stop acts of ultimate cruelty.

"Jerry Heimann, dying of terminal cancer, afflicted with pain, suffering both physically and emotionally," remarked private detective Fred Wolfson, "was killed by a deadly predator who, in the process, also committed the most repulsive and perverse child abuse in contemporary history. Heather's best friend, Marriam Oliver, is the perfect example of a potentially wonderful kid whose entire life was butchered by lies, deception, and the twisted plotting of Barbara Opel."

"I'm in eighth grade at Evergreen Middle School in Everett, Washington," Oliver told detectives. "I get A's and B's on my report card. In my free time, I like to skate and play basketball." She also told police that she had no idea why they wanted to interview her.

"Oliver told us that she last saw Heather at school yesterday," reported the interviewing detectives. "She said that Heather appeared fine. Oliver told us that she was not having behavioral problems in school at the present time, but she did admit to being a troublemaker while in the sixth grade and attending North Middle School. She told us that she has been a suspect in a harassment case in the past [and] that she underwent counseling for that incident. Oliver then suddenly 'recalled' the first name of the male living with Heather's family—Jerry."

"What would you think if I told you that Jerry was dead?" asked Detective Neussendorfer.

"Ohhhhh," replied Marriam Oliver, "that would be scary."

"Why would that be scary?"

"Well, if he were murdered like people on *America's Most Wanted,*" she answered, "that would be scary."

"Marriam," said the detective, "I didn't say anything about Jerry being murdered."

As the questioning continued, Oliver told detectives how mean Jerry was to Heather. "I didn't see him being mean to Heather myself," she acknowledged, "but I heard about it all the time from Heather's mom, Barbara."

Detectives took a brief break from interviewing Marriam Oliver, and discussed Oliver's responses and their suspicions that she was not being completely honest with them. When they returned to the interview room, they confronted her directly.

"At first, she denied any involvement," said Neussendorfer, "but later opened up and told us of her involvement in the homicide. Oliver told us that she had been approached by Barbara Opel to kill Jerry Heimann, but Oliver declined because she didn't think she could do such a thing. She told us how Opel continued to solicit individuals for the murder of Jerry Heimann. Eventually Barbara Opel got Heather's boyfriend Jeff to agree to commit the murder. Oliver agreed to assist in the murder by stabbing Heimann to make sure that he was dead."

CHAPTER 6

According to court records, Marriam Oliver's birth mother suffered from extreme medical issues with problematic behavioral symptoms.

"In simple terms," said Jeff Reynolds, "Marriam's mom was all fucked-up, on booze and other drugs. Little Marriam, named for her grandmother, tested positive for cocaine at birth. Her father is unknown. She and her brother were taken in by her grandmother, who, with love and patience, dedicated herself to giving those kids a good life."

"Me and my sister had the best brother-sister relationship ever," said Marriam Oliver's younger brother, J.P. Marriam attended all of his baseball games, encouraged him in his studies, and helped him with his homework. "We were so close. She was the person I looked up to. She was always there. When I had any problems, she'd be the first person to have my back. She was always there for me, a huge support to me."

Her grandmother was supportive of Marriam and her brother, but when Barbara Opel entered Marriam's life, the grandmother's influence paled next to the domineering style of Heather's mother. She played upon Oliver's sense of loyalty and friendship, plus a twisted sense of justice, to enlist her in the murder of Jerry Heimann.

"Mrs. Opel was a buddy to all of Heather's friends," said Marriam Oliver. "She hung out with us at the local skating rink, took us to the movies, took us out to eat, walked around the mall, and she talked to me on the phone all the time." Heather's friends even called Opel "Mom."

In February, Mrs. Opel hosted a Valentine's party and invited some girls to spend the night. One twelve-year-old guest said Barbara Opel let teens drink beer, smoke marijuana, use the backyard hot tub, and have sex in Opel's bedroom. The girl, who attended Evergreen Middle School with Opel's daughter and Marriam Oliver, said she didn't engage in any illicit behavior that night.

The girl's father, Mike Wassemiller, was furious when he found out weeks later what had gone on at the party. When he dropped off his daughter and her best friend, he had gone into the house and chatted with Barbara Opel to make sure the party would be safe, he said.

"I'm absolutely shocked—I'm ashamed I let my daughter spend the night there," he said. "I trusted her." Marriam Oliver received numerous clandestine telephone calls to her Everett house from Barbara Opel. Heather Opel would be on the phone at first to fool Oliver's grandmother into thinking it was a friend on the phone, when Barbara Opel actually wanted to talk with her.

Many of those conversations were aimed at discrediting Jerry Heimann, she said. Barbara Opel told Marriam, for example, that Heimann threw an ashtray at Heather in a rage. "I got mad because she's my best friend," said Marriam. "I didn't want anyone hurting her.

"Barbara Opel and I talked on the phone all the time," said Marriam, "and she brought up the idea she wanted to kill Jerry. But I thought it was in a joking manner, and I didn't take it seriously at the time."

The telephone call came around March 18 that year, and Barbara Opel persisted with several more attempts at recruitment. "One time she asked me directly, 'Do you want to kill Jerry with us?' I was shocked. I said no."

Marriam Oliver later had a change of mind, and an equally revealing change of story, once detectives gathered more information about her participation.

"If we got caught," confirmed Marriam, "we were told to blame everything on Jeff."

According to Barbara Opel, Marriam offered to kill Jerry Heimann—whether or not anyone helped her. Marriam, of course, believed there were valid reasons to kill Jerry because Barbara Opel fed her nonstop stories of highly fictionalized abuse.

These dramatic vignettes were characterized by such phrases as "he almost hit Heather," "he almost hit Derek," "I was afraid he was going to hit so and so," or "he could have easily hit so and so." Upon reflection, Marriam admitted that she never heard of Jerry actually hitting anyone, only that he "almost" hit someone. She was also told that Jerry strangled Heather. Heather, who confided in Marriam about everything, never mentioned any such incident.

With daughter Heather and Marriam Oliver on board, Barbara Opel wanted an unrelated male presence in her murderous plan. "She offered me ten thousand dollars to kill this guy, Jerry Heimann," said Danny D'Angelo. "She had it all worked out. If things went wrong, she already had someone else all set up to take the blame." That "someone else," according to D'Angelo, was Heather Opel.

"Me? Mom was going to blame me? I thought we were always going to blame Jeff," said Heather.

It was Marriam Oliver who first revealed that there was

an earlier plot to kill Jerry Heimann by the same method, except with different underage participants. Marriam knew those individuals only by their first names: Brandon, Chris, and Danny.

"She told us that she was supposed to assist those individuals by leading them up to Jerry Heimann's room," recalled Detective Neussendorfer, "but apparently Danny decided against committing the murder at the last minute, and called it off."

The "Danny" in the story was Danny D'Angelo, Heather Opel's surrogate "big brother."

"Danny D'Angelo was Heather's best male friend, but not her boyfriend," explained her mother. "She has other good male friends too, such as Brandon Carter and Chris Mathies. When we go to the Skate Deck—and that means the entire family, plus usually Marriam Oliver, Heather's best friend—I sit and watch them skate. When we are at the Skate Deck, Heather and Marriam usually hang out with Brandon, Chris, and Danny."

"Well, I know Barbara from the Skate Deck," Danny later recounted to police. "I know her daughter Heather from school. I actually used to take care of the two younger kids once in a while. Sometimes I would give them money, and other times they would help me out. I used to stay with their family once in a while before they even lived with this Jerry Heimann, and, pretty much, they just helped me out when I needed it."

According to Danny D'Angelo's statement given to police investigators, on or about the first of April, Danny got off the big yellow school bus near his house and started walking home. "It was then that I saw Mrs. Opel driving on her way to pick up Heather from school," said

Danny. "She stopped and picked me up, and then she asked me if I would kill this guy."

Slightly taken aback, Danny inquired as to the underlying motivation for her sudden interest in homicide. "I went, like, 'huh?'" Danny confirmed. "Then she told me that this guy, her roommate—she didn't tell me his name—physically and mentally abused her kids while they were staying there. She didn't tell me anything that he did. She was, like, real vague, except she offered me ten thousand dollars if I would murder this guy. I asked her how I would get paid, and she said she would pay me two hundred dollars a week until the ten grand was paid off."

The young boy was not favorably impressed with Opel's murder-for-hire offer. "I'm a schoolkid, not a hired killer," said Danny. "The whole thing was just too weird, and a bit scary. I figured it was better to play it cool and tell her that I would think it over, instead of calling her a crazy-ass psycho bitch and jumping out of the car. Maybe she would kill me too, ya know?"

Six days later, Danny was essentially homeless. "I needed a place to stay and wound up over at Opel's. Right away, she starts in again about having me kill this guy. She wanted me to do it that night. I told her that I'm a Christian, and I can't really kill anybody. But there was no stopping her nagging me, telling me that Heather and Marriam would help me do it. I finally said that she had to find someone else, because I just wouldn't do it."

Two weeks following Danny's after-school offer of money for murder, he found himself hounded at the Skate Deck by Barbara Opel. "She was once again nagging me to do it," recalled Danny. "This was the Friday before spring break, and she was still offering me all that money, plus a bat and a knife. She really put the pressure on—you know, bringing up the fact that she had helped me in the past and that she wanted me to return the favor. I outright refused altogether, but Barbara wouldn't accept it, and she badgered me at every opportunity—especially when my judgment was impaired. I mean, she may be a crazy bitch," said D'Angelo, "but she knew how to pick vulnerable kids, put on the pressure, and take advantage of their weaknesses.

"The more she got on me, insisting and begging that I do it, the more I got thinking about it," said Danny. "She promised me that I would never get caught, because if the cops were ever involved, she was going to blame everything on her daughter Heather. I got thinking about it because I needed the money, and she was going to pay me out of his bank account, and I was getting high, so I wasn't thinking too clearly. Anyway, we got some weapons. I had a bat and the girls—Heather and Marriam—had steak knives.

"The plan," said Danny, "was pretty much that Heather was supposed to get him, and I was just supposed to watch just in case he tried to get away. Well, I was running it all through my head, and I figured it wasn't really a good idea. So I just stopped the whole thing. I wouldn't go through with it. I told them that I'm not into this. I told them that they could do it without me, but then I talked them out of doing it. I thought after that, it was all over. I didn't think they were really going to go through with it."

Danny saw Barbara Opel with Jeff Grote one week later. It was Friday, April 13, about 10:00 P.M. at the Strawberry Lanes bowling alley in Marysville. "She was in a maroon Camaro, and they also had a gray Firebird. I knew where those cars came from, because I saw them at the guy's house when I went there before. She told me, 'We done it.' When she said that, I knew she meant that they had killed him. She was kind of happy, but then excited and fearful. I can't quite find the right words to describe the expression, but she had a smile when she said it. I kind of thought she was lying about it. I didn't see her after that, and I didn't see Heather either. Honestly, I didn't think they were going to follow through because I got the impression that they needed me," said Danny, "and that without me, they would give up on the whole idea because they wanted someone to help and someone to blame. I didn't help. They got Jeff, obviously, and so they got what they wanted— someone to help do it, and someone they could blame. When it came out in the news, I was shocked that it was real. I was glad that I didn't do it, that I had enough brains or whatever to not do it."

Having the brains to not do it isn't the same as having the brains to not almost do it. When Danny eventually shared his story with Everett Police, they arrested him, charging him with attempted assault.

"That makes perfect sense," said Fred Wolfson. "Danny had a history of run-ins with the law. He stole things, and, at first, he wasn't the least bit cooperative with authorities. Well, it is amazing what a little deal making will do. When D'Angelo agreed to testify against Barbara Opel, a new world of opportunity opened up for him."

"Danny's dependency on drugs and alcohol is the foundation of his problems," said Max Harrison, his defense lawyer. "It was Barbara Opel who snared Danny. She provided a haven for youths without strict guidance from parents. He is certainly not a murderer. In fact, it was Danny who talked others out of killing Jerry Heimann."

"You are at a crossroads," Judge Knight told Danny. "You can become a productive member of society or be warehoused in a prison for the rest of your life." The judge suspended a sentence of between thirty and forty weeks, but warned the youth that if he violated conditions of probation, "I will give you the maximum sentence I can give you, and that's a promise."

* * *

When Tiffany's father, Henry, refused to participate, and young Danny backed down the staircase to homicide, Barbara Opel was not dissuaded. Alternately portrayed as a dim-witted pawn in Barbara's game and the murder's underachieving mastermind, Jeff Grote was the next selected participant and predesignated fall guy.

Those who knew Grote said they noticed a change in him after he started dating Heather Opel. "Yes, that's when Grote began to change," agreed Dianne Groves, owner of the venue where he had skated for years. "Not long before the murder, Barbara Opel and the two teen girls—Heather and Marriam—came to the skating rink to see Grote, and they caused a scene by swearing and harassing my staff and customers. They were pretty scary."

"She tried to get all sorts of different people to kill Jerry," said Jeff Grote, "and when she couldn't find anyone, she finally asked me. I got in touch with Kyle Boston and 'Little Michael.' Barbara told me that we didn't have to kill him. She had someone who would do that, once we beat him up. We were going to beat the shit out of him, and then this other person would finish him off." The "other person" was thirteen-year-old Marriam Oliver.

As with the other youths, Grote first feigned ignorance when questioned by police. "He was given a can of pop and two candy bars, and a short time later he was given a container of soup and some crackers," said Detective Brouwer. "Jeff Grote signed that he understood his rights and signed the waiver portion, agreeing to talk to us. Jeff was asked if he knew why he was here."

"Someone is missing," answered Jeff.

"Who's missing?"

"The guy's name is Jerry. I've never met the guy and wouldn't know him if he passed me on the street."

"Jeff, do you know what we've been doing for the past several hours?"

"No, what?"

"We've been talking to people about Jerry being dead, and people were saying that you killed him."

With no hesitation Jeffrey Grote said that all he did was knock him out.

"Who was supposed to finish him off, Jeff?" asked detectives.

"Marriam Oliver."

"Did she finish him off?"

"Yeah, she beat his head in with a baseball bat."

Further questioning revealed that Jeff Grote had waited in the bedroom of Jerry Heimann's invalid mother. Using an aluminum baseball bat, he had hit Jerry Heimann in the back of the head, knocking Jerry Heimann to his knees. Grote also admitted hitting Heimann a few more times and admitted to trying to cut Jerry Heimann's throat with a knife.

"I hit him at least four times, twice in the head, once in the ribs, once on the back," said Grote. "Heather stabbed him, and so did Marriam. Kyle Boston was hiding in the kitchen, and Michael was upstairs. They punched him at first too, but they ran away scared and took off in Jerry's Firebird. We caught up with them later at the bowling alley and they had Misty with them. We had the body with us in the back of the truck."

"I was at the bowling alley," recalled Jimmy Burleson, brother of Michael Smathers and cousin of Kyle Boston. "My sister and I were there bowling. Anyway, my sister comes in and says Kyle and my brother are outside in a stolen car, and they're covered in blood."

"I was standing outside the bowling alley," confirmed Jimmy's sister Desiree, "because I didn't have enough money to get in. I was standing there with my friend Seanna when my brother Michael and Kyle Boston drove up in a gray Firebird. Also in the car was a girl named Misty, who was sitting in the backseat. I got permission to go in the bowling alley and get Jimmy."

"They weren't covered in blood," said Jimmy, "but I told Michael to get out of the car."

"They argued," Desiree remembers, "and Jimmy threatened to tell their mother. At that point Michael got out of the car. About twenty minutes later, Jeff Grote and his girlfriend, Heather, arrived in a black pickup truck. I noticed something in the back of the truck, but I didn't get close enough to see what it was. When I approached the truck, Jeff told me to get away."

A second vehicle, which she described as a maroon car, entered the parking lot behind the pickup truck driven by Jeff Grote. In the car was Barbara Opel, Marriam Oliver, and what she believed were Barbara Opel's children in the backseat. "I couldn't see the kids clearly in the backseat, but I could hear them."

"My brother comes into [the] bowling alley with me," said Jimmy, "and then Jeff Grote pulled up in a truck with a reddish Camaro following him."

"Kyle," yelled Grote, "get in the car and follow me."

"I asked my brother what was going on," said Jimmy. "He said he would explain it later when we got home. He was kind of shaky, and he said they did some crazy shit."

"When my brothers do anything wrong," said Desiree, "they never tell me, because they know I'll tell our parents right away. Because of that, they don't tell me anything."

"The next morning," recalled Jimmy, "they were all telling me that [they] regretted doing it and they wished that [they] wouldn't have done it. They were feeling bad, and they didn't really want to do it. They were all calling Jeff and trying to get a hold of him to come give 'em money or whatever, and then, like, about three o'clock or so, they got a hold of him. Jeff came over and then we got in the car. . . . Jeff was letting me drive and we drove a couple blocks away, and Jeff was telling me what happened. . . . He said that the body was in the back of the truck while they were at the bowling alley, and then the truck broke down and they had to put [it] in the back of the gray Firebird, and they drove away and went and . . . I don't know exactly what they did with it, but Jeff told me that they poured acid on his face."

Burleson's information was essentially accurate. Jerry Heimann's body was transferred to his Pontiac Firebird because the pickup stalled and wouldn't start. The body was then driven to the Tulalip Indian Reservation, where the kids removed it from the car, and Jeff Grote kicked it down a hillside in the woods.

"People are always dumping bodies here," said Scott Keeline, who has lived on the reservation for twenty-seven of his thirty years. "Who knows how many they haven't found?" At least seven bodies have been found on the reservation in the past decade.

"Basically, we're a rural location right outside an urban location," said John McCoy, the Tulalip Reservation governmental-affairs director. "Unfortunately, we're an easy target for people wanting to dump things." Forensic experts say criminals are often drawn to such places— sparsely populated but easy to get to—when choosing where to dispose of bodies.

"I've been here nineteen years, and there are bodies left all over," said Leon Reichle, chief investigator for the county medical examiner's office. "Jerry Heimann's killers, for example, drove to the reservation to drop off his body after beating him to death in his Everett home."

After dumping the victim's body, Jeff Grote, Heather Opel, Barbara Opel, Derek Opel, Tiffany Goudeau, and Marriam Oliver, along with Misty, drove to Denny's, on Pacific Avenue in Everett, and had something to eat.

"Misty?" Jeff Reynolds raised his hand at the Everett Denny's where KRKO's Tony Stevens, famed Hollywood private investigator Fred Wolfson, and he were discussing the case in retrospect. "Excuse me, but remind me where this Misty comes into the picture. Where did she come from, and what does she have to do with any of this?"

CHAPTER 7

Misty Moore, 3½ months pregnant, lived with her mom on McDougal Street. For a young girl, Misty had a backlog of experiences outstripping women twice her age. "I was smoking meth when I was eleven," she admitted, "and I've been locked up in juvenile detention three times. My dad is dead and my mom is in prison on nine felony charges. I had never met or heard of Barbara Opel or Jeff Grote in my entire life until that night. I only knew Kyle and Marriam because we went to the same school. I hadn't seen Kyle in about six months. The only reason I went with them is because I was bored and tired of staying home. I wish I had never gotten into that car.

"That was between ten and eleven at night," recalled Misty. "And Kyle's cousin Mike was with him. I knew the car he was driving wasn't his, because first of all, he's not even old enough to have a driver's license. First he tells me that the car belongs to his uncle or his cousin, but he lies all the time so I didn't pay much attention. Anyway, they were looking for my brother," said Misty, "but he wasn't home. I was really bored sitting home alone, so I went along for the ride to the Skate Deck. Long story short, they drove me home to get some money for gas so we could drive around more. We went to the Skate Deck, the bowling alley, and by Michael's dad's house. The bowling alley is in Marysville—Strawberry Lanes. When we were driving, that's when Kyle told me that Jeff Grote beat a guy with a baseball bat."

She said both Kyle and Michael bragged about the incident, and both claimed that they hit the victim "upside the head." They also told her that they thought the victim was dead. "I didn't pay much attention to what they were saying, because I know Kyle brags and lies all the time, so I don't believe anything he says. They told me that the guy they beat up was beating this lady and her kids, and that Jeff was tired of the man's behavior and wanted to beat the guy down with a baseball bat. They said that the car we were in belonged to the man they beat up, and that they thought he was dead, and that Kyle was supposed to take the Firebird back to the guy's house, but that he didn't do it."

"Later on that night," she explained, "after, like, a half an hour to an hour passed, Barbara and her children pulled up, and so did Jeff Grote. I was still sitting in the gray Firebird. Kyle was in the front seat, talking to a friend. Barbara was in a maroon Camaro and Jeff was in a black truck. She told Kyle to get the car back to the house, and all of us wound up back in Everett, and some people followed Kyle or Tony back and gave Kyle and Michael a ride back to Marysville.

"I wanted to go home," said Misty. "I told Barbara that I wanted to go home, and asked for a ride. She said she would take me home, but she had something she had to do first."

Misty had no idea that "something" meant disposing of Jerry Heimann's dead body. She didn't hear anything about an actual murder until Marriam Oliver filled her in. "I found out when the truck wouldn't start. I asked what was going on, and Marriam told me, and then Jeff told me more."

The essential exposition of the action so far was provided

during the impasse in automotive inertia. Jeff Grote told Misty that there was a dead body tucked in the truck bed.

"C'mon, help us move it, Misty!"

"No, I'm not touching it," she replied nervously. "I don't want anything to do with any of this!"

Misty was as stuck as the pickup. Perplexed and panic-stricken, the pregnant teen decoded the unspoken message that she was going along for the ride—whether she liked it or not.

"At the dump site," said Misty, "Jeff threw the victim's body down a hill, and then threw away the baseball bat and a bloody plastic bag. Then we went to dinner at Denny's, and they talked about how far down the hill the body went. I didn't have much of an appetite."

According to Misty, Barbara paid for the meal, while Misty went to the restroom. She also used Denny's pay phone to call home. There was no answer. "I was scared and confused," said Misty. "They told me not to call the police, and I didn't. I was really scared. They said to me, 'Don't call the cops, 'cause if you call the cops . . .' They didn't say exactly what they would do to me, but I got the message."

Back at the Heimann residence, Misty was assigned to the cleanup crew. "My job was to help wipe up the blood in the back of the Firebird. I used paper towels to try to soak it up. That didn't work too well." With that task completed, Misty again timidly pleaded for a ride home. "Barbara kept promising me a ride," said Misty, "but there was always something that had to be done first."

One of those "somethings" was cleaning up blood and brain matter from the kitchen floor and walls. "Heather and her mom finally told me the reason they killed him," Misty explained. "They said the reason why they did it was because he wouldn't let them do what they wanted in their life, like he would only let them go out once a week, and that was on Saturdays, and that he was doing things to her daughter, like hitting her daughter and stuff."

Misty finally convinced Jeff Grote and Barbara Opel that she had to be taken home because she had an important doctor's appointment. "That was a lie," said Misty, "but I was scared and wanted to get out of there. Jeff gave me a ride home early in the morning, and he was talking about putting some acid on the guy's face, or something. I just kept quiet and wanted to get away from them. I was really scared. I mean, Jeff pretty much threatened me more than once, and Barbara was right there backing him up. I didn't dare call the cops."

Misty didn't call the cops, but she did confide in her mother. "She didn't believe me at first," said Misty. "But she said that if it was true, it was my problem."

Misty's story altered slightly each time she recounted it. In her first version she didn't help dump the body. In her next retelling, she told detectives that she "touched the blanket" in which Jerry Heimann was wrapped. She then changed her story again, admitting that she picked up Heimann's legs by the blanket and helped move the body to the Firebird.

"She told me that she was standing in the back of the truck when this occurred," reported Detective Kiser. "She said that she could not lift it further and she told the others that the victim was too heavy for her to lift. She said that Jeff Grote then picked up the victim by his torso and moved the body over the top of the tailgate. She said someone else assisted in moving the victim's body into the back of the Firebird, but she did not know who that person was. She thought perhaps it was either Marriam Oliver or Heather."

Two days after the incident, on Easter Sunday, Misty received a phone call from Heather's mother. "Barbara Opel took me out to eat at the Royal Fork Restaurant in Marysville. The others were there too. We didn't talk about what happened, because this girl named Desiree was also with them, and they didn't want to say anything in front of her."

After telling detectives what she knew, Misty was transported to the Denny Youth Center and booked for rendering criminal assistance, first degree. "What the hell was the poor scared girl expected to do," complained Reynolds. "It seems horribly unfair to arrest her for being trapped in a vehicle with murderers and a dead body, about which she knew absolutely nothing."

Detectives had bigger fish to fry than the unfortunate teen caught up in the investigatory net. "Detective Fortin and I began preparing the paperwork to book Barbara Opel," recalled Joe Neussendorfer. "I went into the interview room where Barbara Opel was being held. I had her put all of her personal property into a paper bag. In Barbara Opel's wallet I located two hundred and seventy dollars in cash and a check made payable to Jerry and Evelyn Heimann. The endorsement on the back of the check was signed over to Barbara Opel. During the interview Barbara Opel acknowledged that she was not employed and she had been stealing money and forging checks from the victim's account after the murder. I impounded the check and the cash as evidence.

"I asked Barbara Opel about the check found in her wallet," said Neussendorfer. "She told me that the check was old and that Jerry had signed it over to her because he owed her some money. She said she didn't cash it because she didn't have a bank account."

She told Neussendorfer that the cash found in her wallet was part of the $410 in child support she received from Derek and Heather's dad. She said that she received his support check and cashed it on April 18.

"Amazing, isn't it," remarked Jeff Reynolds, "that

she didn't cash the check from Jerry because she didn't have a bank account, but she did cash the check from her ex-husband."

Kyle Boston and Michael were located and arrested by the Marysville Police Department. When Neussendorfer began reading Boston his rights, young Kyle said, "I want my dad here."

Detectives allowed Boston to call his mother and she agreed to come to the station for the interview. "We also attempted to locate Kyle Boston's father, but were unable to do so at that time because Kyle Boston did not have any phone numbers where his dad could be reached. While we waited for the arrival of Boston's mother, we took a lunch break. While on the lunch break we were advised that both Kyle Boston's mother and father arrived at the police department. Detective Fortin contacted them and arrangements were made for Boston's father, Steve Boston, to be present during our interview of his son."

Because Boston had not waived his constitutional rights during the first attempt to interview him, they again started reading him his constitutional rights from Everett Police Department form PD-06.

"Kyle, wait a minute," said his father, Steve. "I want you to get an attorney."

"Detective Fortin and I planned on ending our interview at that time," said Neussendorfer. "However, Kyle continued talking and making unsolicited remarks."

"I didn't do anything, Dad," insisted Kyle.

"It's your right to have an attorney present," Neussendorfer told him. "Your father can advise you, but it is up to you whether or not you want to talk to us."

Kyle turned in confused despair toward his father. "Dad," he said, "I don't know what to do."

"Can I ask you one question?"

"Sure, Dad."

"Were you there?"

"Yeah," Kyle replied.

"Okay," Steve Boston told his son, "then don't say anything."

Kyle continued to talk. "I don't want to go to prison for the rest of my life because I decided not to say anything. I want to tell my side of the story."

"I told Kyle that we could not continue talking," said Neussendorfer, "because of his earlier statement about an attorney. I then informed Kyle that he would need to make up his mind whether or not he wanted to speak with us."

Kyle paused and thought about it for a little while. His father reminded him that he could stop the interview at any time. "Is that true?" Kyle asked the detective.

"Yes, that's true, Kyle."

"Well, I want to keep talking, even if there isn't an attorney here."

Kyle Boston signed the form indicating that he understood his rights. He also signed the waiver portion of the form indicating that he wanted to speak with the detectives. Steve Boston signed the form as a witness.

"I was there when Jeffrey Grote attacked Jerry Heimann, but I didn't participate in the attack," said Kyle Boston. "I know Jeff Grote real well, and he called me up one night and invited me to go skating. After Jeff picked me up, he brought me to Heather Opel's house and told me that we had to wait until the man living there came home. When Jerry came home, Jeff Grote attacked him with a white aluminum baseball bat.

"Jeff hid in a bedroom just inside the entry door," explained Kyle. "As Jerry walked through the door, Jeff came out of the bedroom and hit him from behind. He fell to his knees, and Jeff kept beating him. Jeff asked me to help, but I refused. I just grabbed the car keys and took off."

Kyle Boston denied participating in the assault, and also claimed that it was Jeff Grote alone who attacked Jerry Heimann. "I was sitting on the couch in the living room when this happened," he said. "I got scared and left when Jeff began hitting the guy, and told him to stop. After we left, me and Michael drove to the bowling alley in Marysville. The next day Jeff threatened to kill me if I said anything.

"He paid me for keeping my mouth shut," said Kyle. "Jeff came to Michael's house the next day with Heather's mom. We went to Wells Fargo bank, and Jeff cashed a check and gave Michael and me each a hundred and ten dollars."

Steve Boston asked his son if Jeffrey Grote had threatened him when Kyle told Grote to stop the assault. "No, Jeff just told me to shut up."

"Listen, Kyle," said Detective Neussendorfer, "we've talked to all the other people involved who were there at the house that night. They all gave statements describing their participation in the assault. They all talked about what you did. You did hit the victim in the face, didn't you?"

Kyle began to nod his head up and down in an affirmative manner. At this point Kyle Boston's dad told his son to get an attorney. Neussendorfer continued by asking Kyle if he had struck the victim with a souvenir bat. Kyle Boston did not answer the question, but replied, "I want an attorney."

Detectives ended the interview and allowed the youngster a few moments alone with his father while they prepared the booking paperwork. Once the paperwork was completed, Boston was transported to the Denny Youth Center, where he was booked on the charge of murder in the first degree.

Prior to securing for the evening Detectives Fortin and

Neussendorfer went to the crime scene and checked on the progress of the Washington State Police (WSP) lab technicians and the Everett PD personnel who were processing the crime scene.

In solving crimes, physical evidence is critical. All experienced investigators and attorneys know that eyewitnesses have never been 100 percent dependable. Only physical evidence—properly recognized, studied, and interpreted—is infallible.

"Of all responsibilities shouldered by the forensic scientist," remarked Brent Turvey, forensic scientist and criminal profiler, "the reconstruction of the circumstances and behaviors involved in a crime is one of the most important. In conjunction with agreeable witness accounts, a crime reconstruction may be a powerful instrument of corroboration. In the face of conflicted witness accounts, it may provide an objective view that points to one possibility over another. In the absence of witness accounts, it may be used to investigate and establish the actions that occurred at the scene of a crime. The role that crime reconstruction can play investigatively and legally should never be underestimated."

"The biggest problem with crime reconstruction," said Fred Wolfson, "is that it can be performed by someone who is overconfident. All the training doesn't mean a thing if you don't put it into consistent practice. On the witness stand many so-called experts will cite all their training and experience as a substitute for actual facts from the case file. Experience should make the expert more responsible for justifying his or her opinion with scientific facts."

Conclusions regarding the circumstances and behaviors elicited from the physical evidence are not always accurate and correct. "It is an intense process with imprecise results," insisted Wolfson. "That doesn't mean that crime reconstruction isn't valuable. The real value is in establishing the general circumstances of a crime, demonstrating links between victims, suspects, and offenders, corroboration of witness statements, providing investigative leads, and identifying potential suspects."

Forensic analysis in general, insisted Wolfson, and crime reconstruction in particular, is concerned with those conclusions that can be logically drawn from the evidence, as well as with those that cannot. As such, the consideration of both the strengths and limitations of available physical evidence is an important part of crime reconstruction.

Dr. Edmond Locard's work formed the basis for what is widely regarded as a cornerstone of the forensic sciences, "Locard's Exchange Principle." This doctrine was enunciated early in the twentieth century by Edmund Locard, the director of the first crime laboratory, in Lyon, France. Locard's Exchange Principle states that with contact between two items, there will be an exchange.

"In other words," explained Wolfson, "anyone who enters a crime scene leaves something and takes something away. There is always an exchange. That's why you want to keep a crime scene as pure as possible."

By recognizing, documenting, and examining the nature and extent of this evidentiary exchange, Locard observed that criminals could be associated with particular locations, items of evidence, and victims. The detection of the exchanged materials is interpreted to mean that the two objects were in contact. This is the "Cause and Effect Principle" reversed; the effect is observed and the cause is concluded.

Forensic scientists also recognize that the nature and extent of this exchange can be used not only to associate a criminal with locations, items, and victims, but also with specific actions.

Crime reconstruction is "the determination of the actions surrounding the commission of a crime." Dr. Edmond Locard, in speaking similarly on the subject of physical evidence and crime reconstruction, maintained that "the criminologist re-creates the criminal from traces the latter leaves behind, just as the archaeologist reconstructs prehistoric beings from his finds."

"The physical evidence left behind at the crime scene," stated Dr. Richard Saferstein, retired chief forensic scientist from the New Jersey State Police Lab, "plays a crucial role in reconstructing the events that took place surrounding the crime. The collection and documentation of physical evidence is the foundation of a reconstruction."

Crime scene processing is a very intricate and interwoven task. As each crime scene is different, a variety of approaches may be used. There is, however, a basic crime scene protocol adhered to in all crime scenes. These basic functions or tasks are as follow: (1) interview, (2) examine, (3) photograph, (4) sketch, and (5) process.

The crime scene technician must interview the first officer at the scene or the victim to ascertain the "theory" of the case—what allegedly happened, what crime took place, and how was the crime committed. This information may not be factual information, but it will give the crime scene technician a base from which to start. Next the technician examines the scene to ascertain if the "theory" of the case is substantiated by what is observed in the general layout of the crime scene.

Photographing the crime scene is the third step in the protocol, the purpose being to record a pictorial view of what the scene looks like and to record items of possible evidence. Crime scene photographs are generally taken in two categories, overall views and items of evidence.

A "sketch" is completed by the crime scene technician

to demonstrate the layout of the crime scene or to identify the exact position of the deceased victim or evidence within the crime scene. In the "old days" a sketch was exactly that—a hand-drawn representation. A sketch may not be completed on every case; however, some form of sketching usually occurs in most cases, i.e., on a fingerprint lift card to identify exactly where the latent was recovered.

The Everett Police Department utilizes sophisticated techniques far surpassing the old sketching methodologies. "The data collected from the crime scene by Officers Whatley, Davis, and I," said Mark Zehnder, "was downloaded into our CAD program, which allowed me to draw a diagram of the scene."

The computer-aided design (CAD) program Zehnder mentioned is for investigators who need to create 2-D and 3-D crime scene diagrams. With these new computer programs, it is easy to create accurate, realistic, 3-D views of any scene, which are ideal for aiding in the investigation and also for courtroom presentations.

The last step in the protocol is to actually process the crime scene for physical and testimonial evidence. It is the crime scene technician's responsibility to identify, evaluate, and collect physical evidence from the crime scene for further analysis by a crime laboratory.

All this technology and sophistication, however, does not make the process immune from error. Evidence may have been altered prior to or during its collection and examination. The integrity of the evidence must be established. The physical evidence in the Heimann homicide was subject to significant movement, alteration, and other influences.

Barbara Opel and her young henchmen may have used sponges, mops, and bleach to remove physical evidence, but they accomplished only superficial cleaning. WSP forensic scientist Margaret Barber found "heavy deposits of blood" after she removed the molding strip and baseboards from the kitchen cabinets and also the carpet tack strip between the kitchen and dining area.

The area where there is the least amount of blood is usually the area where the assault began, and the area where there is the most amount of blood is usually where it ended.

"The carpet in the dining room also had a large area of bloodstaining near the kitchen doorway," she said, noting that stains were also found on the east wall of the kitchen, the south kitchen floor, and on the living-room carpet. Barber's efforts also revealed two blood swipes on the front door, and another near the door hinge, approximately thirty-five inches above the floor.

The more they looked, the more bloodstains they found. Spatter stains with a shallow angle of impact were on the east wall of the kitchen and living room in an arcing pattern originating from the kitchen, just west of the doorway to the dining area. In this same pattern of impact spatter were bloodstains on the south doorjamb of the bathroom and on the north-facing projection of the north doorjamb of the bathroom. These stains impacted nearly perpendicular to the doorjamb surface. Some had a slightly upward trajectory.

"The highest stain on the east wall, north of the bathroom, was approximately ten inches south of the diningroom doorway and sixty-one inches above the floor," stated the scientist. "The highest stain on the entire east wall of the kitchen was on the lower edge of the wall clock, at the south end of the kitchen. This stain was approximately sixty-nine inches above the floor and sixty inches south of the dining-room doorway."

South of this area, the pattern begins a downward trajectory. Bloodstains were also found on a four-by-four support beam on the east wall of the living room. One of these stains was 127 inches south of the dining-room doorway, and similar bloodstains were located on the south wall of the dining room extending to the east as far as the stairway in the southeast corner of the room, which led up to the second floor. This was approximately 102 inches east of the kitchen. The highest stain on the south wall of the dining area was approximately forty-eight inches east of the kitchen and fifty-nine inches above the floor.

In the kitchen blood splatter stains extended from the floor almost to the ceiling, and were found on the topmost part of the kitchen cabinets. "The angle of impact of these stains indicated an area of origin a few feet south of the cabinets in the doorway between the kitchen and dining room."

Barber observed several indications that an attempt was made to clean up. "The areas of carpet in the dining room and living room that were within a few feet of the kitchen floor had brushlike marks that appeared consistent with the use of a carpet-cleaning machine," she reported. "General swabbings of all areas of the kitchen floor tested positive for blood, though no stains were obvious in the swabbed areas. The wallboard below the north kitchen cabinet appeared to have been wiped or washed, as the blood deposits were mainly in the recesses of the textured surface. The base of the floor lamp just north of the support beam in the east wall of the living room had been wiped on one side. A sponge mop was propped against the north counter in the kitchen. Bloody smears were on the lower part of the handle, up to approximately the center of the handle."

Each stain tells a story, depending on the angle and the placement. "Several bloodstains having a downward and slightly eastward trajectory were on the north wall of the dining room," she reported. "These stains may be from an event close to the north wall, such as dropping or moving a bloody person or object on the floor.

"A single stain was on a glass panel of the chandelier in the dining room. In its present orientation, the area of origin was apparently from the west.

"Small spatter bloodstains were on the side of the dining-room table at one end. However, the origin of these stains could not be determined reliably, since the table is moveable and may not be in its original position at the time of the event."

When Heimann's body was moved from the kitchen to the back door, bloodstains were left behind. "A horizontal bloody swipe was on the leading edge of the sliding door between the dining room and the backyard," reported Barber. "The swipe was between fourteen and twenty-seven inches above the floor and indicated motion of a bloody object from the dining room into the backyard.

"Passive blood drips were on the floor of the upstairs bedroom between the bed to the north and the microwave oven and dresser to the south. No blood trail was found leading either to or away from these stains."

All the mops, Clorox, and sponges were no match for the knowledge, perception, and education of forensic scientist Margaret Barber. The crime fighters weren't the only ones calling in qualified, knowledgeable help.

CHAPTER 8

The family of Kyle Boston retained attorney Doug Ricks to represent him, and Ricks encouraged his client to cooperate with the police in their investigation. Detective Neussendorfer called Ricks and scheduled an appointment with him to interview Kyle Boston at the Denny Youth Center.

"Boston told us that Jeff Grote called him approximately one week before the murder and asked him if he would ever kill someone," said Neussendorfer. "Boston reportedly said no to killing anyone but agreed to help beat somebody."

"Thursday night, the twelfth, Michael came up, stayed the night with me, and Jeff called me when I was in the bathtub," said Kyle. "Michael answered the phone and he knocked on the bathroom door and said, 'Jeff's on the phone,' and I said, 'I'm in the bathtub,' and he goes, 'Well, dry yourself off,' and he slid the phone under the door. Jeff asked me to come beat up this guy, and I told him that we couldn't do it tonight because we just got home. He asked about the next night, and I said, 'That might work.'"

On Friday, April 13, Grote picked him up and took him to Jerry Heimann's home in Everett. "Jeff was gonna hide in the bedroom. Me and Michael were gonna hide by the fridge, but I hid on the stairs, and everybody else was behind me. Jeff was gonna hit him after he walked through the door, and then I was gonna come up and hit him. Marriam had a knife in her hand that she got out of the kitchen drawer.

"Heather's mother told us that we better not chicken out," said Kyle. "I just thought we were gonna beat the guy up, that's all. I had a pellet gun with me that I brought along to maybe scare the guy, 'cause it looked like a real gun. I was just trying to look cool, but I never used it."

Michael had a small wooden bat, Grote had an aluminum bat, and, according to Kyle Boston, Derek Opel had a small souvenir bat. "Jeff hit the guy with the baseball bat in the back of his neck, and when he fell to his knees," said Kyle, "I ran over and punched him in the nose as he was trying to get back up. That made his nose bleed, and I got blood on my tennis shoes. Later I cleaned them up and gave them to my cousin Jimmy."

According to Kyle Boston, things spiraled out of control after he swung his one and only punch. "It wasn't the way Michael and I thought it would be," he lamented. "We thought all that was gonna happen was that we were gonna beat the guy up for being mean to Heather. When we saw it getting more than that, we just ran out of there almost right away, because this wasn't the way I thought it would be. I didn't see Marriam use the knife at all, and I didn't see Jeff's girlfriend, Heather, do anything either. I mean, even later, when I talked to Jeff about all this, even Jeff said, 'I thought they were just gonna beat him up,' but then Marriam said that she was gonna beat him to death with a bat, or cut him or something, but she didn't, at least not while I was there. I didn't see Heather do anything either. I thought all we were gonna do was beat the guy up a bit, teach him a lesson, but not anything like what happened. That's why me and Michael got out of there right away.

"As we were leaving," Kyle recalled, "I looked back and I could see the guy on the floor with his legs moving, and there was blood everywhere in the kitchen. Well, we ran outside, but then I went back inside [and] asked Jeff to give me the keys to the car."

Grote tossed him the keys to the Firebird, and the two youngsters—Kyle and Michael—drove away. "We drove the Firebird to my friend Mark's house in North Everett," said Boston. "I don't know his last name, but he's fourteen and we went to North Middle School together. Mark wasn't home, but we did talk to his sister, Misty, and we took her with us. We left there and went to the Marysville bowling alley. We were there about forty-five minutes when Jeff showed up in the guy's truck."

Behind Grote was Barbara Opel in Heimann's maroon Camaro. "Marriam got out of the Camaro and began yelling at us about returning the Firebird," said Kyle. "I had my friend Tony drive the Firebird back to Everett, following Jeff and Mrs. Opel in the other two vehicles."

Tony asked his pal Geritt to follow along in his Honda. The killers now had an entourage of innocent bystanders participating in a ghoulish caravan.

"We get back to Everett," recalled Kyle's friend Tony, "and Barbara Opel is circling the block, looking for us. She told me where to go and we pulled in front of the house and parked it. Then she pulled up behind us, we got out and gave her the keys, and she said, 'If you boys want to borrow the car anytime, just give me a call, and you can borrow it anytime you want.' She wrote her number down and [gave it] to Kyle. Before we walked away, Kyle walked up to her car and started whispering to her."

"He had a gold watch," Kyle whispered to Barbara Opel. "Did you take it?"

"No," replied Barbara. "If you want it, go down there and get it."

"Fuck no, I'm not gonna touch the body."

"Well, if you want the gold watch, you have to tell Jeff and maybe he'll get it for you."

Before the conversation about who would get the ghoulish glee of stealing Jerry Heimann's wristwatch could reach its conclusion, Heather Opel came running up from down the street.

"Mom," called out Heather, "the truck broke down. It won't start."

At this juncture in the posthomicide adventure, Tony's friend Jared came around the corner in his Honda, rolled down the window, and told Tony and Kyle to get in the car. Jared drove them back to Marysville, where, in the Strawberry Lanes parking lot, he told them to get out.

"Kyle," said Jared, "I don't want you to ever talk to me or come around me again!"

"Tony had asked me if I'd follow him and give him a ride back," recalled Geritt, "so me and a couple guys, Bud and Josh, buddies, followed along to give Tony a ride back. I had no idea where we were going, why, or anything. In the other two rigs was a heavyset blond lady in the Camaro, and a guy and a girl in the truck."

Everyone pulled up in the front of a white house, "kind of up something of a hill," as Geritt described it, where the primary participants exited their vehicles and huddled together for consulting. "The truck's down the street, right around the corner. They're just parked right there and the guy and the girl were still in it. The truck is still running, and everybody else was just huddling up, talking and something."

Geritt stayed in his car, but he could catch bits of the

animated conversation. "You can take the car anytime you want," Barbara Opel told Kyle Boston, "just keep your mouth shut, understand? You just let me know when you want to use the car, and I'll give you the keys. Just keep your damn mouth shut."

Why Kyle was supposed to keep his mouth shut did not remain a mystery for long. Kyle immediately began bragging about his participation in the homicide.

"I didn't take him seriously at first. He's got a lot of stories. Pretends that he's like a little gangbanger guy. You know, likes to rock people all the time, but I've never seen him rock anybody. It's all talk and hearsay."

When Kyle showed off the flecks of blood on his shoelaces, Geritt was neither impressed nor alarmed. The young driver became uneasy, however, when Kyle revealed details of Heimann's demise. "Little bats," said Geritt, "that's all I remember. A Mariner bat, I think he was talking about. Like a little souvenir bat or something, and they said they were gonna get rid of the body with sulfuric acid or something. They were going to put it in his mouth, I think."

As they pulled into the bowling alley, Kyle announced that Jerry Heimann's body had been in the pickup truck, underneath the wheelbarrow. "I started believing him, like, later that night when I was dropping him off and he wasn't gonna go home, he was gonna stay at Tony's house."

The following day, according to Kyle Boston, Jeff Grote cashed a check at Wells Fargo bank and gave "hush money" to Michael and to him. "I don't know where Jeff got the check," said Boston, "or who it belonged to, but the money we got was to keep Michael and me from talking to the cops. Jeff went back to the bank another time and got more money for me and Jimmy. He gave Jimmy a hundred dollars," Kyle explained, "because Jimmy was supposed to buy Jeff some hydrochloric acid."

"Yeah, I told Grote that I could get the acid, but I wasn't really going to get it," confirmed Jimmy. "I just wanted to have the car to drive around in. So they gave us the keys to the red Camaro and told us to hurry up and go get the acid. Well, we didn't go get the acid. We just drove around all day, and then I called him the next day, Sunday, and told him that we had to run from the cops and that the acid was up in Darrington. It was all a lie."

Jimmy wasn't the only character with a fascination for motorized vehicles. "After Jeff gave us the money," said Kyle Boston, "we drove to a gas station to put some gas in the Firebird. When Jeff went in to pay for the gas, I just took off with the Firebird and left him there. After I stole the Firebird, I dropped off Jimmy, then I picked up two other friends and we went to the Everett Mall. That's where I ran away from the security guard, and the car, I guess, got impounded."

Piecing together the diverse versions of events from primary participants, Detective Fortin finally and flatly told Barbara Opel that police had no doubt that she was directly involved in the death and disappearance of Jerry Heimann.

"But I'm not," protested Barbara Opel. "I didn't actually do anything. It was Jeff. He beat the shit out of Jerry with a baseball bat, and Heather stabbed him once.

"Of course," she added, "I don't know that for a fact, because I didn't actually witness it, but that's what Jeff told me. I never hit Jerry," Barbara said. "It was all Jeff. It all started with Jeff. Jeff was tired of Jerry yelling at us. Heather was scared of Jerry too."

The reason Grote knew of Heimann's abuse was because he had heard the stories from Barbara Opel—stories confirmed by his new girlfriend. By the time Jeff Grote entered the basement with Heather, Barbara Opel had already decided that Jerry Heimann deserved death.

"I knew something had to be done," Barbara Opel told detectives, "when Jerry actually threw something at Heather. When I came home, she was standing in the corner, crying. That was [in the middle of] March. That's when I decided that we had to get rid of him. To kill him."

"Marriam wanted to do it first thing," explained Barbara. "Jerry had called Marriam profane names, really bad names, and asked me to take her home right then and there. He didn't want that black bitch in his house, and Marriam said, well, we all said that we wished that he was dead." Barbara Opel didn't explain that it was Marriam attacking Jerry with a baseball bat that prompted his angry outburst. "We wanted to kill him or beat him up extremely bad."

In Barbara Opel's version of events, all acts of violence were instigated by Jeff Grote. It was Jeff, Barbara insisted, who fired up Kyle and Little Mike with diatribes about Jerry's dreadful abuse of Heather and the other youngsters. According to Barbara Opel, Jeff Grote was so outraged by the abuse perpetrated against his new girlfriend that he murdered Jerry Heimann, ran roughshod over her and the other children, and even forced her beloved child to mop up afterward.

"Jeff wanted to beat the shit out of him, and the two boys agreed to help," said Barbara, who pinpointed the day of the murder as Friday the thirteenth. "Marriam arrived between three and five in the afternoon. Kyle and Michael arrived at around seven P.M.

"I admit that I encouraged them at first," she told detectives, "because I'd already planned to move out, but the night that it happened, I had second thoughts. In fact, I told

Kyle and Michael that they should leave before Jerry got home so he wouldn't be angry, but they said, 'No, fuck him. We'll just beat his ass.'"

Asked about the disposal of Heimann's body, Barbara Opel's answer was direct and clear: "Jeff dumped him. It was Jeff who wrapped the body in green sheets. Jeff even complained that the body was too heavy for him, so he used a wheelbarrow. Jeff even made Heather and Marriam help clean up the blood!"

"If the murder of Jerry Heimann was all Jeff Grote's doing," asked detectives, "why did you ask Henry to kill Jerry?"

"Oh, that was a joke," explained Barbara. "I was kidding. I told him that he could leave his wife and move in with me and the kids if he killed Jerry, and that if he did it, I would pay his parking tickets. It was a joke, really, just a joke."

Neither Henry nor the detectives found Barbara Opel amusing. Henry, as detectives knew, derived less than minimal amusement from her invitation to murder. "At first, everyone directly involved had somewhat similar stories," recalled Detective Neussendorfer, "but as we asked more and more questions, the stories began changing. Bit by bit, we were able to get a better idea of what actually took place. Barbara also claimed that three or four days prior to our interview, she and her family were confronted by Kyle, Michael, and Jimmy. She said that she and her family were threatened with bodily harm if they said anything to the police. Opel told us that Michael's brother Jimmy was known to carry a gun."

"They came back," Barbara told detectives, "and said that people had been talking about what Jeff had done, and Jeff would be the one to get in trouble. That nobody would say anything on them because of their brother. You know, 'cause of Jimmy there would blow them away. He would kill anybody, and Jimmy and Kyle both had guns on them that were loaded when they came, and they threatened me and the children and even Jeff that if their name was even brought up anywhere 'round this situation, that we would be killed."

The convoluted and constantly changing versions of events were sufficient for arrest, but conviction requires extensive, convincing documentation. Everett Police began the painstaking work of compiling all physical evidence, including relevant paperwork.

Detectives Zehnder and Garcia were assigned to collect Visa receipts from various local businesses where Jerry Heimann's charge card was used after his death. They collected a receipt from the Skate Deck for $20, signed with Jerry Heimann's name, and another from the Rodeway Inn. Barbara Opel's room rent was paid for on April 19 by a Visa card belonging to Jerry Heimann.

There was a charge of $30.70 to his card at the Denny's on Pacific Avenue, and the rental fee for the Rug Doctor used to clean blood from the carpet was also charged to the account of the man who bled to death.

Sunday, April 22, 2001

Detective Fortin drove to the Safeway store on Broadway. "I wanted to talk with Mr. Richard Paige, the store's manager," recalled Fortin. "When I showed up, he had a Rug Doctor carpet cleaner with him."

"This is the machine Barbara Opel rented," said Paige, "and here's the receipt book."

Receipt number 4456381 indicated that machine #OM16082 was rented to Barbara Opel on April 13, 2001, at 10:02 P.M. After comparing the serial number on the machine and the serial number on the receipt, Fortin took the white copy from the receipt book, along with the machine, and impounded them both at headquarters. A few hours later, Fortin received a message: *Contact Cheryl at Safeway.*

"I called and spoke to Cheryl," recalled Fortin. "She said that if I called Mike Rush, in Phoenix, Arizona, he would be able to get me the original copy of the charge slip that was signed when the carpet cleaner was rented. I was given a phone number and a fax number."

Rush asked for the account number, date and time of the rental, and the store number.

"Cheryl at Safeway, she gave me the store number, 474, the amount of the rental, $56.67, the date and time, 04-14-2001 at 2151 hours, and the account number, 4428680002542442. I immediately asked why the date and time were different, and Cheryl explained the reason that the date and time are different than what I saw on the receipt was that they process these a day later."

Detective Fortin next examined an Everett Police report, 0001-8151, entitled "Suspicious Circumstances." The report, filed by a Mrs. Pohren, told how Barbara Opel tried renting an apartment from her on April 18 and 19.

"I asked her if she remembered whose name was on the check," said Fortin, "and she said that one of the names was Jerry and the other was Evelyn."

Fortin next spoke with both Wells Fargo and Bank of America regarding Heimann's checking and savings accounts, and faxed a "fraud information sheet" to each of them in order for the police to receive activity reports on the various accounts. Wells Fargo faxed back fifteen pages of activity on Heimann's accounts from December 2000 to February 2001.

"I next called Jerry Lush at Bank of America," said Fortin, "and asked him about getting a copy of Jerry Heimann's account activity. I was told that the easiest way would be to have the executor of Heimann's estate file a claim with customer service."

The executor of Heimann's estate was his son Greg. "Three bank accounts," recalled Heimann, "had fraud committed on them on and after April thirteenth, the day my father died. The extent of the fraud was around fifteen thousand dollars."

As forensic scientist Margaret Barber discovered, the automobile used to transport and dump the body of Jerry Heimann was a barely operational bucket of bolts. The flaked paint and overworn interior were not the worst aspects of its cosmetic deficiencies. Heavy blood deposits were noticeable on the hatchback door, the latch itself, on the rubber seal running along the trunk's rear lip, and under the jack. Barber also found bloodstained paper towels stuffed under the jack in the bottom well.

Already a clutter of old food wrappers and other disposable waste, the car's interior contained two quart-size bottles of muriatic acid and some safety goggles. Evidence of blood wasn't limited to the trunk. Barber found bloodstains on the car's center console, parts of the passenger-side seat belt, and the driver's shoulder harness.

"Everything about Barber's report," recalled investigator Fred Wolfson, "was indicative of a bloody body being in the trunk, and that whoever put the body in the trunk got it on themselves and into the front seating area."

Barber's expertise was next applied to Jerry Heimann's Dodge pickup truck. The scientist found Heather Opel's diary on the passenger-side dashboard, and copious bloodstains on the tailgate, frame, and bumper. Under the tailgate's release handle were the type of bloodstains found when someone with bloody hands opens the release hatch.

After comparing blood samples and DNA taken from stains found at the Heimann residence and on the kitchen mop used to clean up the house, Barber concluded that Jerry Heimann was a possible source of bloodstains found in the home and in both of Heimann's vehicles.

All evidence items from both vehicles were returned to the Everett PD. The extracted DNA was retained in the WSP Marysville Crime Laboratory. Aside from bloodstains and DNA, another item of interest was retrieved from one of Heimann's vehicles—an item subject to significant scrutiny and evaluation: Heather Opel's diary.

The diary contained nursery rhymes, thoughts on sports, and mundane happenings: *Today, I brought a lunch from home,* she wrote at one point. The next entry, a month before the murder and in apparent reference to the promised dirt bike, was, *So my mom said if I helped kill Jerry I can go get one.*

If murder was equal to nursery rhymes, observed psychologist Marty Beyer, who later read the diary, it's probably because Heather thought of it as fantasy. She "didn't believe that the murder was going to occur. And then as it started to happen, she felt that it wouldn't have made any difference if she had spoken up. . . . She did what her mother told her to do." Once again, we return to Heather Opel's life lesson number one. Be it on the basketball court or in the bedroom, playing sports or committing murder, always mind your mother.

Truth may or may not be stranger than fiction. The evident truth in the Heimann homicide was that truth is more stupid than fiction. "Fiction has a plot," remarked investigator Fred Wolfson, "but Barbara Opel's gang of underage underachievers was commanded by a woman too shallow for a plot. In fact," insists Wolfson, "the various plots to kill Jerry

Heimann were devoid of plot. There was no plan, no thought of how they were going to kill Jerry and not get caught."

"If you look at the Heimann homicide, and ask yourself, 'What was the plan?' you won't find one," agreed Jeff Reynolds. "Every preplanned murder, with few exceptions, is plotted by someone who egotistically believes they can get away with murder, cover their tracks, manipulate the crime scene, et cetera, and place themselves above suspicion. In this case, we have a preplanned murder with absolutely no plan—no thought as to anything beyond the event of death."

The lack of rational thought within the irrational framework of cold-blooded murder was not merely an unusual characteristic of the case, but a matter of exceptional importance. "Maybe Barbara Opel never watched a murder mystery," offered Tony Stevens. "When it came to hiding and destroying evidence, she was clueless. Consider what she did with Jerry Heimann's checkbook."

CHAPTER 9

"I found the dead guy's checkbook," said Mr. Lansing to the officer on duty at the Everett Police Department.

"What are you talking about?"

"My cousins Joan and Debbie were visiting from out of town, and they were staying at the Rodeway Inn, room 126," he explained. "Well, before they checked out, they wanted to make sure they didn't leave anything behind. They found this checkbook and check card under the mattress in their motel room. They didn't want to give it to the motel manager because of the check card. So they gave it to me to return to the guy because they were on their way back out of town.

"I went to the address on the checkbook to give this Jerry Heimann guy his checkbook," said Lansing, "but when I got there, a neighbor told me what had happened at the house, so I brought the checkbook here to the police station."

The officer sealed the checkbook and check card and impounded it to the regional property room.

"Who conceals damning evidence by hiding it under the mattress? Either a child or an adult who has the thinking abilities of a seven-year-old," insisted Jeff Reynolds. "If seven-year-old Tiffany stashed it there, it would make sense. If Barbara Opel stashed it there, she has the brain of a seven-year-old."

Funeral services for Jerry Heimann were private; the obituary succinct:

Jerry D. Heimann, 64, born January 5, 1937 in Valley City, North Dakota, graduated from Rogers High School in Spokane, WA. He worked for Boeing in Everett, WA and in the Minute Man Program. He was preceded in death by his father Vernon Heimann; two brothers, Robert and Gene Heimann and his son Mitchell Heimann. His mother Evelyn Heimann; a sister Joy Korsno; two sons, Greg and Michael Heimann; one daughter Colleen Muller and six grandchildren survive him.

"Back in September 1982, his son Mitchell Heimann, then twenty-two, was killed when the motorcycle he was operating was struck by a car," recalled Teresa Heimann. "The death haunted Jerry and plunged him into deep grief for about ten years. But he managed to find joy again. Yes," said Teresa, "he was married five times, including twice to the same woman, and at the time of his death was on good terms with all of his former wives. He'd planned ahead for death and had arranged to be cremated. He actually told the family to flush him down the toilet," she said, "but we vetoed that. His ashes were placed near his son's grave in Machias."

While Jerry Heimann's relatives and friends mourned his death, Heather Opel sat in the Denny Youth Center watching the murder's news coverage on television.

"I never met anybody so proud of something so sick,"

remarked Amy T. who, for twenty-four hours, was with Heather Opel at the Denny Youth Center. "She was bragging about it the whole time. All she ever wanted to do was watch the news because she thought she would be on there. I told her, 'Listen, little girl, you're not on the news. If anybody is, it's your mother.' Oh, that made Heather so mad when I said that!

"Heather said it was her boyfriend who actually killed him," recalled the girl. "She said that she stabbed him twice after he was dead. She said she did it for her mother, and she said that she was gonna get a dirt bike if she did it, and her boyfriend was going to get two hundred and fifty dollars, and that Marriam Oliver would get free skating tickets."

Amy was not favorably impressed by Heather's attitude toward the murder of Jerry Heimann. "That girl, Heather," she remarked, "is one sick fuck."

Her opinion of Marriam Oliver was far more sympathetic. "I didn't even want to ask Marriam about what happened." According to Amy, her demeanor was one of despondency and despair over her actions. "She can't sleep at night," said Amy, "because she can't stop thinking about it all the time."

While the kids waited at the Denny Youth Center, Barbara Opel was tossed into the overcrowded Snohomish County Jail. In 2001, the Snohomish County Jail was famed for its substandard facilities for females: eighty-plus women, fifty-three beds, and two toilets. Women had no sick rooms, no psychiatric units, and no separation of minimum- and maximum-security offenders.

"There are so many women, they have to be locked down twenty hours a day," said Corrections Officer Lourie Happy, a veteran of the jail's two female units. "Tensions run high, and there's no outlet for their frustrations. Women behind bars are an afterthought. They're second-class citizens in a system designed for men. Some of them call their families, screaming, 'Get me out of here! I can't take it anymore!'"

"Twenty years ago, when people were designing jails, they didn't think women would be committing more serious crimes," said Susan Neely, public safety program manager for the Snohomish County executive's office.

"The Snohomish County Jail was built back in 1986," recalled Tony Stevens. "Back then, it had twenty beds for women, and it was rare if they had five female residents. By 2001, the daily population would sometimes hit as high as ninety, the cells were double bunked, and the women who didn't have beds slept on the floor, head to toe, on plastic cots. It was worse than a second-rate dog kennel."

While doggedly pursuing all forms of evidence against the suspects, authorities placed Barbara Opel's two youngest children, including Bill Opel's eleven-year-old son, in protective custody. "It struck me as strange," said Jeff Reynolds, "that little Michael was arrested, but Derek wasn't. According to Kyle Boston, Derek was armed with a baseball bat during the assault."

Teresa Heimann said she and others in the family don't hold Derek or Tiffany responsible for any wrongdoing. "We don't hold any grudges against those two little ones," she said. "We feel so bad for them."

"Derek and Michael were close in age," said Jeff Reynolds. "Derek admitted that it was he who got the sheets for wrapping Jerry's body. Aside from the Heimann family's attitude, I'm still not sure why Derek skated."

Patrons of the Everett Skate Deck, familiar with Grote as an athletic speed skater of decent reputation and no previous history of crime or violence, were horrified by his involvement in the Heimann murder. So was Jeff Grote.

After hitting Jerry Heimann three times, Grote dropped his weapon to the ground. In a state of shock and panic over what he had just done, Grote sat down on the stairs with his head in his hands.

"People were saying things, but I didn't much hear them,"

he later told police. "I panicked, and just sat there, with it all going on around me. That's when Heather took the bat and whacked him a few times, then Marriam Oliver got the bat. She hit him with the same bat I had, but I had thrown it down. I had to stop."

"I never would have suspected that Grote would be involved in anything more slippery than oiling his Rollerblades," commented a fellow patron. "I used to see him speed skate, and he was a worthy competitor. The Skate Deck is a fun family place—has been for years—it's the kind of place where good kids have a good time. You just don't think of healthy, active, sports-minded youngsters, such as Jeff Grote and Heather Opel, being cold-blooded murderers. I find it very difficult to think of Jeff Grote as someone who would think of this on his own, and convince others to go along with him, or that he would be so selfish and shallow that he would murder someone in exchange for some money."

It wasn't just money. The first lure that hooked Jeff Grote was sex. "It's a classic femme fatale scenario," remarked Jeff Reynolds. "This is just like something out of film noir. A flawed, susceptible teen is lured into murder by irresistible sex. If you think having sex with Jeff Grote within hours of directly approaching him was Heather's idea, wise up."

Seattle attorney Michele Shaw, Heather's court-appointed attorney, insisted that Barbara Opel urged Heather to sleep with Grote so he could be recruited for the killing. "Her mother used her as payment for murder," said Shaw, "then commanded her to kill too. She is a victim herself."

"It sounds stupid to say he's a good kid," Grote's attorney said. "But this was shocking to everyone who knows him because there was nothing in his background to suggest he was some kind of predatory teenager."

PART II

CHAPTER 10

When Jerry Heimann was murdered in 2001, the phrases "predatory teenager" and "superpredatory youth" were not uncommon. Although juvenile crime in America had dropped approximately 40 percent since 1994, two-thirds of Americans believed that juvenile crime was rising, out of control, increasingly violent, and "worse now than forty years ago." Running throughout news stories was the stereotype of the "superpredator" youth.

"The youth crime wave has reached horrific proportions from coast to coast," stated John J. Dilulio, who, at the time of Heimann's murder, served as assistant to the president of the United States and first director of the White House Office of Faith-Based and Community Initiatives. Although he had access to accurate information, Dilulio spawned the blatant lie known as the "superpredator myth."

"No one in academia is a bigger fan of incarceration than I am," stated Dilulio in 1996. "Between 1985 and 1991, the number of juveniles in custody increased from forty-nine thousand to nearly fifty-eight thousand. By my estimate, we will probably need to incarcerate at least one hundred fifty thousand juvenile criminals in the years just ahead. In deference to public safety, we will have little choice but to pursue genuine get-tough law enforcement strategies against the superpredators."

Within a year Dilulio's estimate for the growth in violent juveniles had escalated to 270,000, painting a horrific scenario of "fatherless, Godless, and jobless juvenile superpredators flooding the nation's streets."

All of these dire predictions proved inaccurate. Juvenile crime rates began a steady decline beginning in 1994, reaching low levels not seen since the late 1970s. According to Franklin Zimring, a leading legal authority on juvenile justice and director of Boalt's Earl Warren Legal Institute, "The evidence of a juvenile crime wave—either current or on the horizon—is no more substantial than the evidence that supports the existence of the Loch Ness Monster."

Voters and legislators across the country, of whom 82 percent derived their assessment of youth crime severity from news stories, were approving increasingly punitive measures to address this imaginary increase in youth crime. Policies advocated as a direct result of consistent media misinformation ignored the founding principles of America's juvenile justice system: prevention, intervention, and rehabilitation.

It was into this climate of fear-based misinformation that decisions were made regarding the futures of Heather Opel, Kyle Boston, Marriam Oliver, and Little Michael.

"At the state level the superpredator myth played an important role in amending laws on juvenile crime to get tougher on youthful criminals," recalled Tony Stevens. "Legislators modified state laws to permit younger children to be tried in adult criminal courts. More authority was given to prosecutors to file juvenile cases in adult courts."

During the 1990s, rates of juvenile incarceration increased, and more minors were sentenced to adult prisons and jails. "Proponents of harsher penalties frequently and consistently claimed that rehabilitation had either failed or should not be available to young people who commit violent crimes," said Jeff Reynolds. "The portrayal of rehabilitation strategies as failures, and incarceration strategies as successful, went unchallenged. It is difficult to run a tough-on-crime political campaign if there isn't a crime wave, and good news doesn't make for exciting headlines or gripping television news stories."

"As a newsman, it rather embarrasses me to admit the role media played in scaring the hell out of the public in the big lie," said Stevens. "Real crime was down, but crime news was way, way up."

"It is mean-spirited and just plain wrong to portray youth as criminals," added Jeff Reynolds, "when, in fact, they are much more likely to be victims of crime. Making scapegoats of young people doesn't make us safer, and it doesn't help our youth. It only blinds us to the abuse, neglect, and mistreatment so many kids suffer in our country today."

In Everett, Washington, there were two simple facts in play: (1) Jerry Heimann was brutally murdered by youngsters, and (2) the public saw this as confirmation of the "Predator Youth Epidemic." Everyone, from prosecutors and defense counsel, to the presiding judges and the defendants themselves, were all impacted—some more than others—by prevailing attitudes and altered public policy.

"Kill the little bastards," barked an outraged Everett resident. "They killed an innocent man, they should get killed too. That will teach them a lesson, and it will send a message, that's for damn sure."

Sending children to the gas chamber, strapping adolescents in the electric chair, hanging them by the neck until dead, or subjecting them to lethal injection are among the punitive actions forbidden under international law. The

United States signed and ratified the International Covenant on Civil and Political Rights (ICCPR) in 1992, but reserved the right to execute children and those who committed crimes while they were under eighteen. The only other countries known to execute underage offenders between 1990 and 2000 were Iran, Pakistan, Saudi Arabia, and Yemen. The United States executed more juveniles than the other four countries combined.

"Jeff Grote was charged as an adult with aggravated first-degree murder," recalled Damian Klauss, his attorney, "and that would have meant life behind bars if he was convicted. Given the facts of the case, that was a very strong possibility. He was too young for the death penalty to be considered," confirmed Klauss. "I had expected the case to go to trial, but then prosecutors offered a plea agreement."

Jeff Grote pleaded guilty to first-degree murder in Snohomish County Superior Court on September 10, 2001, agreeing to a fifty-year sentence in exchange for his testimony against everyone else.

As for the rest of "Opel's Little Helpers," the prosecutor's view was clear and concise. "We don't think juvenile punishment is enough," deputy prosecutor Chris Dickinson said. "This was basically a cold-blooded assassination for money. We're going to wait to see whether Judge French rules in favor of trying these teenagers as adults before we decide about charging them with aggravated murder."

Dickinson didn't intend for Misty Moore, the young girl who accepted the posthomicide ride from Kyle Boston, to face more than thirty days in juvenile detention for her coerced participation. The judge, however, felt different.

"The girl was not accused of helping kill Heimann, or of having any knowledge of the murder plan," recounted Sergeant Boyd Bryant, "and Misty wept as she told the judge why she didn't go home that night."

"I thought my mother would be mad," she said tearfully. "So I stayed and helped Barbara Opel. She asked me to do something, so I helped her do it." The girl broke down sobbing before completing her explanation. "I helped her clean up the blood."

Snohomish County Superior Court judge Ellen Fair gave the girl a five-month sentence, saying circumstances called for a more serious penalty than the prosecutor's recommended standard sentence of up to thirty days in jail. "There is something going on with a child who isn't so horrified by being asked to help cover up a murder that the first instinct isn't to run far and fast," said Judge Fair.

Wednesday, September 26, 2001

Superior court judge Charles French opened hearings to determine whether or not he should waive jurisdiction over the four accused teens. In Washington State, juvenile court judges clear the way for prosecuting juveniles as adults by waiving jurisdiction over individual juveniles. Under state law a case against a juvenile must begin in juvenile court; it cannot be channeled elsewhere without a juvenile court judge's formal approval.

In an attempt to keep the cases against these kids from going to adult court, experts in child psychology were brought in to evaluate the youngsters and testify before Judge Charles French. Exceptionally significant was the testimony of Marty Beyer, a clinical psychologist and independent consultant in Washington, DC.

Beyer's professional focus is on adolescent development: understanding how a youth's cognitive, moral, and identity development and trauma affect the commission of offenses, and designing developmentally sound dispositions. In addition to developmental assessments in individual cases, training, and improving services in juvenile facilities, she is also a consultant in statewide child welfare reform.

"Heather Opel was so in her mother's thrall she couldn't even consider refusing," Beyer told the court. "Her mother was the center—the only center—in her life, and her mother's control was unquestioned."

Beyer reviewed records of Heather Opel's life and summed it up succinctly: "chaotic." Child Protective Services fielded repeated reports of abuse and neglect. Barbara Opel's relationships with men were marred by domestic violence, the woman was destitute and moved her children twenty-two times in seven years.

"Opel was extremely controlling of her daughter," Beyer reported, "and a unique type of closeness developed between the two. As a result, the girl remained unusually immature in some areas, and to this day does not question her mother.

"In all the time I've spent with Heather Opel, she has said nothing but positive things about her mother," the psychologist added. "The girl is a youngster who does not have violent thought processes or a delinquent mentality, but instead views herself as an athlete and a good student. The teen would benefit most from treatment in a juvenile setting, not a lengthy prison sentence," Beyer said.

The entire purpose of the juvenile justice system in the United States was designed to protect children from close association with criminals, and to foster healthy transformation of the individual prior to adulthood. The United States Congress enacted the Juvenile Justice and Delinquency Prevention Act to remove juvenile offenders from adult jails, and separate juvenile offenders from adult criminals in correctional settings.

These provisions were based on the realization by Congress and the states that many juveniles were being confined in facilities where they simply did not belong, including jails and lockups for adult criminal offenders. "Sometimes this was done using the twisted justification that the kids would be taught a lesson," explained Shay Bilchik, administrator of the United States Office of Juvenile Justice and Delinquency Prevention (OJJDP).

"For example," related Bilchik, "a fifteen-year-old girl who voluntarily returned to her parents after having run away from home was placed in a county jail by a juvenile court judge to teach her a lesson. On the fourth night of her incarceration, a deputy jailer sexually assaulted her. Subsequent litigation revealed that the juvenile court judge routinely followed this punitive policy even with first-time truants. It was discovered that over the previous three years, more than five hundred juveniles—many younger than fifteen years old—had been locked up in the county jail, often for status offenses. On the day on which the trial was scheduled to begin, the county signed a consent judgment under which it agreed to stop confining children in the county jail for any reason."

Similar stories, some involving suicide, led Congress and many state legislatures to conclude that "in no instance should young people be detained in an adult jail or lockup," Bilchik said.

Young Heather Opel should not be charged as an adult, asserted expert Marty Beyer, because Heather was incapable of reasoning as an adult. "Adolescents do not think or act like adults because the juvenile brain is often incapable of adult reasoning because of its long maturation process," Beyer explained.

"Immature thought processes, difficulty with comprehension, unstable identities, moral values that are overshadowed by a sense of loyalty, or the effects of childhood trauma can make a young person incompetent to participate in his or her own defense," said Beyer. "The effects of immaturity are evident from the time the juvenile becomes involved in a crime, through the police interview, planning for hearings, and considering a plea.

"Telling a twelve- or thirteen-year-old child that they have the right to a lawyer may mean absolutely nothing to them," Beyer submitted. "They may not even know what a lawyer is, or what 'right' means in the context of the sentence."

For example, a fourteen-year-old was asked to explain "You have the right to remain silent." He answered: "Don't make noise." Asked to explain "Anything you say can be used against you," he said, "You better talk to the police or they're gonna beat you up." Asked to explain "You are entitled to consult with an attorney," he said he did not know. When told it meant he could call a lawyer, he said, "I never heard of a lawyer before. Now I know what it means to have a lawyer, but back then, I wouldn't know a lawyer to call and you have to have money for a lawyer."

A sixteen-year-old had similar comprehension problems. Asked to explain "You have the right to remain silent," he said, "The police are telling you when not to talk. I never could see why they said 'right' in that." Asked what would happen if the judge heard later that he would not talk to the police, he responded, "The police would tell the judge I was lying. I would get in more trouble by saying I didn't do it. Then the judge would say I must have did it."

A seventeen-year-old was asked to explain "You are entitled to consult with an attorney." He said it meant he could get a lawyer to help him in court, but he did not understand why the detective told him about getting a lawyer then. Like many young people, he had no idea that he could ask to have a lawyer present before he responded to police questions.

As for Heather Opel, Beyer was insistent that a professional analysis of her maturity, or lack thereof, pointed directly to an inescapable point: "The girl can't think like a healthy adult because she is a child who has been shaped by a life of trauma."

An examination of Heather Opel's diary provided more validation of the child's immaturity. Mixed in among entries about what the teen ate for lunch or her basketball games were nursery rhymes and frank discussions about plans for Heimann's killing, followed by a party. "The diary," said Beyer, "provides a good tool for the girl's therapy and could later help her reflect back on her childish minimizing of a brutal murder."

Prosecutors described the role of Barbara Opel's daughter, who had just turned fourteen, as "particularly striking" and her attack on Heimann "particularly savage." They said she told police that Heimann "had yelled and cursed at her and her younger siblings, and once threw something at her." Michele Shaw, her lawyer, said the girl had "a tremendous amount of remorse for her role in the incident." She "was directed to participate in this offense by the only adult who she knew in her life at the time—her mother, her caretaker, her protector," Shaw said. "Heather Opel is a very well-behaved girl outside this incident."

CHAPTER 11

"Heather has always been well-behaved," testified William Tri, her sports coach for over three years. "I never saw her get in arguments with any kids. I never saw her in any physical fights. I always saw her interact well with her brother and younger sister, both of whom really looked up to Heather. And she was always really loving and caring with her younger sister, Tiffany. And Heather and my two younger daughters just, you know, really delighted in doing things with Tiffany."

Sibling squabbles are not uncommon, but Tri never noticed any between Heather and her younger brother and sister. "Heather was always well-behaved and got along well with my two younger daughters, particularly my daughter Karissa."

A local attorney with a passion for sports, Tri vividly remembers his first meeting with young Heather Opel. "When I first saw Heather in the fourth grade, I remember walking into the gym and actually, I could tell I had a very strong group of kids—immediately—but Heather stood out particularly. And she was probably the finest basketball player at age fourth grade that I had ever seen or coached. She was not only a great player, very strong, aggressive, talented, but she fit in—she was new to the area and fit in well with the other kids. The other kids, at first, seemed to—including my own daughter, who was a year younger—seemed initially to be a little intimidated by Heather and felt that for several years, because she was so good, that perhaps she was a bit of a take over, control everything, and whatnot. But it didn't take long—Heather seemed to adjust well, and it didn't take long for her to assimilate into that group of kids, work well with them, and earn their respect and their friendship.

"After that season," recalled Tri, "I then had Heather on my softball team. She was an exceptional ten-year-old softball player. Heather was always a very enthusiastic kid, at least initially. I thought her enthusiasm really spilled out. She truly loved the sports that she was involved in, and I had a sense that that was one thing that she could really throw herself into with everything she had, and it was one thing that she excelled at. And I could tell also that her mother really pushed that."

Her mother also pushed buttons, and raised serious concerns about her behavior. "Barbara was difficult, if not impossible," said Tri. "I was around Barbara a lot, and when I asked her questions, how are things going or whatnot, she would not really respond."

Try as he might, Mr. Tri had difficulty explaining Barbara Opel's disconcerting nature. "I'm having a hard time putting this into words, because she made me uncomfortable. Barbara's way of talking to someone would be to blurt out extreme, over-the-top praise."

Overenthusiastic praise that rings hollow makes people uncomfortable, as do sudden angry outbursts of uncontrolled temper. "I know that the other parents were uncomfortable around her," said Tri, "not knowing if she was going to explode and yell something loud and inappropriate at her daughter or perhaps at an umpire at any second, and they just didn't feel comfortable speaking to her."

Barbara Opel didn't sit near the other parents: "She was standing around by herself, very close to us or the kids, where she would be able to yell out something at Heather, if she felt the need arose."

Dianara Slate, mother of one of Heather's teammates, also found Barbara Opel both intimidating and disconcerting. "I remember walking into the gym, wondering if I should say 'Hi' or smile at her, or if I should duck out of the way and get up to the bleachers as high as I could before she noticed me," said Slate. "She was very intimidating. She had a stern look to her. You knew that she would be up yelling at Heather and yelling, I would say, almost, even at the coach about how Heather was going to play. And that's not a parent's decision. That's the coach's decision, on where he's going to put the kids. She would pace back and forth, screaming at Heather during the game, yelling out things like 'How could you let them do that,' 'knock them out,' and things that were not encouraging words to be yelling to your children as they are playing a sporting game."

Coach William Tri also found Barbara's yelling off-putting. "She would get on Heather anytime she was less than perfect," he testified. "And although Heather was a gifted athlete, she made her mistakes, like everyone else. And Barbara would—whenever [Heather] made a mistake—Barbara would not only jump on Heather, but she would jump on her immediately, loudly, inappropriately, embarrassing to anyone who would have heard it. And I believe that affected Heather. And there were times that I tried to get Barbara to stop, but it was just—it was almost the type of thing that she could not control, being loud and overbearing and controlling. After the basketball season, the first year I had Heather as a player, I had seen Barbara make these types of yelling, inappropriate comments toward Heather in basketball games. And she would do this when they were beating teams, you know, thirty to nothing, or forty to two. And if Heather still missed a shot, she would get yelled at by her mother to the point that it was having a negative effect on Heather."

Mrs. Slate found Heather crying after a game because she feared her mother. "I remember one time after a game at the Evergreen Middle School," said Slate, "they had lost, and Heather was over in the corner crying. My daughter tried to console her. She was hugging her in the locker room, and trying to stop her from crying, and Heather just kept saying that she knew she was going to get in trouble on the way home.

"There was an awards ceremony," recalled Slate, "and it was a potluck affair for the basketball players. I remember Ms. Opel was sitting by herself with the youngest daughter, and I remember looking at her. She had flip-flops on and sweatpants and an old T-shirt. And when she stood up, I know she had no bra on. And, as a parent, you wouldn't come to an awards banquet just like that. You would take more pride in your child and in yourself for an important affair like that."

When Heather and her family were living at the Motel 6, prior to moving in with Jerry Heimann, Karissa Tri asked Heather why they were staying at the motel. "Heather told Karissa that it was because they were staying there while their family was building a new home, or getting a new house, or something to that effect," William Tri said. "The story changed as the months went by. Karissa pressed Heather a little bit about why they hadn't moved into the house yet, or when were they going to be moving, or why was she still living at the Motel 6. And Heather told her, at that time, to basically just drop it. She didn't want to talk about it anymore."

Tri also financially rescued the Opels on more than one occasion. "One time Barbara approached me and asked for a loan," confirmed Coach Tri. "This is when they were living at the motel. I gave her the money. Then Heather asked me for money after Barbara had. But Heather came to me in the dugout during a game, a Little League game, softball game, and handed me a note. And I didn't open the note until I walked outside. I believe I had walked over to the third-base coach's box there, to start doing whatever you do when the game gets going, with the batters and whatnot. I just kind of unfolded it to see if it was something I should show around to the other kids, but it was a note that was written in which Barbara was saying, 'Bill, we need seventy-five dollars or we will be thrown out on the street tonight,' something to that effect. I talked to Barbara about it later and told her that I simply wasn't in a position to be giving her seventy-five dollars here and there."

Tri was able to help out in other ways, he said. "I knew enough about their home life to know that money had to be a problem for her. I knew that Barbara didn't work. The checks that she had written for Heather's entry into Little League for the first couple seasons had bounced. I went to the board people who were involved and asked that they give her a scholarship. And in order to do that, they gave me a little form for Barbara to fill out, which described briefly her finances and her expenses that justified the giving of a scholarship, which was granted. I knew they were pretty much either on the street or living in the motel."

Although his daughter and Heather were close friends, there reached a point, admitted Tri, that his wife and he didn't want their daughter going over to the Motel 6. The problem wasn't so much the motel, it was Barbara Opel.

"That was more my wife than me, but we talked about it," he said. "I think one time we let Karissa go spend the night with Heather and her family at the room in the Motel 6. It was one of those situations, though, where my wife wasn't comfortable with the fact that they were living in a motel, and living there long-term. I don't think she had ever been there and seen the room. But I think the time that Karissa did stay there, she didn't get any sleep.

"My wife," explained Tri, "didn't like the lack of structure and discipline. Barbara would let the kids run across Highway 99 to get snacks at the store, at the supermarket across the street, in the middle of the night, and things like that. She did not want our daughters going over there, and preferred and always offered that if the kids were—whenever a game would get over and it was, like, a Friday night or a weekend night, the kids always wanted to go spend the night at invariably one place or the other, and they'd all start forming their little plans. And my wife would always try to encourage, you know, if you're going to spend the night with Heather, she's welcome to come over and spend the night here."

Barbara preferred a motel room full of kids, including her, staying up all night, watching TV, and eating junk food. "I remember," William Tri said, "there were times that the stipulation got to be 'If you want to spend the night with Heather, it was going to have to be at our house,'" said Tri. "Barbara did not want Heather to do that, but my wife would not allow Karissa to go over and spend the night at the motel anymore."

Well aware of Heather's living situation, her family's financial distress, and the overall weirdness of Heather's mother, Coach Tri attempted to set up some aid and intervention through a friend who worked with Child Protective Services.

"I had talked to this friend of mine," he testified, "who is a parent of another child that was on our same select softball team and she had observed Heather, and I believe had Heather out to spend the night at her house at times, and knew Heather and Barbara and their situation fairly well. And I knew with her position with Child Protective Services that she might have an idea of how to help Barbara with her living and financial situation. So I had told her that, about Barbara sending Heather to me with a note and that I had loaned the money and that, as I talked about, I wasn't comfortable loaning her the money, and my wife certainly didn't want me to continue to do that. And she suggested that I have Barbara contact her. She actually went so far as to line up assisted housing for Barbara and the family."

Coach Tri shared this good news with Barbara Opel, and told her that all she had to do was contact his friend Sandi. "I gave her Sandi's work number and said Sandi is waiting for you to call, you should jump on this right away, it's all set up."

Barbara never called Sandi, despite being evicted from the motel. Heather and the other kids were seen panhandling in the mall and living out of a car.

William Tri cared deeply for Heather Opel's well-being, and her involvement in the brutal slaying of Jerry Heimann was terribly out of character. On the witness stand in Judge French's courtroom, Coach Tri offered additional comments.

"The thing that's different about this," said Tri, "and that has to be considered, from my standpoint, is that her mother was the one that at least allegedly planned it and somehow arranged this group of kids to do this terrible thing. And I've struggled with, you know, would I be capable of actually influencing my twelve-year-old or soon-to-be thirteen-year-old to do this, if I tried to convince her it was something that we needed to do? I would hope that I would not be able to. I would hope she would look at me, like, 'You're nuts, there's no way I'm going to do that,' and then she would run to the first teacher or coach or police officer or something and say, 'Hey, my dad's wacko, he wants me to participate in this crazy, terrible scheme.'

"I've often wondered," he told the court, "how the heck did Barbara really have that type of influence over Heather? But I know Barbara had a very strong, close relationship with Heather, and that, coupled with the type of environment that Heather grew up under, I think those are factors that have to be considered."

Prosecutor Chris Dickinson asked Tri, "Were you aware that Heather had been plotting this murder for approximately a month before it occurred? It's in her diary, which we have a copy of here."

Heather's lawyer immediately objected. "Your Honor, I'm going to object to this line of questioning. Mr. Tri hasn't seen a piece of discovery. I haven't sent him anything from my office, purposefully, not to influence his testimony, and I'm going to object to him rendering an opinion about Mr. Dickinson's characterization that Heather was involved in the planning."

"The diary speaks for itself," said Dickinson, "and this witness is being asked to offer some insight into Heather Opel's character, and that's what we are here to discuss."

"Your Honor," said Michele Shaw, "the other basis for my objection would clearly be that Dr. Beyer's opinion is different from Mr. Dickinson's representation about the content of that March nineteenth entry. I did not call this witness, nor was there any testimony on direct about his opinion of any piece of evidence that has been presented to the court. He testified about his observations of Heather, of Barbara, their interaction together, the time Heather spent—nothing to do with the discovery in this case. I just think it's not appropriate."

Judge French overruled Shaw's objection. William Tri asked for Dickinson to repeat the question. "Well, I'll make it simple," he replied, "I'll show you the diary itself."

"Your Honor," objected Shaw, "if Mr. Tri is going to be asked questions about the diary, then I'm going to ask that we recess, that he be allowed to read several pieces of discovery and be allowed to read the diary in its entirety, because to take that out of context is not a fair representation of the diary."

French disallowed Shaw's request, and Dickinson drew attention to the diary entry for March 19, 2001. Tri asked Dickinson to read it aloud for him.

"*Today I told Danny my situation with Jerry. So Danny is going to kill him tonight, then we will have forty-one thousand dollars just to mess around with. I hope I get what I want. I want a new dirt bike.* Does that sound like the Heather Opel you know?"

"Well, no," replied Tri, "that's alarming. I don't understand that to say that she planned it, though. My reading of it is that someone else has arranged this. But still it is alarming, regardless of how you read it."

William Tri gave the matter more thought and offered another comment. "I can envision, in my mind," he said, "her mother putting her in a situation and encouraging her to get involved with the older kids having started it, and Heather getting involved because she is loyal to her group, and particularly loyal to her mother. Do I think she would be capable of doing something like this? That seems out of character for her, because she was a good kid. The Heather that I knew, I did not think was capable of committing first-degree murder."

* * *

Tuesday, October 2, 2001

"Unlike twenty other states, defendants under the age of eighteen cannot be sentenced to death in Washington State," said a Snohomish County prosecutor. "If Judge French decides we can try them as adults, they would receive a mandatory sentence of life in prison without the possibility of parole if convicted."

Twenty-five juveniles were executed in the United States between 1976 and 2005; seventy were awaiting execution on death row when the United States Supreme Court ruled that execution of children violated the Eighth Amendment's prohibition of cruel and unusual punishment. The state of Washington had previously reached that conclusion, and although Washington has the death penalty for adults, children could not be executed.

Speaking of the death penalty in general, United States Supreme Court justice Scalia stated, "The Fifth Amendment provides that no persons shall be held to answer for a capital . . . crime, unless on a presentment or indictment of a grand jury . . . nor be deprived of life . . . without the due process of law."

This clearly permits the death penalty to be imposed, and establishes beyond doubt that the death penalty is not one of the "cruel and unusual punishments" prohibited by the Eighth Amendment. One other issue is that the United States has not abolished the death penalty for youths. Juveniles do not have the same moral reasoning as adults, so there should be an alternative way of punishing them.

All the participants in Barbara Opel's murderous plan and the subsequent disposal of Jerry Heimann's body were between the ages of seven and seventeen. The ability of thirteen- and fourteen-year-olds to grasp the implications of such legal proceedings is, research proves, highly doubtful.

Courtroom onlookers were taken aback by the defendants, chained in leg irons, giggling childishly. The inability of the immature to "properly express" remorse or shame for a crime, such as that committed against Jerry Heimann, is both baffling and upsetting to mature adults.

"The more emotionally immature a young person, the more difficult it is for him/her to face shame about an offense," Marty Beyer explained. "When they cannot or do not express their guilt feelings, an erroneous conclusion can be drawn that they do not feel sorry for the offense."

Defense attorneys said the thirteen- and fourteen-year-olds were just as they appeared to be: "children who need help." Prosecutors said they were "cold-blooded murderers, among the most savage we've ever seen. Adult prison is society's only hope for security given the severity of the crime." Defense attorneys argued that the four were "basically good, redeemable youths who were led astray by an adult."

Both prosecutors and the children's defense attorneys agreed, however, that Barbara Opel was the mastermind behind the murder plot, and seventeen-year-old Jeffrey Grote was the foreman who played the lead role in carrying it out. But what Grote described in Judge French's juvenile justice courtroom could hardly be called a plot, being as sloppy in design as it was brutal in execution.

In a mumbling monotone Jeff Grote told how he became involved, described beating Heimann with an aluminum bat, and admitted that he thought no one would ever find out. "We had no plan on what we were gonna do after he was dead," admitted Grote.

Grote's statements were stereotypical of the immature and unrealistic mind-set of troubled teens studied professionally by psychologist Marty Beyer. "They don't anticipate," confirmed Beyer. "Adolescents often fail to plan or follow a plan, and get caught up in unanticipated events.

They view as 'accidental' consequences that adults would have foreseen. After an offense they say, 'It happened so fast, I couldn't think.'"

Grote was asked: "What did Kyle Boston say when you asked if he would ever kill someone?"

"He said that he wouldn't kill someone, but he said that he had no problem beating someone up. When I told him Mrs. Opel would pay him to beat Heimann up, he said that was fine. He just wanted enough to buy a gun. When him and his cousin came to the house, she just asked them where they were going to hide, and if they were really willing to beat him up."

By Grote's account, the cousins, armed with miniature bats, each hit Heimann twice and then fled from the house before the man was dead. The youngest boy, reportedly about four feet eleven inches and ninety pounds at the time, was quiet and shaking during the attack, Grote testified.

The boy about whom he spoke gave quizzical, confused looks to his lawyer during these proceedings. "Young people who have been abused or abandoned have difficulty believing that adults, including their lawyers, will protect them. Their apparent compliance is a learned survival strategy, but they tell their lawyers little of what they are thinking and may not believe their lawyers are really on their side."

Little Mike's lawyer, Steve Garvey, who was assuredly on his side, argued, "If he is kept in the juvenile system, the state will have eight years to reform him. Remember that he was only twelve at the time of the crime. In prison," said Garvey, "inevitably he will be ruined beyond whatever he is now."

Cousin Kyle was only one year older than Mike, and his maturity level was not significantly higher. Kyle Boston was already assuming a hardened public persona. Whatever prison would do to Mike, it would do even more to Kyle. "Acting tough," explained Beyer, "can be the young person's only way to avoid overwhelming feelings of sadness and shame. Adolescent bravado should not be misinterpreted as a lack of remorse."

The entire "tough guy" facade, common to Kyle, Mike, and numerous adolescent male participants in this tragedy, is sadly stereotypical of youths who adhere to the "Boy Code"—those unwritten rules reinforced by society that boys cloak their emotions and hide their fear, shame, and compassion behind macho exteriors. According to experts on the development of boys into men, boys are misunderstood, their reticence is mistaken for a lack of feelings, their hands-on learning patterns are mistaken for unruliness, and their physical forms of bonding and endearment are mistaken for aggression.

"A boy may be struggling with loneliness, divorce in the family, death of a pet, or the illness of a friend," said Donna McCooke, a health care professional in Great Britain with extensive experience working with the United Kingdom's volatile male prison population, assertive military men, and sensitive truck drivers with characteristic difficulty processing highly emotive content. "When boys encounter life-altering events, or circumstances with intense emotional components, several things can occur," states McCooke. "Because he has been taught not to show emotions other than anger, he may lash out in anger. If anger isn't an option, he may appear near comatose, unresponsive, or withdrawn. This self-imposed emotional isolation may give a false signal that he doesn't care when, in truth, he cares deeply. And, as caring deeply is a violation of the Boy Code, he may actually say, 'I don't give a shit,' when, in fact, he's being terribly torn up inside."

Brain-based research shows basic gender differences, in

particular in processing emotion. The female brain processes emotion more completely, using more of the senses than the male brain, and females typically verbalize emotive information quickly. Boys can sometimes take hours to process emotive information. This difference may affect a boy's ability to learn and his academic performance if he is not able to process emotional stress quickly.

Brain scans of males after a crisis show brain activity in the area where emotion is processed, rather than in the four lobes at the top of the brain where thinking occurs. So, contrary to popular belief, a boy's reaction to a crisis tends to be more emotional than logical.

"There is an excellent expression," says Donna McCooke, "'If we don't let our boys cry tears, they'll cry bullets.' This means that boys may respond to their fragility by hurting themselves and others, even those they love the most. Keep in mind there are exceptions, some girls may react aggressively to stress, and boys may be better learners after a crisis because they can shut off emotions, so brain differences and personalities also make a difference."

"Little tough guys, such as Kyle and Michael," commented investigator Fred Wolfson, "don't exactly have a history of male high achievers as role models. There are two schools of thought about why boys fail. One is the lack of positive role models. Many boys are raised without a strong male role model in the family, and our schools have so few male teachers that many kids can go from preschool to high school without having had a male teacher."

"Another problem," added Tony Stevens, "is media presentation. Not so much on radio, but in television and movies it's either the tough-guy ultramacho image, or it's the fool. You often see the TV male who is a fool, and whose wife is the bright partner who puts up with him out of loving pity, mercy, or amusement."

Peer pressure contributes to boys' poor performance in the classroom and even their early exit from the school system. "It's seen as more cool to be a fool than to achieve. Girls are allowed to excel. That's cool. But even a smart guy who's sensitive to peer pressure from the wrong peers would rather pretend to be stupid than to stand out as a nerd or a wuss."

The situation for young females is remarkably different, and Marriam Oliver's academic record indicated that she was blessed with remarkable potential but offered no indication that she was a potential murderer.

CHAPTER 12

Marriam Oliver's school performance was exceptionally impressive, especially in contrast to the horrors of her family situation and upbringing. "She is a good student who dreamed of studying marine biology in college someday," Mickey Krom, her attorney, said.

In French's courtroom, prosecutors asked Everett Police detective Joseph Neussendorfer about a curious word Marriam Oliver used during her police interrogation. "Cerebellum," Neussendorfer said. The girl used the anatomical term, which he found oddly sophisticated for a fourteen-year-old, for the part of the brain that her bat struck.

Asked where she learned the term, she said she had studied the human body in fifth grade, Neussendorfer said. She landed a blow there "because she realized that would cause brain damage."

The interrogation of children, and the validity of their confessions, is a contentious topic. There are no cannon of police ethics, no standardized policy for prosecutors. What is acceptable in one state is against the law in another.

Some states have what is termed the "interested adult test" when evaluating the voluntary nature of a juvenile's confession. "The court must consider whether the juvenile had an opportunity to consult with an adult interested in his or her welfare," explained the OJJDP, "either before or during the interrogation."

The concerned adult rule is particularly relevant in situations where a juvenile has obvious trouble understanding the interrogation process, has asked to speak with parents or a concerned adult, or where the police have prevented parents from speaking with the child. "The thinking," according to the OJJDP, "is that parents or other adults are in a position to help juveniles in understanding their rights, acting intelligently in waiving them, and otherwise remaining levelheaded in the face of police interrogation."

Another rule often in effect is the age test, meaning that courts cannot admit the confession of a juvenile under a specified age unless the youth is permitted consult with a lawyer or other adult, preferably a family member, who is personally interested in the child's well-being: "The adult acting on behalf of the juvenile must also be informed of the child's constitutional rights."

The state of Washington uses a combination of the two different rules, plus others, in what is termed the "totality of circumstances" test. This test requires the court to consider a number of factors before concluding that the juvenile has knowingly and willingly waived his or her rights. These factors include the juvenile's age, education, knowledge of his or her rights, and the substance of the charge against them. Also considered is whether the juvenile is allowed to consult with relatives, friends, or an attorney, fair treatment by the police, and the juvenile's prior experience with the criminal justice system and police interrogation.

The four youths in the courtroom of Judge French were garnering extensive experience with the Snohomish County's criminal justice system. "The hearing before

Judge French lasted more than a month," commented Sergeant Bryant. "To a thirteen-year-old in leg shackles, that must seem like a year."

The teens sat nervously while their lawyers tried to persuade Judge Charles French that casting them out of juvenile court would be inappropriate, counterproductive, and unduly harsh. "If those aren't reasons enough, it would be unconstitutional too," said Heather Opel's attorney, Michele Shaw.

She believed a 2000 U.S. Supreme Court ruling on criminal sentencing invalidated Washington State law on determining when teens could be tried as adults. In a motion joined by the other defense attorneys in the case, she argued that "state law allows judges to make decisions that could ultimately add years or decades to juveniles' sentences based on a burden of proof that is too lenient under the Supreme Court decision."

The Supreme Court ruling Shaw addressed, *Apprendi* v. *New Jersey,* told judges that they could not increase maximum sentences based on factors that weren't weighed by a jury or proven beyond a reasonable doubt. The state of Washington did not require "proof beyond a reasonable doubt, and weighed by a jury" in determining whether or not to try juveniles as adults.

Since that Supreme Court decision, criminal sentences in courts around the country had been thrown out or decreased. Several federal appellate courts found that the new Apprendi rule applied to federal drug cases, and legal experts predicted Apprendi would become widely used in death sentence appeals, among other kinds of criminal appeals.

According to juvenile justice experts, it had not yet been commonly used in cases involving youths facing the prospect of longer sentences because they might be tried as adults. "But I plan to use it in such hearings," said Simmie

Baer, attorney supervisor for the juvenile division of the Public Defender Association in Seattle.

"How far Apprendi reaches is really unknown right now," said John Strait, a Seattle University law professor. "I don't think anybody knows what the current Supreme Court would do when a novel application of Apprendi comes up."

Snohomish County prosecutors contended that Shaw's case might be a novel attempt at applying Apprendi, but not a suitable one. "Apprendi is about making sentences longer," said Deputy Prosecutor Chris Dickinson. "Heather Opel and the other teens have not even gone to trial. Shaw and the other teens' lawyers are seeking to put the cart before the horse. There isn't anything in this hearing about increasing her client's sentence."

"Nonsense," insisted Shaw. "The judge's decision could directly affect Heather Opel's maximum sentence. It would raise it from about seven years if she is convicted in juvenile court to at least twenty if she is convicted as an adult," said Shaw, "and as much as life without parole if prosecutors upgrade the girl's charge to aggravated first-degree murder.

"Heather Opel deserves a chance to take advantage of the services that are available to her through juvenile rehabilitation," Shaw said. "Because of the Supreme Court ruling, Judge French should make his decision based on 'beyond a reasonable doubt.'"

Exasperated, Dickinson insisted the higher burden of proof was not called for in this situation. "The U.S. Supreme Court didn't talk about this kind of thing, or anything to do with juvenile court hearings," he argued. "It is just not applicable to what we call 'decline hearings,' where juvenile courts decline a juvenile and turn them over to adult courts."

"What Heather Opel's attorney was doing was both daring and smart," commented crime writer Jeff Reynolds.

"Defense attorneys had long complained that applying adult-sentencing guidelines in juvenile cases was excessive. It certainly looked like all of a sudden the U.S. Supreme Court had come to the rescue. Of course, the decision in the matter of Heather Opel, Kyle Boston, Marriam [Oliver], and Little Mike [Smathers] was up to Judge Charles French."

Friday, November 9, 2001

Wearing orange prison jumpsuits and leg shackles clamped over their orange prison socks, the four youngsters shuffled into Judge French's packed courtroom. Each child had high hopes and deep fears.

Judge Charles French announced his decision on whether or not Heather Opel, Marriam Oliver, Kyle Boston, and Mike Smathers were redeemable youths who could be saved. "This case is not about saving children," said French.

He declined juvenile court jurisdiction over three, putting them at the mercy of an adult court system that would provide little in the way of rehabilitation or counseling. Only Mike Smathers would stay in juvenile court.

"Legal grounds exist to move the murder cases against Marriam Oliver, Kyle Boston, and Heather Opel to the adult system," French ruled. "Ultimately the choices these children will continue to make will determine whether or not they succeed."

As French voiced his decision, sobs and gasps from family members broke the courtroom's stillness. All four children broke into tears. Recalling outbursts from earlier hearings, French said he would call upon courthouse marshals to remove anyone who got out of line.

"The difficulty of this case," explained Judge French, "lies in the contrast between the young age and development level of each of the respondents and the vicious and gruesome nature of the alleged offense. I was torn between the need for understanding, compassion and hope of rehabilitation, and the substantial risk to the public that release at age twenty-one could threaten. The court's role is to balance the best interests of the children with that of the public."

Seattle court-appointed attorney Michele Shaw had argued that Heather Opel was a good candidate for rehabilitation, and psychologist Marty Beyer said that the girl participated in the killing because she was severely abused and had learned over the years not to question her mother's orders.

"To put Heather in an adult prison is to abuse and write her off the way her calculating mother did," argued Michele Shaw. "This girl was manipulated most of her life—especially in the days prior to the murder, when she was urged by her mother to sleep with a boy Barbara hoped to recruit for the killing. Her mother used her as payment for murder," said Shaw, "then commanded her to kill too. She is a victim herself."

The nature of Mr. Heimann's death, wrote Judge French, *suggests there is more to Heather Opel's behavior and personality than loyalty to, and manipulation by, her mother. It is the violent, "hands-on" aspect of this killing that remains unexplained.*

Shaw spent much of the hearing stroking her client's back and hair as the girl wept and sobbed. "I am deeply disappointed with the ruling," said Shaw, "but grateful that the judge had ordered that the teens will remain in juvenile detention, instead of adult jail, while awaiting trial. I'm disappointed the court thinks Heather Opel would not embrace the services available to her in the juvenile system."

"My decision," said French, "caused me a great deal of sadness, but I'm not convinced that Marriam Oliver,

Heather Opel, and Kyle Boston would be rehabilitated in the juvenile system."

Oliver's attorney, Mickey Krom, disagreed. "I presented evidence that my client, despite an early childhood marred by neglect, had become a good student and had no history of trouble," recalled Krom. "She was an excellent candidate for rehabilitation."

"How does rehabilitation occur," asked Judge French rhetorically, "for a young girl whose only apparent behavior aberration is senseless killing?"

"Hell, it serves the little bitch right," snapped a citizen in angered agreement. "She killed that poor man with a baseball bat. I don't care if she is thirteen years old or three years old. Can't the judge strap the kid in the electric chair or something?"

"As in any crisis," commented Shay Bilchik, "the crisis of juvenile violence and victimization presents both dangers and opportunities. The danger is twofold. First, some may see locking up kids and throwing away the key as the solution. Second, others may lose patience with the grueling, often thankless, labor of working for long-term solutions instead of the quick fix—which is no fix at all."

"Kyle Boston," French noted sadly, "has a history of scrapes with the law and continued to make violent threats after his arrest. He is an angry and aggressive young man who likely won't benefit from rehabilitation efforts."

Attorney Stephen Garvey represented Mike Smathers, Boston's younger cousin. "My client's case will remain in juvenile court," he said. "We were fortunate that the psychologist was able to make a strong case that the teen and community will benefit from his receiving help in a juvenile setting.

"While the state of Washington has a spotty record on rehabilitating juveniles, it excels in turning problem

children into highly disturbed and dangerous adults,"
Garvey said.

Packed with family and friends of the accused, the court-
room was filled with sobs when Deputy Prosecutor Chris
Dickinson announced, "I expect to file adult charges against
Oliver, Boston, and Opel by Wednesday."

Even though they were to be tried as adults, Judge French
ordered that they be kept at the Denny Juvenile Justice
Center rather than the Snohomish County Jail. "Heather
Opel begged me not to have the judge send her to the big jail
tonight," said Michele Shaw. "Her hands were freezing.
She's in shock."

Thursday, November 15, 2001

Marriam Oliver and Kyle Boston once again stood
in front of a judge in Snohomish County Superior Court.
Despite being the same age as they were six days previous,
they were now officially "adults"—adults charged with first-
degree murder.

"How do you plead?" asked the judge.

"Not guilty," replied Kyle Boston. Marriam Oliver gave
the same reply. Bail was set at $500,000 each, payable
only in cash. Marriam Oliver's lawyer had already filed an
appeal of Judge French's ruling.

"The issue of kids in adult prisons is a very interesting
one," said Representative Mary Lou Dickerson, Democrat-
Seattle, "and we've looked at what's happened with this
across the country. The research has shown us nationally that
public safety is not served by that practice," she said. "Juvenile offenders sent to the adult system are almost eight times
as likely to commit suicide and five times more likely to be
sexually assaulted." They are also 200 percent more likely to

be beaten by staff, and 50 percent more likely to be attacked with a weapon than youth in a juvenile facility.

Jim Krider, a Snohomish County prosecuting attorney who made juvenile crime his priority, said that "declining juvenile crime rates show that getting tough works. Kids are getting the message, and they should be getting the message."

"Most young people aren't getting any message at all," countered Bill Jaquette, the county's chief public defender. "Most young people are clueless about their risk of facing adult prison for crimes committed as juveniles. They are not aware of anything. Consequences don't seem to be something they think about.

"Judges need more discretion to fashion sentences that reflect the defendant's age and chances for rehabilitation," Jaquette said. "Something similar already is allowed for some drug offenders who are considered good candidates for treatment, instead of just being sent to prison."

Friday, December 7, 2001

Based on evidence that fourteen-year-old Kyle Boston participated in the brutal murder of Jerry Heimann, the state charged him in juvenile court with first-degree murder. The juvenile court declined jurisdiction. Boston moved for discretionary review of the declination order. While that motion was pending, he pleaded guilty to second-degree felony murder predicated on assault. The plea agreement stated in part that Boston agreed not to challenge the conviction. He didn't have to challenge the conviction because on October 24, 2002, the Washington State Supreme Court, in deciding another case, ruled that particular version of felony murder (second-degree felony

murder predicated on assault) did not rightfully exist as a
crime. Boston had to be recharged.

On November 21, 2002, Boston turned sixteen. Charged
as an adult, Kyle Boston pleaded guilty to second-degree
murder. "I am sorry Mr. Heimann died," he said, "and
sorry for my participation in this crime." His sentencing
would be delayed until after he had testified against all the
other defendants.

Saturday, December 22, 2001

Stephen Garvey's client Michael Smathers was only
twelve years old when he punched Jerry Heimann in the
nose, then ran away with his cousin Kyle Boston before returning to get car keys and, later, cash. The only one of the
youths tried as a juvenile, he was found guilty of first- and
second-degree murder. Little Mike couldn't bring himself
to speak in court the day of his sentencing.

"I know he's remorseful," his mother, Tina Wagner, tearfully told Snohomish County Superior Court judge Charles
French. "I talked to Mike last night, and I asked him what
he wanted to say. He doesn't know what to say, except he's
sorry."

"I'm holding out hope that the boy will start making
good decisions in his life," said Judge French. "Neverthe-
less, it is appropriate to give the boy the maximum sentence for juveniles allowed under the law." He ordered
the Marysville boy to be confined until he's twenty-one,
leaving open the possibility that the boy could spend the
last year of his sentence in a transitional program.

"I recognized the inevitability of it without agreeing with
it," the boy's lawyer, Stephen Garvey, said of French's decision. "I'm pleased that he was kept in the juvenile system."

The Washington State Police mobile crime lab at the Heimann residence in Everett. Barbara Opel and her children lived in the basement.

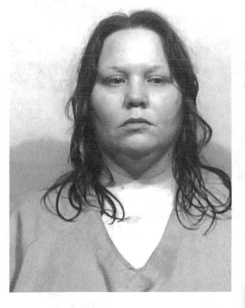

Barbara Opel on the day of her arrest.

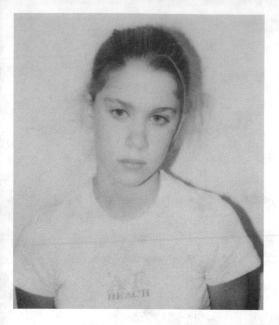

Heather Opel on her first visit to the Everett Police Department.

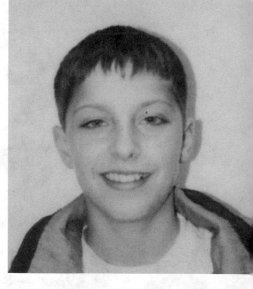

Michael Smathers (right) took off with Kyle Boston in the Firebird when the beating got out of hand.

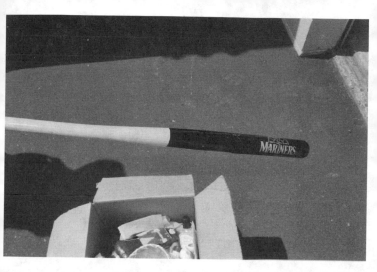

Miniature Seattle Mariners souvenir bat used in the
assault on Jerry Heimann.

Detectives search the Tulalip Reservation for Jerry Heimann's body.

Heather Opel tossed the murder weapon used by Marriam Oliver into the bushes by the side of the road.

After using a Rug Doctor to clean the bloodstained carpet, Opel tossed this bottle of anti-foam out with the victim's body.

Interior of Jerry's Firebird. Note latex gloves used when pouring acid.

Jerry Heimann's body, wrapped in his comforter.

Heimann's body was driven to the bowling alley
in the back of his black truck.

Strawberry Lanes bowling alley parking lot, where Opel and
Grote chased down Kyle and Michael.

A bottle of corrosive acid found near Heimann's body.

Marriam Oliver crushed Jerry Heimann's skull with a baseball bat. (Photo courtesy of the Washington State Department of Corrections)

Jerry Heimann died in the kitchen of his Everett home.

Mopping the floor didn't remove the deep blood stains under the kitchen baseboards.

Little Tiffany helped her mother clean the carpet, but their attempt to remove bloodstains failed.

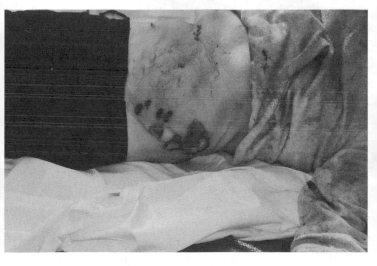

Stab wounds inflicted by Heather Opel on the body of Jerry Heimann.

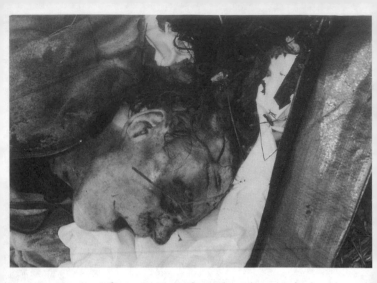

Jerry Heimann's face was "an ashen white" because hydrochloric acid was poured on it in an attempt to conceal his identity.

The blood-stained trunk of the stolen Firebird.

After stealing the Firebird, Kyle Boston stopped at McDonald's on the way to the mall. Note the empty bag of French fries on the car's floor.

Kyle Boston told his dad that he didn't do anything. (Photo courtesy of the Washington State Department of Corrections)

Seventeen-year-old Jeff Grote had sex with 13-year-old Heather Opel and then offered to help kill Jerry Heimann. *(Photo courtesy of the Washington State Department of Corrections)*

Interior of the U-Haul truck crammed with Opel's possessions.

Opel and Grote rented the U-Haul from this location on
Evergreen Way.

Detective James
Brouwer found the
body of Jerry
Heimann.

Heather Opel's official inmate photo, taken five years after the murder. *(Photo courtesy of the Washington State Department of Corrections)*

Barbara Opel forged this check for $6,000 on Jerry Heimann's account to rent a new apartment for her family.

Officer Joe Nuessendorfer was an Everett Police Department detective at the time of the investigation.

Inspector Peter Grassi of the Everett Police Department.

Snohomish County Deputy Prosecutors George Appel and Chris Dickinson.

Little Mike appealed the conviction, arguing that his Everett lawyer, Steve Garvey, was ineffective, and claimed he was prejudiced at his trial by his lawyer's failure to contest his issue of guilt.

"A review of the record in this case shows that the defense strategy had to take into consideration the unusually shocking nature of the murder, the boy's confession and the strength of the state's case," said Judge Mary Kay Becker. "Garvey also tried vigorously to suppress the boy's confession," Becker said.

The appeals court upheld Snohomish County Superior Court judge Charles French, who imposed a stiff sentence. The three-judge panel said the judge took into consideration the need for rehabilitation and to protect the public.

In the middle of March, Marriam Oliver agreed to a stipulated trial in Snohomish County Superior Court on a first-degree-murder charge, meaning a judge would render a verdict based on police reports and other documents, but not hear testimony. If guilty, she could serve at least twenty years in prison. The advantage of a stipulated trial instead of a guilty plea is that it preserves the defendant's right to appeal. Oliver's lawyer immediately began preparing her appeal.

CHAPTER 13

Tuesday, March 26, 2002

Prosecutors offered a twenty-five-year prison sentence to Heather Opel if she would plead guilty to first-degree murder. If she refused, they would upgrade the charge to aggravated first-degree murder and thereby she would face possible life in prison. Her attorney, Michele Shaw, consulted with juvenile psychology experts who expressed reservations about Heather Opel's ability to even comprehend the complexities inherent in such an offer.

"Because adolescents often have a limited future perspective and ability to anticipate," said psychologist Marty Beyer, "they may not be able to think strategically about the comparative risks of decisions, and they may be cognitively too immature to assist in their defense."

Most juvenile law experts doubt that young teenagers have the capacity to make decisions on certain legal matters. "It's not up to the attorney, even for a fourteen-year-old, to substitute their judgment for the client's," said Stephen Garvey, the attorney for Kyle Boston's cousin Mike. "If they want to make a horrible decision, it's the job of the attorney to convince them it is a horrible decision," he said. "But ultimately, it's their decision."

An essential part of meaningful decision making is the ability to foresee the consequences of a decision, stated noted expert Thomas Grisso. *Defendants must be able to imagine hypothetical situations, envisioning conditions that do not now exist and that they have never experienced, but which may result based on the choices they make. They must then evaluate these potential outcomes, comparing them with what they know or imagine to be more or less desirable or painful in life.*

Validation of Beyer and Grisso's scholarly opinions came in the form of a letter to prosecutors from young Heather Opel, penned without her lawyer's knowledge or approval. Written on notebook paper, the missive informed prosecutors that she wanted to accept a plea offer to avoid the possibility of a stiffer sentence.

The only reason I haven't taken the plea, wrote Heather Opel, *is because Michele Shaw, my attorney, has been telling me that she doesn't want to talk about it, so that's how I think she doesn't want me to take it.*

"I'm not sure that my client, Ms. Opel, is competent to decide whether she wants to enter a plea at this point," said Michele Shaw. "It would be pretty difficult for an adult to make that decision, let alone a fourteen-year-old with a history like hers," Shaw said, referring to Heather Opel's troubled home life, which was the subject of numerous investigations by Child Protective Services.

In explaining her wish to prosecutors, Heather Opel wrote, *I figured that I still have a chance to succeed in the career I want to have in the future. I also want to graduate from college.*

Shaw thought her client was influenced by Marriam Oliver's decision a week earlier. "Heather envisions she will be with Marriam if she pleads guilty," Shaw said. "In her childlike way, she thinks, 'I can do twenty-five years. That's not very long.'"

Prosecutors immediately scheduled a hearing. "We want to find out what Heather wants to do," said Chris Dickinson, "and to make sure Heather understands the offer and what the consequences are if she does not accept it. If she doesn't take the plea, she faces a mandatory life sentence with no chance of parole if convicted of aggravated murder."

In Washington State, a child as young as eight years old can receive a mandatory life sentence with no chance of parole. Only Washington, DC, Indiana, and Oregon expressly prohibit courts from imposing life without parole on offenders younger than age sixteen at the time of their offense.

"I've consulted with juvenile psychology experts," said Michele Shaw, "and I'm going to ask the court to give her more time to consider her options." Shaw said it would be inappropriate to comment on whether Heather Opel had ever expressed a desire to plead guilty. "I find the letter very surprising," she said.

One reason Shaw was reticent to discuss a plea agreement was that she was busy formulating an appeal of Judge French's decision that Heather Opel be tried as an adult. "Heather Opel was only thirteen at the time of the crime," Shaw reiterated. "Of all the mistakes that adults have made in Heather's life, none can top sending a mother's compliant little daughter to prison for following orders."

Shaw did more than appeal French's decision; she requested French step down as judge in the case of Heather Opel. Barbara Opel's lawyers were expected to make a similar motion, as Judge French was originally scheduled to adjudicate both cases.

Shaw challenged French on the grounds that he had presided over a lengthy Snohomish County Juvenile Court hearing in which he found that all but one of the teens should be tried in adult court.

Shaw said she thought long and hard about asking French to step aside, and did so only after consulting with an expert in judicial ethics. She said French had done nothing to show bias or prejudice, but a reasonable person could conclude he might be biased after hearing extensive details about the case in the juvenile court hearing.

Prosecutors wanted French to stay on the case. *Essentially, what the defendant is really arguing is that she did not like the court's decision in this case so far, and is afraid she will not like other decisions this court may render,* wrote George Appel, deputy prosecutor. *Heather Opel only read certain things into your honor's decision, and her attorney has not shown any evidence of actual or potential bias. Stepping aside might be viewed by some as a successful effort at judge shopping.*

French said it's sometimes difficult to assess the significance of decisions that are made on a daily basis and the effects they have on people involved. "My only concern is whether there would be an appearance of unfairness to Heather Opel because I ruled against her in juvenile court," responded French.

After serious consideration Charles French removed himself as judge in the case of fourteen-year-old Heather Opel. "Heather wanted to be in another court, and Heather's pleased with the judge's decision," said Michele Shaw.

Brian Phillips, Barbara Opel's attorney, followed immediately with a request for French to step down as judge in his client's case as well. "French has too much knowledge about the case after presiding over a lengthy proceeding in Snohomish County Juvenile Court where attorneys for the juveniles kept throwing blame at Barbara without giving her a chance to respond.

"French will have to make numerous decisions on evidence and on pretrial motions in my client's case," said Phillips, "and although I don't believe Judge French would be deliberately unfair, it could appear to a reasonable person that Ms. Opel will not get a fair trial. Maintaining appearance of fairness is fundamental to the rule of law in our society." Phillips frequently appeared before French, and didn't enjoy asking the judge to recuse himself.

"I don't believe there is an appearance of fairness problem in either the Barbara or Heather Opel cases," said deputy prosecutor George Appel, "and it makes sense for just one judge to handle all the remaining defendants in the case because of its complexity."

Because French stepped aside in the Heather Opel case, Appel suggested that French do the same with her mother so the same new judge could handle both cases. The judge said that he would take it all under advisement and he would let the attorneys know his decision in writing the following week.

Less than seven days later, Judge Charles French wrote a short letter to attorneys: *In view of the claim of an appearance of unfairness, my involvement in court proceedings in Juvenile Court . . . and the offense with which she is charged . . . I am recusing myself from further proceedings.* The judge also noted that deputy prosecutor George Appel had suggested it might make sense for the same judge to handle the cases of both Barbara and Heather Opel.

"I'm pleased that Judge French recognizes how important it is that people believe the trial is fair," said Appel. "And we hope, despite the nature of the case, Barbara Opel will be able to receive a fair trial." Appel and his associates were still mulling whether to seek the death penalty for Opel.

"My God," wailed Heather Opel, "can they really kill my mother?"

"Heimann was mean and abusive to Heather," asserted Barbara Opel's lawyer. "That abuse caused the teenagers, out of loyalty to their friend, to act by themselves without her direction. It was Jeff Grote who developed a plan to attack Heimann, offering to recruit a couple of young thugs to help beat him up. Others intended to hurt Heimann, but not kill him, until Grote decided to go one step further."

Barbara Opel had no explanation why her daughter Heather rushed up from the basement and stabbed Heimann, or why Marriam Oliver returned to smash Jerry Heimann's skull. "She'd better come up with explanations for more than that," said a prosecutor off the record. On the record the Snohomish County Prosecutor's Office spoke with deadly intent: "We've reached a decision. We're going for the death penalty."

"I'm going crazy locked up in a cell by myself," said a distraught Heather Opel. "I want somebody to talk to, somebody I won't get bored with, and somebody who will help the time pass." Staff at the juvenile detention center wouldn't allow Heather Opel a cellmate. Her official designation was "dangerous." Heather Opel put imaginary quotation marks around the words with her fingers. "I'm not dangerous," she said. "I'm depressed."

Heather Opel had good reason for depression, not only after incarceration, but before. "Take one look at her life," remarked a defense psychologist, "it's miraculous she even did as well in school as she did. Her life was one trauma right after another."

"Depression is a common reaction to trauma," said Marty Beyer, "but often is not diagnosed in delinquents. Aggression can be a defense against the helplessness common among traumatized children, but aggression in victimized young people is often misinterpreted as offensive rather than defensive."

Heather Opel's stabbing of Jerry Heimann—when he was already bloody and unconscious—was both cruel and sadistic. "Although sadistic offenses can sometimes be traced to the cruelty of an adult earlier in the child's life," Beyer explained, "more often traumatized delinquents present a passive account of having no choice but to defend themselves when they felt threatened."

Heimann was continually defined as a threatening presence in Heather Opel's life. Whether that definition was based on real-life experience, parental influence, or adolescent fantasy is irrelevant. She had enough actual threat and trauma in thirteen years to infuse virtually any situation with a threatening presence. "Typically, the delinquent is unaware of his/her long-standing pattern of reflexive self-protection in response to perceived threat," said Beyer.

Due to Heather Opel's depression and anxiety, the evening of April 13, 2001, kept replaying in her mind. Over and over, she relived plunging that ten-inch knife into Jerry Heimann. But she still sometimes lost it, banging her head against the wall.

Long before her mother's trial, Heather Opel was suffering from such severe depression that the county put her on medication as an antisuicide preventive. "I'd give up my life right now for Jerry to come back," said Heather, "I seriously would."

Jerry Heimann wasn't coming back, her mother possibly faced the death penalty, and a murder trial was inevitable. "All eyes were on her, her mom, the rest of those kids, and the Snohomish County Courthouse," recalled newscaster Tony Stevens. "Every time the case was mentioned, tempers would flare, opinions would fly, and emotions would run wild. Everyone had something to say, and anyone who knew nothing at all assumed they knew the whole story."

"It's all Barbara Opel's fault," voiced an Everett homemaker. "She is nothing but a monster." That monster is the mother of three children, one of whom already announced his plans for the future. "I want to go to jail," said Derek Opel, "so I can be with my mom and my sister."

"Derek was arrested for performing oral sex on other young boys, if I remember correctly," said Jeff Reynolds. "They didn't lock him up with his sister, but he wound up in juvenile detention just the same."

"She wasn't a very good mom," said Terrica Goudeau, wife of Henry Goudeau. "She constantly was yelling at her kids. She did good in terms of getting up each day and getting them to school. She did the sports thing, but she yelled at them and let them do whatever they wanted. They didn't have any discipline. They stayed up all night watching TV and sometimes didn't go to school.

"When she and the kids were living in a motel before she met Jerry Heimann," said Terrica, "she didn't even have a kitchen. How was she feeding them? She wasn't working, but I know she got child support from Henry and the other kids' father, and may have gotten money from her family.

"When Henry heard all the details about what happened, he had to leave the courtroom," Terrica said. "He was just bawling. We were both in a state of shock. I can't even imagine what that little girl is going through. On Tuesday night Henry cried himself to sleep. He's so scared for her. Right now, we're like blinded mice, running around trying to find the end of the tunnel. We haven't been able to talk to her, see her. We don't know what's going on."

The suffering of children in this case was beyond severe, noted investigator Fred Wolfson. "Not only Henry's daughter, but all the young people involved had to have experienced some emotional damage. And how damaged were the youths that willingly participated?"

"We get all eager to punish those who may deserve

punishment," remarked Tony Stevens, of KRKO radio, "but we overlook the simple fact that everyone facing a death sentence is someone's child, brother, sister, mother or father, daughter or son, relative or friend. Family members experience a profoundly complicated and socially isolating grief process. It is especially devastating when your mother or father is on death row, or actually executed by order of the state."

Prosecutors were seriously considering going for the death penalty, and Barbara Opel's court-appointed attorneys were obligated to give her the best defense. "One thing about Mrs. Opel was obvious," Stevens remarked. "I don't know the medical and legal terms, but the long and short of it is that the woman was nuts."

"Nuts" may not be either medical or legal terminology, but almost without exception, men and women on death row have damaged brains, according to research by Dr. Dorothy Otnow Lewis, a professor of psychiatry at New York University. Her studies focus on some of the most violent criminals; she has interviewed 150 to 200 murderers, sorting through their medical histories and, as much as it can be done, their brains. Dr. Lewis "has revolutionized the way people think about criminal behavior," said Elyn R. Saks, who teaches forensic psychiatry at the University of Southern California Gould School of Law.

Legal scholars say new findings on brain dysfunction are finally gaining attention, at least where they matter most: in death penalty cases. In the same year that Jerry Heimann was murdered, four states banned executions of the mentally retarded, bringing the number of the thirty-eight death penalty states that have made that exception to seventeen.

Lewis's longtime collaborator, Dr. Jonathan H. Pincus, the chief of neurology at the Veterans Administration Hospital in Washington, DC, administered the neurological examinations, from simple reflex tests to EEGs and brain scans, that supplemented the interviews. The researchers also combed whatever medical records they could find.

In 1986, Dr. Lewis and Dr. Pincus published a study of fifteen death row inmates that found all had suffered severe head injuries in childhood and about half had been injured by assaults. Six were chronically psychotic. Far from invoking an "abuse excuse," Dr. Lewis said, all but one had minimized or denied their psychiatric disorders, figuring that it was better to be bad than crazy.

Through these comprehensive assessments, Lewis and colleagues found that all fourteen had sustained head injuries as children. Nine had major neuropsychological disorders, seven had had psychotic disorders since early childhood, and seven had serious psychiatric disturbances. Seven were psychotic at the time of evaluation or had been diagnosed in early childhood. Only two had IQ scores above 90 (100 is considered average). Only three had average reading abilities, and another three had learned to read on death row. Twelve reported having been brutally abused physically, sexually, or both, and five reported having been sodomized by relatives.

Many of these factors, however, had not been placed in evidence at the time of trial or sentencing and had not been used to establish mitigating circumstances. The time and expertise required to document the necessary clinical information were not available. Furthermore, the attorneys' alliances were often divided between the juveniles and their families. On several occasions attorneys who chose to make use of the evaluations requested that information regarding parental physical and sexual abuse be minimized or concealed to spare the family.

Many of those on death row had been so traumatized that they could not remember how they had received their scars.

The answers had to come from childhood medical records and interviews with family members.

"No one suggests that abuse or brain damage always causes someone to become a murderer," commented Jeff Reynolds, "and Dr. Lewis acknowledged that most damaged people do not turn into killers, but almost every killer is a damaged person."

Dr. Lewis concluded that most murderers are shaped by the combination of damage to the brain, particularly to the frontal lobes, which control aggression and impulsiveness, and the even more complex damage visited by repeated violent child abuse.

"These findings," said Dr. Lewis, "cast doubt on legal definitions of insanity." Many legal experts agree, and Dr. Lewis and her colleagues study savage and bizarre murders, which she says are almost by definition the most crazed.

"In capital cases," Dr. Lewis said, "the elaborate balancing of aggravating and mitigating factors—those that may be taken into account by judge or jury—actually frustrates the inquiry because the grisliness of the crime is in proportion to the craziness of the act."

"No matter how crazy their acts," noted Reynolds, "not very many defendants actually qualify for the classic insanity defense. For purposes of determining sanity, the test is whether the defendant knew what he was doing and knew it was wrong, although some states also require that the defendant be capable of 'conforming his conduct' to the law."

"Responsibility is so wedded into centuries of tradition," said Deborah W. Denno, a Fordham University law professor who researches consciousness and its influence on defining degrees of culpability. "Unconscious thought is more important than we ever thought," said Denno. "I'm suggesting that the criminal law is way out of line with what constitutes conscious thought. There's this dichotomy in criminal law: either you're responsible or you're not. If you're a sleepwalker or something like that, you're not held responsible at all."

Dr. Lewis, like Ms. Denno, focuses not on guilt but on punishment, and she typically works for defendants who ask only the dispensation of life in prison. "Most of the people I see, I would not want running around again," she said. Lewis and her colleagues are studying serial killers, children who have killed their parents, and capital defendants who represent themselves. "Then," she said, "it's up to the public who they want to kill."

A significant portion of the public wanted to kill Barbara Opel, and the prosecutors Dickinson and Appel agreed. No woman had ever been sentenced to death in Washington State, but on July 11, 2002, the Snohomish County Prosecutor's Office made its official announcement: "We will seek the death penalty against Barbara Opel."

"Prosecutors wanted the death penalty for Barbara Opel," commented investigator Fred Wolfson, "and she's a woman whose entire lifestyle and behavior were textbook examples of mental illnesses, either inherited or acquired. This brings us back to the old problem," Wolfson said, "sane, rational people don't plan murders, nor do they encourage others to commit murder. The very fact that someone is accused of planning a homicide should require a brain scan of the accused. The new technology will reveal brain impairment with over eighty percent accuracy. You don't execute the mentally ill. Now, you tell me, do the mentally healthy commit murder?"

The American Psychological Association (APA), in August 2001, drafted a resolution on the death penalty in the United States, noting that death penalty prosecutions may involve persons with serious mental illness or mental retardation. In such cases procedural problems, such as assessing competency, take on particular importance.

"Basically," recalled Fred Wolfson, "the American Psychological Association asked that there be no death penalties carried out anywhere if that jurisdiction could not show by solid psychological and social research that any previous shortcomings in assessing competency had been fully addressed."

If defendants were mentally retarded, demented, or suffering from a traumatic brain injury, they should not be given the death penalty, insisted the APA. They also stressed that people who had a severe mental disorder or disability significantly impairing their capacity to appreciate the nature, consequences, or wrongfulness of their conduct, to exercise rational judgment in relation to conduct, or to conform their conduct to the requirements of the law, should not get the death penalty.

In a landmark issue the *Archives of General Psychiatry,* June 1996, focused largely on one controversial topic: are mental illness and crime strongly linked? The inescapable conclusion, according to associate editor Peter Marzuk, was "yes."

The extensive studies of crime and violence among the mentally ill are well designed and quite convincing, according to Marzuk. Most persons with mental illness are not criminals, and of those who are, most are not violent. However, there is a direct link between crime and mental illness. While most people with mental illness are not criminals, most criminals are mentally ill.

"I always thought she had psychiatric problems," Barbara Opel's sister, Shirley, admitted. "I think my whole family tried not to think about what was going on with Barb. I called her 'brain dead,'" said her sister, "because she couldn't act rationally."

Rational people don't commit murder, and irrational

people rationalize that murder is rational. As previously noted, Opel couldn't use the classic insanity defense, because she knew murder was wrong and/or illegal. However, as Tony Stevens noted, "if the defense didn't have that woman's head examined, they were missing their best chance of keeping her alive, and I don't mean alive on death row awaiting execution."

No one is executed quickly. Death row inmates in the United States typically spend over a decade awaiting execution. Some prisoners have been on death row for well over twenty years. This raises the question of whether death row prisoners are receiving two distinct punishments: the death sentence itself, and the years of living in conditions tantamount to solitary confinement—a severe form of punishment that may be used only for very limited periods for general-population prisoners.

Barbara Opel's defense attorney wasted no time in calling in experts to give his client every conceivable psychological and psychiatric evaluation. Her attorney would bring out Barbara's own abuse as a child, including the damage inflicted prebirth by her mother's excessive alcohol consumption. The argument, not unreasonable, was that Barbara Opel suffered irreparable damage—damage denying her the ability to think and reason with an accurate and "human" moral compass. Either this was good science, or a legal long shot to save Barbara Opel from becoming the first woman in Washington State history to wind up on death row.

The court closed some proceedings and sealed thousands of pages of the state's child welfare documents related to Barbara Opel's attempt to use the children in her defense. The defense hired four experts to study Barbara's behavior and to interview her three children and others associated with the case. A. Shulamit Glaubach, a child and adolescent psychiatrist in Seattle, interviewed Heather, Derek, and

Tiffany, while a guardian and possibly two attorneys—
representing Heather and her brother—watched through a
two-way mirror.

"Dr. Glaubach was instructed to form an opinion on the
psychological effects an execution could have upon the children and present it to prosecutors," recalled Jeff Reynolds.
"The defense wanted to demonstrate that the harm to the
kids would be so severe that they would never recover."

The kids, especially the two younger ones, were
exposed to more suffering from the questioning demanded
by their mother's defense strategy. "It is expected," admitted Barbara Opel's attorney, Brian Phillips, "that the children may experience distress by the very nature of the
matters to be discussed."

The defense also looked for life-saving mitigating factors from Barbara Opel's own erratic childhood and adolescence. Barbara was examined by psychologists and by
experts in fetal alcohol syndrome (FAS) and toxicology.
One researcher determined that her parents and other relatives suffered from mental and alcoholic illnesses.
"Opel's family history of severe psychiatric illness requires neuropsychological testing in order to determine if
Ms. Opel has any indicators of mental illness," said Dr.
George Woods. "There are also indications of significant
alcohol abuse by her mother during her pregnancy, and her
mother was also employed in a dry cleaner during the first
eight months of pregnancy." Dr. Woods requested that Barbara Opel be tested for possible "behavioral consequences
of any chemically related deficits."

Sharren Wells, an Everett social worker who interviewed
Barbara Opel, said, "I think there is neurological damage
there. Opel has thought blockage, misfiring motor skills, and
possible brain trauma. She is disconnected from the world."

She was also disconnected from her own family history.

"The man everyone thought was Barbara's father wasn't Barbara's father." According to the sister, Barbara's real dad was an itinerant racehorse fancier whom Barbara's mother followed around to racetracks while drinking and carousing.

The FAS influence on Barbara Opel's chaotic, irrational life is, in light of recent research, difficult to dispute. Studies of FAS, not only in America, but in Canada and the UK, portray horrific social consequences for those so afflicted.

Children afflicted with full-blown FAS display both physical and mental characteristics. Those with partial FAS may not have the physical abnormalities, but they display the same behavioral and psychological problems.

The effect of alcohol on the fetal brain is such that this region does not develop sufficiently to allow the FAS individual to appropriately control his or her actions. As such, FAS patients tend to be impulsive, uninhibited, and fearless. They often display poor judgment and are easily distracted. Difficulties in perceiving social cues and a lack of sensitivity often cause interpersonal problems. FAS patients have difficulties linking events with their resulting consequences. These consequences include both the physical—e.g., getting burned by a hot stove—and the punitive—e.g., being sent to jail for committing a crime. Because of this, it is difficult for these individuals to learn from their mistakes. Lacking sufficient cognizance of the threat or fear of consequences, the FAS patient is less likely to control his or her impulsive behavior. Similarly, FAS individuals have trouble comprehending that their behavior can affect others. As such, they are unlikely to show true remorse or to take responsibility for their actions. These are the very attributes that can lead to crime.

"They are very impulsive and do things that are not well-thought-out, and they get into significant difficulty from that. The malicious intent is seldom there. I find they're exploited by more talented criminals to do some of the running, if you like, and they're more likely to get caught."

According to Royal University Hospital psychologist Josephine Nanson, as many as half the young offenders appearing in court may be there because their mothers drank during pregnancy. Her assessment has tremendous implications for how the criminal justice system handles youth in custody, University of Saskatchewan law professor Tim Quigley observed. "It's analogous to the mental disorder defense, in the sense that we've said that people who are affected should not be punished in the usual criminal justice sense," he said. "Are these victims just as much affected by something over which they have no control, and are they deserving of punishment?"

Legal Aid Commission lawyer Kearney Healy said Nanson's suggestion strikes to the basic principles of criminal justice. "The criminal justice system is based on the premise that people understand there are rules, why they have to be obeyed, and if they aren't obeyed, then society has the right to come up with any number of options," he said. "All of those things are irrelevant to these kids. It's got nothing to do with good or bad—they just don't see it the same way. Planning, organizing, and learning from past mistakes are not in their repertoire. They are egocentric, impulsive, and very concrete in their thinking. Typically, they do not make connections between cause and effect, anticipate consequences, or take the perspective of another person.

"There are an increasing number of cases reaching the courts because we've been diagnosing this for about twenty years. Those individuals are now in adolescence and adulthood, and at a prime age for when they're going to be involved in the court system," Nanson said.

"It presents tremendous challenges, and I'm not sure the courts always understand," said Dr. Brian Habbick, professor emeritus at the University of Saskatchewan College of Medicine. Habbick added that, given the strict diagnostic criteria used in the study, "you're only looking at the tip of the iceberg. For every full case of fetal alcohol syndrome, there are four out there with the partial effects."

"All too often I find there are children who aren't able to moderate their behavior in even the most obvious ways, even when there are strong rewards," said Healy. "Instead, they are doing things that are going to cause them a great amount of personal pain, for no gain. When I see them, I've got to think there's something going on there."

Shirley LeClaire, of Social Services' Family Service Bureau, said, "There's been a long-standing history in our community of not giving this the attention it needs. It's one of the areas where there's not a lot of attention paid, especially fetal alcohol effects, because you don't have the physical attributes."

"The whole area of FAS and fetal alcohol effects is significant because the way that our system is set up to deal with kids is obviously not going to work for them."

One of the ironies is that children with FAS often make model prisoners, Nanson said. "In terms of the justice system handling individuals with this, one of the things they fail to understand is that FAS people do very well in structured environments," she said. "Often people are fooled in the early stages of treatment into thinking somebody is doing really well, not realizing that they're doing really well because all the opportunities for them not to do well are taken care of in a structured program. There is a point where the individual with FAS falls apart again."

Suffering from mental illness isn't against the law, but murder is a capital offense. When the one accused of murder is mentally ill, a variety of factors immediately come into play.

"Popular misconceptions about mental illness are partially

responsible for the railroading of mentally ill persons through the criminal justice system," stated Jeff Reynolds. "From arrest to the determination of competency to stand trial and beyond, a person's mental illness affects every stage of passage through the criminal justice system."

"Behavior associated with mental illness is often perceived as bizarre and suspicious," insisted private investigator Fred Wolfson, "thus drawing police attention, even if the person has not committed a crime. Untrained to recognize and handle mental illness, arresting officers and other staff inappropriately assume the arrestee understands such things as their Miranda rights. Mentally ill people are more likely to give a false confession, especially if they are delusional."

The concept of culpability is an important aspect of who is sentenced to death. Culpability signifies qualities such as consciousness, reason, and responsibility. It is precisely these qualities that are disabled and distorted by mental illness and therefore a gap exists between a mentally ill offender's behavior and his culpability.

"In death penalty cases, such as Barbara Opel's," said Wolfson, "the issue of mental illness can be raised as a mitigating factor. Mitigating factors are particular circumstances that are legally recognized to decrease a defendant's culpability and result in a non–death penalty sentence. Since untreated brain disorders can cause individuals to act in inappropriate or criminal ways, certain aspects of mental illness, such as a defendant's diminished capacity to appreciate the criminality of his conduct, and to conform his conduct to the requirements of the law, are codified as mitigating factors in capital cases."

In a majority of cases dangerous or violent behavior exhibited by persons with brain disorders is the result of neglect and inappropriate, or insufficient, treatment of their illness. Therefore, mentally ill offenders are by definition not the worst of the worst offenders.

What is exceptionally problematic is that crimes are primarily committed by criminals, and criminals share certain thought disorders common to sociopaths. Among these are traits of manipulation, dishonesty, and lack of empathy. They never recognize the rights of others, and they see their self-serving behaviors as permissible. They feel entitled to certain things as "their right."

"Verbal outbursts and physical punishments are normal for them," commented Donna McCooke. "Based on my experience working with convicted criminals, they don't really see others as people—they see them as either targets or accomplices—and both of those become victims. They also tend to have no sense of guilt or remorse. They are unable to empathize with the pain of their victims, having only contempt for others' feelings of distress and readily taking advantage of them."

Sociopaths are not concerned about wrecking others' lives and dreams, are oblivious or indifferent to the devastation they cause, do not accept blame themselves but blame others—even for acts they obviously committed. Psychopaths, of course, are an even worse and more severe version, and comprise a minority of sociopaths.

Most parents of children with sociopathic or psychopathic behavior are well aware that something is wrong even before the child starts school, according to Dr. Robert Hare. "They are different from normal children—more difficult, willful, aggressive, and deceitful. They are harder to relate to or get close to. The parents are always asking themselves, 'What next?'"

Dr. Hare, who conducts training seminars for the FBI, pinpointed certain school-age traits as prime indicators of young psychopaths. "As I mentioned in my book *Without*

Conscience, these hallmarks include repetitive, casual, and seemingly thoughtless lying, apparent indifference to, or inability to understand, the feelings, expectations, or pain of others, defiance of parents, teachers, and rules. [They are] continually in trouble and unresponsive to reprimands and threats of punishment, persistent aggression, bullying, and fighting, a record of unremitting truancy, staying out late, and absences from home." The dangerous psychopath will often have, Hare explained, "a pattern of hurting or killing animals, early experimentation with sex, vandalism, and fire setting."

"Put a brain-damaged, vindictive adult as authority figure for sociopathic and easily misguided youngsters," remarked Tony Stevens, "and what we have is kids not old enough to get into an R-rated movie sentenced to more time in prison than they have been alive, an addled and allegedly murderous mother of three facing a possible death sentence, and Jerry Heimann—one hell of a nice guy—murdered. They didn't just kill Jerry. They also tore the heart out of his kids, grandkids, brothers, and sisters. All the prisons and punishment, electric chair and gas chambers put together, won't bring Jerry Heimann back for that joyous reunion with his son."

CHAPTER 14

While Barbara Opel sweated out the prosecutors' decision in her county jail cell—and the families of Oliver, Boston, Grote, and Opel wrestled with the nightmare of their beloved children being murderers—the family of Jerry Heimann dealt with the horrid emotional pain of his senseless death.

Adding daily insults to the trauma of Heimann's death, creditors throughout Everett were calling constantly, complaining of bounced checks written on Jerry Heimann's account—checks written after his murder. "Barbara Opel just helped herself to Mr. Heimann's bank cards and checkbook," remarked Sergeant Bryant. "But then again, the motive for the murder in the first place was, according to Grote and all the kids, all about money."

"That doesn't mean Grote and the kids were telling the truth," stated Jeff Reynolds. "Let me play devil's advocate for a minute. What if Barbara Opel, in truth, never plotted the murder of Jerry Heimann, never bribed the teens to stab and beat him to death? What if Barbara Opel wasn't some evil, murder-plotting woman, but instead was just a stupid, vindictive woman and a rotten mom who got sick and tired of an offensive drunk named Jerry Heimann abusing her daughter? What if she bitched and moaned about the way Heimann treated the kid so much that the idea of having the shit beat out of him seemed like a fine idea, and that beating just got out of control?"

Reynolds's hypothesis—a concept put forth for consideration as a viable alternative to prevailing assumptions, and an obvious position for Opel's eventual defense—was one that the family of Jerry Heimann found exceptionally offensive.

"Offensive or not," countered Reynolds, "maybe the reason they didn't have a plan as to what to do with the body was because there wasn't supposed to be a body. Maybe no one ever planned on killing Jerry Heimann. Let's assume he was just supposed to get beat up as payback for treating poor little Heather like a piece of crap, payback for bossing her and her little brother and sister around when he got drunk, payback for throwing things at her and calling her names. Offensive or not, it's a possibility you are going to have to accept as true if you serve on the Barbara Opel jury."

When you plead not guilty in America, you don't have to prove you are innocent. You are presumed innocent. The burden of proof is on the prosecution to prove you are guilty beyond a reasonable doubt.

The moment Barbara Opel pleaded "not guilty," the law required that any potential juror accept her innocence as a fundamental assumption unless proven otherwise. Not simply suggested otherwise, but proven otherwise beyond a reasonable doubt by evidence in a court of law.

"After all this publicity," asked broadcast journalist Chet Rogers, "how does anyone expect Barbara Opel—our alleged manipulating, murderous mother of the year—to get a fair trial? These are still juveniles pointing the finger at an adult. From a defense standpoint—and there will be a defense standpoint—they could all be saying this out of fear and intimidation by an adult system hell-bent on portraying Barbara Opel as some sort of monster, when, in reality, she is just another victim."

"I am a good mother," insisted Barbara Opel. "I'm nothing like the way I've been portrayed. I scrimped and saved so my kids could participate in their school bands, play on sports teams, go roller-skating once a week, and wear Tommy Hilfiger clothing. Do you think Heather would have been such a good student, so admired by teachers and classmates, if I hadn't encouraged her and supported her at home?"

Barbara Opel insisted that Jerry Heimann was an abusive drunk, that she never intended for him to get killed, and she was not guilty. "The abuse was starting to occur on a daily basis," said Barbara, "if Jerry came home, and maybe his dinner was not put in the refrigerator on the right plate, if maybe that wasn't what he had said that morning when he left that he wanted for dinner, if something was not in the right place, if maybe he didn't have cigarettes up on top of the refrigerator or a beer in the refrigerator—pretty much anything."

According to Barbara Opel, it didn't take a lot to set him off. "He would start yelling at whoever happened to be around, myself, my children. 'What in the hell is this crap that you cooked for dinner? That isn't what I said I wanted this morning, that isn't what I told you to cook.' He would yell at me, Heather, or whoever happened to be around when he came in."

It didn't do any good to reason with Jerry, insisted Barbara. The next day he wouldn't even remember what he said or did. "Jerry Heimann drank, and when he drank, he became verbally abusive and occasionally violent. He threw things. I was tired of Jerry Heimann being verbally abusive to my kids," she said. "And, yes, I said many times that I wished someone would kill that SOB, but people say that sort of thing all the time when they are fed up with someone. I never seriously requested anyone murder Mr. Heimann. I never paid anyone to kill him. I never asked anyone to kill him. I never thought anyone would really kill him. I just thought the boys were going to beat him up to get even for the way he treated Heather."

A review of Kyle Boston's statements lent credence to Barbara Opel's position. As with Oliver, Kyle Boston was convinced that he was giving Heimann "what he had coming" for the way he mistreated Heather Opel. He hadn't witnessed any mistreatment firsthand, but had heard about it from Grote. It was a continual downline of distorted misinformation fed by Mother Opel to Jeff Grote, then from Grote to Boston.

It could be argued that Jeff Grote was acting out the Boy Code and protecting his weaker sex partner. There were times when Grote said that, albeit in different terms. On other occasions he claimed the motivation was money. Due to his own conflicting statements, it was never clear whether he did it for money or out of loyalty to Heather.

"The entire issue of loyalty, and adherence to higher moral principles," said expert Marty Beyer, "can lead to tragic outcomes for youngsters."

"What is the higher moral principle," asked Jeff Reynolds, "in executing men, but not women?"

"There is a gender bias when it comes to capital punishment," said Victor Streib, a professor at Elon University who tracks death penalty cases involving female offenders, "probably stronger than a race bias."

Women account for about one in eight murder arrests nationally, but only about one in seventy-two people on death row. Of more than seven hundred people executed in the United States since 1976, only seven have been women. Even advocates of capital punishment sometimes balk at the notion of executing women.

"I've had politicians say to me, 'We don't treat our women that way,'" Streib said. "It's like in a football game. If you knock down a guy, you're a hero. If you knock down a girl, you're a guy who hits girls."

"There was a national outcry back in 1998," recalled Jeff Reynolds, "when a good-looking thirty-eight-year-old white woman named Karla Faye Tucker was executed in Texas. After she killed two people with a fifteen-pound pickax, she found Jesus on death row. Hell, I didn't even know He was incarcerated."

"It's like there's something more valuable about women's lives," Streib said. "Women are also treated differently when they're victims. You always hear about the women and children killed in fatal crimes."

John Junker, a University of Washington criminal law professor, doubts prosecutors would hesitate to charge women with aggravated murder when warranted. "But they might be reluctant to ask for the death penalty, either because of their own attitudes about women or because of their assessment of what community attitudes might be," he said.

Other death penalty experts insist a gender bias does not exist, claiming the discrepancy is more due to the kinds of murders women tend to commit. "They rarely murder in the course of violent crimes against strangers," said Elizabeth Rapaport, a University of New Mexico law professor and one of the nation's foremost experts on women and the death penalty. "I am not going to argue that there never has been a break cut for somebody because she's a woman, but the huge explanation is eligibility. Women very rarely commit the kinds of murders that statutes treat as aggravated."

"Rapaport's theory could account for the disparity between the numbers of men and women executed," admitted Reynolds, "but that doesn't explain why here in the Pacific Northwest no woman has ever been hung by the neck until dead, put in the electric chair, or given lethal injection. You may as well not have the death penalty for women. And if you don't have it for women, you have no explanation or justification for having it for men."

Juries have traditionally been less likely to sentence women to death because of juries' and judges' preconceived ideas of women. In some of the older cases, noted Victor Streib, judges from the bench would say, "If you had committed this crime as a man, I would have sentenced you to death. But women are the source of all life—so how can I take your life?"

Lesbians don't get the same breaks as straight women, research shows. The less traditional the woman, the less special consideration she receives for her femininity. In some countries, Streib says, it is illegal to execute women. Russia is one of them.

In Washington State, out of 252 people convicted on aggravated-murder charges, eight are women. Of those eight convictions, five were murder-for-hire cases. Their victims: three husbands, one ex-boyfriend, one 59-year-old mother. Prosecutors sought the death penalty for only one, Susan Kroll, who hired two young men to kill her husband.

"That particular murder was exceptionally grisly," recalled Jeff Reynolds. "Her husband was repeatedly stabbed, smacked in the jaw with a crowbar, and his throat slit. She didn't get the death penalty because she had four kids."

Women always get a better deal than men in capital cases. Only about 11 percent of women sentenced to death nationally are executed. For men, it is about 24 percent. In the mind of Chris Dickinson, Barbara Opel was 100 percent guilty of

Jerry Heimann's murder, and 100 percent worthy of death under Washington State's statute, revised in 1998.

Washington State's first execution, in 1904, occurred under a statute that called for a mandatory death sentence. The statute was revised in 1909 to give discretion over the death sentence to the judge. The death penalty was abolished in Washington in 1913, and then reinstated in 1919. In 1972, the U.S. Supreme Court ruled capital punishment unconstitutional, and then reinstated it in 1976. Washington State began executing people again in 1977. The statute presently in effect was last revised in 1998.

"Unless there was a made-for-TV movie about them," remarked Jeff Reynolds, "you probably couldn't name one person on death row. Then again, even if there were a TV movie, you probably still couldn't name who is on death row. Most folks think that the death penalty is handed out to only the worst, but that isn't true at all."

Washington State had ten inmates on death row in 2007, and none of them murdered as many people as Gary Ridgeway, the confessed "Green River Killer," who took the lives of forty-eight people. Ridgeway didn't get the death penalty. He received a sentence of life in prison.

Washington State's present death penalty law allows a death sentence to be imposed only in cases of aggravated first-degree murder where a jury unanimously finds that no reasonable mitigating circumstances exist to allow the alternative sentence of life imprisonment without the possibility of release or parole. The jury is asked not whether they will impose the death sentence, but: "Having in mind the crime of which the defendant has been found guilty, are you convinced beyond a reasonable doubt that there are not sufficient mitigating circumstances to merit leniency?" If the jury responds "yes," a death sentence is imposed.

Mitigating circumstances include, but are not limited to,

mental disturbance, age, role in murder, inability to understand the illegality of the act, whether the defendant was under duress or domination, and the likelihood of the defendant posing future danger.

The trial of a capital offense occurs in two parts. The jury first decides whether the defendant is innocent or guilty of the crime with which he or she is charged. The jury then decides whether to impose the death sentence or a sentence of life without the possibility of parole.

In order for someone to be charged with aggravated first-degree murder, there are thirteen criteria that must be met.

1. Victim was a law enforcement officer, corrections officer, or firefighter performing official duties.
2. Defendant was in prison, had escaped, or was authorized or unauthorized to leave incarceration at the time of the crime.
3. Defendant was in custody at county or county-city jail at the time of the crime.
4. Defendant entered into agreement to receive money or item of value for committing the crime.
5. Defendant solicited another person to commit murder and agreed to exchange money or item of value for the crime to be committed.
6. (1995 Legislation) Defendant committed crime to maintain membership or advance in the hierarchy of an identifiable organization or group.
7. (1995 Legislation) Defendant committed crime with a firearm shot while inside a motor vehicle.
8. Victim was a judge, juror, former juror, prospective, current or former witness, prosecutor, deputy prosecutor, defense attorney, sentence review board

member, probation officer, or parole officer and the
murder(s) was related to the exercise of victim's official duties.

9. Murder committed to conceal the commission of
   another crime or to conceal defendant's identity.

10. More than one victim and murders were part of
    a common scheme.

11. Murder committed in the course of, furtherance of,
    or flight of: first- or second-degree robbery, first-
    or second-degree rape, first- or second-degree
    burglary, (1994 legislation) residential burglary,
    first-degree kidnapping, first-degree arson.

12. Victim was news reporter or journalist and murder
    was committed to hinder investigative, research,
    or reporting activities of victim.

13. (1998 Legislation) Victim had an official Order
    of Protection against the defendant at the time
    of the crime.

Each death sentence is reviewed by the state supreme
court during which the court considers whether sufficient
evidence of mitigating factors was presented at trial, whether
the death sentence is excessive or disproportionate to similar cases, and whether the sentencing was affected by feelings of passion or prejudice.

Execution in Washington State used to be by hanging.
Now inmates may choose the method of their own demise.
The menu includes two items: lethal injection of sodium
thiopental, or a rope around the neck.

On January 6, 2003, Barbara Opel's defense team claimed
that Washington State's death penalty was unconstitutional

because the final decision, under appeal, was not left to a jury, but to judges. A judge denied the motion.

"Next," recalled Tony Stevens, "the defense requested a change of venue, arguing that there was no way that Barbara Opel could get a fair trial in Snohomish County."

Getting a fair trial in America, regardless of venue, has become progressively more difficult. According to twenty years of public-opinion polls, Americans are less apt to think of people accused of a crime as innocent until proven guilty than they were two decades ago. "This trend," said Rick Busselle, Washington State University assistant professor of communication, "is an indication of the American public being less aware of how our court system works."

One reason for the shift in public opinion may be the way crime is portrayed in the news media. Consumers of media tend to focus on names associated with the crime, then automatically associate guilt with that name. It is precisely for this reason—media publicity—that a change of venue is requested.

"Mass media is everywhere," commented Tony Stevens. "That's why they call it mass media—it reaches the masses. Prejudicial media coverage saturates communities, and courts struggle to balance the Sixth Amendment's guarantee of an impartial jury and the First Amendment's protection of freedom of the press."

For a defendant such as Barbara Opel, the real issues are the presumption of innocence versus the presumption of guilt and the right to a just trial untainted by outside influences. The concept of presumed prejudice, and not merely actual prejudice, is a useful weapon in the fight against "trial by newspaper."

When Barbara Opel, charged in an obviously high-profile case, requested a change of venue, three factors were critical in evaluating the issue. The first factor was the existence of knowledge about the case in the community of jurors. This includes awareness of facts or rumors that would not be admissible or are going to be contested by the defendant at trial.

The second factor was the "opinion of guilt" that existed within the community. Finally the third factor was the strength of such opinion.

Trial courts have traditionally relied on the voir dire process to measure the extent of juror bias. However, empirical studies have demonstrated that the voir dire process is not effective in uncovering significant biases and prejudices that jurors may bring to a courtroom after exposure to pretrial publicity.

"A good public opinion survey, properly conducted," explained Fred Wolfson, "can directly address the critical factors of the impact of pretrial publicity prior to the voir dire process." Such a survey must employ the highest level of scientifically accepted standards for the market research industry, including skilled practitioners in survey design, "best practices" techniques for unbiased inquiries, and ethical considerations throughout the research process. For this reason, though not frequently used, public opinion polling has been recognized as an important tool in assessing the need for a change of venue in high-profile cases since at least the 1970s.

Fairly recently these surveys have proven to be a critical tool in evaluating motions for change of venue in high-profile cases in federal district courts in certain states, including Alaska. Washington State, however, kept things more simple. The court simply refused a change of venue—and soon the trial by newspaper and trial by jury converged in the Snohomish County Courthouse.

"She was the supervisor of this whole grisly scenario," insisted Dickinson. "Even if she wasn't in charge, she clearly knew what was going to happen. She even admitted that she knew that these kids were going to attack Jerry Heimann. However, she didn't leave the house before it happened, immediately before, she didn't leave the house while it was happening. Why was that? Because she was in charge—she wanted to make sure it got done and it got done right. She went with the kids to go get the Firebird back from Kyle and Michael. Why? Why if she was not supervising? Why would she go back to make sure that the job got done, that they got the car back. And why did she go along to dump the body if she wasn't in charge? Why did she do that? Because she was the supervisor. She wanted to make sure that these knucklehead kids did it and did it right. She even went so far as to bring her two young children, Derek and Tiffany, with her."

Barbara Opel could argue that she brought Derek and Tiffany along when they disposed of Heimann's body because it is not good parenting to leave children alone at night. Some commentators were actually surprised that she didn't use that line of reasoning.

"I can hardly wait to hear what the defense is going to say to prove that she's innocent of murder," said an Everett resident unfamiliar with American justice. The resident was reminded, as was the jury at the trial, that in the United States of America, the defense does not have to prove anything. The defendant is presumed innocent. The prosecution must prove guilt beyond a reasonable doubt. When it came to the role of Barbara Opel as a mastermind of any kind, there was room for doubt.

The family of Jerry Heimann was understandably devoid of objectivity. "My dad was doing his best to take care of Grandma," said Colleen Muller, Jerry's daughter.

"He refused to send her to a home, and he wanted her to be with him at his home. Right or wrong, that was the most important thing in the world to him. Barbara Opel, Jeff Grote, Heather Opel, Marriam Oliver, Kyle Boston, and Michael Smathers took his life in the vilest ways in front of his beloved mother. Now we are all left with the devastation and the fallout. We are left without our father, our grandfather, and our friend."

Trial and Error

Thursday, March 20, 2003

Snohomish County prosecutors Chris Dickinson and George Appel sought the death penalty, insisting Barbara Opel had Jerry Heimann murdered. She planned it, she encouraged it, and she pursued it with relentless zeal. The motive, repeatedly hammered by the prosecution, was money.

"It is all about this," Chris Dickinson told the jury in his opening remarks. "This" was a dollar bill. The evidence, Dickinson assured jurors, would prove that Barbara Opel wanted the good life, and her creative control of Jerry Heimann's sudden death benefits gave her unprecedented wealth.

"This trial was worthy of pay-per-view," said Jeff Reynolds. "Both the prosecution and the defense were comprised of brilliant, knowledgeable lawyers who did absolutely the best job they could. The prosecutor's office isn't going to pursue a case they don't believe in, and no defense attorney who values his reputation or career is going to offer ineffective counsel. This trial was a battle royal between two teams, both committed to justice, and each determined to give the jury what it needed to make an informed and thoughtful decision."

"Right off the bat," said Tony Stevens, "Dickinson referenced money as a motivation. This was going to be a bone of contention. For sure, the defense was going to say that if she killed him to loot his bank account, she would have looted his bank account. She didn't. She took enough to rent a U-Haul, stuff five people into one cheap motel room, and eat at Denny's. If she was captured on her way to the Bahamas in a late-model Benz, then you might conclude she did it for money—a Grand Slam breakfast from Denny's is not a windfall extravagance, exactly spending like a drunken sailor, or like someone who just got away with murder."

Barbara Opel's attorneys, Peter Mazzone and Brian Phillips, insisted that Barbara Opel didn't murder Jerry Heimann. She wasn't present for the crime, nor did she see it take place. The true culprit, the defense alleged, was Jeff Grote, who swept Heather and Marriam up in a frenzy of violence. What began as an act of retribution became bloody murder—a murder in which Barbara Opel did not participate.

"I will demonstrate," promised Peter Mazzone, "that it was Jeff Grote who by himself decided to kill, rather than just hurt, Jerry Heimann. I will demonstrate that, from the time that Heather met Grote, there was no plan to kill Jerry, but only to hurt him."

This approach wasn't a desperate attempt to free Barbara Opel by manipulating perception. The defense would draw upon the specific, pointed testimony of Jeff Grote himself.

The prosecution, in contrast, would portray Barbara Opel as a mastermind of murder. The defense, while not terming her "mindless," would point out that she did not handle situations in a mature, adult manner. Jerry

Heimann, they would argue, was an abusive drunk of poor judgment whose rude and insulting behavior prompted an immature response—a beating to "teach him a lesson."

To buttress their defense, Barbara Opel's attorneys sought expert medical testimony concerning Barbara's alleged impaired brain functioning. That was easy. "It was no problem demonstrating that Barbara Opel was quick to anger, slow to forgive, and mentally challenged," recalled Tony Stevens. "More difficult, perhaps, would be impeaching the prosecution's primary witnesses against Barbara Opel, including Marriam Oliver, Danny D'Angelo, Kyle Boston, and Jeff Grote—all of whom agreed to testify against Barbara Opel as part of their own plea bargain deals. What was potentially problematic," said Stevens, "was that most of those kids were so crooked, they couldn't lie straight in bed."

CHAPTER 15

The trial began, as all do, outside the presence of the jury. Judge Gerald L. Knight was on the bench, George Appel and Chris Dickinson represented the state of Washington, and Barbara Opel was represented by Peter Mazzone and Brian Phillips.

On the first day of the trial, and prior to testimony, Barbara Opel's attorney raised questions regarding photographs of both Jerry Heimann and Evelyn Heimann, who died in the hospital shortly after Jerry's murder.

"Photo number two is a picture of Evelyn Heimann, an in-life picture of Evelyn Heimann," said Peter Mazzone. "We don't see the relevance of that."

"I think it ought to be admissible," said Chris Dickinson, "to show Evelyn Heimann as she looked in the approximate time frame when this crime occurred. This photo was taken around Christmastime of 2000. Count Two involves Evelyn Heimann, she's the victim in it, and I think the jury ought to be able to see who she was and what she looked like."

Judge Knight agreed, and the photo was allowed. The defense also sought to exclude any reference to a mysterious man named Steve. Jeff Grote would testify that on the first

Monday he stayed with the Opel family, he went with them to Steve's house on Colby Avenue. According to Grote, Barbara Opel told him that she went there to get supplies to kill Jerry Heimann.

"This was supposedly another one of Opel's plots," recalled Jeff Reynolds. "The prosecution wanted to show Barbara's dedication to the murder of Jerry Heimann. The defense thought this was pretty far-fetched hearsay, but Judge Knight ruled to allow it."

"That stuff about Steve is nonsense," groused Barbara Opel, who was more than eager to talk about that Monday visit to "Steve's house."

"Steve lived probably about three, four minutes away from us by car," said Barbara. "Jeff drove the car, and Heather was sitting up front. Derek, Tiffany, and I were in the back. Steve was someone that I had known for a few months, due to his son had come over before and was an ex-boyfriend of Marriam's and a good friend of Derek and Heather's, and at that time I had loaned him two hundred dollars that I couldn't afford to loan him for his utilities, and my purpose in going over there was to talk to him about that loan. When we showed up, his daughter came out. There were dogs there, and Heather and Tiffany got out of the car to talk to the daughter and play with the dogs. He told me that he didn't have the money at the time and he would call me in about a week. I took him at his word because he never tried to dodge me when I went over there or called him."

As for this meeting having anything to do with Jerry Heimann, Barbara Opel was emphatic in the negative. "This had nothing to do with Jerry, had nothing to do with buying supplies of any kind, had absolutely nothing to do with the situation at my house in any way—it was simply a visit to find out about him paying me back the money I lent him to pay a utility bill."

Mention this "mystery man Steve" to Chris Dickinson, and his eyeballs roll back in his head in exasperation.

"Jeff Grote said that Barbara Opel was talking to this black man by the name of Steve," recalled Dickinson, "and something about getting supplies to kill Jerry Heimann, and that it didn't work out, and that he was basically playing her, or ripping her off. Barbara Opel said Steve had nothing to do with the murder. 'I hadn't offered him any money. I was just collecting a debt, some money that I loaned this guy that I had known for a few months. I'd even gone down to the PUD and paid his PUD bill with him.' I asked her, 'Well, what's Steve's name?' She said, 'I can't remember!' She knew him well enough to go with him to the PUD (Public Utility Department) and pay his utility bill, but didn't remember his name."

"Mystery man Steve," commented Fred Wolfson, "was supposedly another plot hatched by Barbara Opel, and plots were popping up with wild abandon. They may have all been true—far-fetched and stupid, but true. It would be for the jury to decide."

The judge also denied the two other defense motions, but he granted that there would be no mention of the state's witnesses having been subjected to lie-detector tests prior to testimony. If the defense brought up the issue, then the prosecution could present the results of those tests.

Denied was the exclusion of testimony by the waitress from Denny's restaurant regarding wisecracks allegedly made by Barbara Opel about being suddenly unemployed, and information regarding missing checks and money from the account of Jerry Heimann.

With all that out of the way, Gregory Dean Heimann, age forty-four, father of four children, and son of Jerry Heimann, took the stand. Step by step, incident by incident, he recounted his heartbreaking trip to visit his ailing father, including his dismay at discovering his father's personal papers scattered across the kitchen counter.

Barbara Opel's attorney Peter Mazzone asked if it were possible that Jerry had been looking through them and simply left them out, perhaps due to a deteriorated mental state.

"No," responded Greg, "I know my father. He wouldn't leave them out."

"Do you know how far your father had gotten into drinking in the last five years?" asked Mazzone. "Do you think that might affect his ability to do certain things?"

"No. I know he drank a lot. He had been drinking all his life. He knew [how] to handle his beer. He doesn't drink hard liquor."

Mazzone then brought up former caregiver Diane Jensen's battles with addiction. The impression was that Jerry hiring a woman with an unpopular medical problem indicated a lack of judgment. Greg Heimann stood by his father.

"I don't believe Dad was aware of her problem with that until after she wasn't Grandma's caregiver anymore."

"But," countered Mazzone, "hadn't you warned your father about having such a person as a caretaker?"

"No," replied Greg, "I warned him about having her as a girlfriend. My dad told me about her problem once they started going together. Well, once you have a girlfriend, you tend to overlook things, I think. Knowing my dad, he was probably trying to help her get over it. He's a nice man."

When Greg Heimann finished his testimony, the judge spoke to the jury. "Ladies and gentlemen of the jury, you are stopping for the day. This is not a typical day. A typical day, we will be going to four-thirty, but not today. Do not read about the case, do not hear anything about it, don't talk about it to anybody. Please do not do any investigation on your own, driving to where this house is. If you were thinking about that, don't do that. I'm trying to think if there's anything else I should tell you not to do. But I told you I'll be telling you that every day, not reading about it. You know that there was a photographer here, and you know that there was—I'm not sure if you know, but there was a motion camera here as well, so that it's more likely than not it's going to be in the newspaper and on TV as to what happened here today. You know what happened here today, so stay away from it. Have a good afternoon. We'll be starting at nine A.M. tomorrow morning."

The jury was taken out, and the attorneys continued their arguments over what pictures of Jerry Heimann would be used in court. The defense objected to a few of the more shocking and grisly photographs.

"Your Honor," said Mazzone, "we are not disputing any of the facts of the case. We are not disputing that the man is dead, we're not disputing that he was found in a ditch someplace in a ravine, we are not disputing the fact that he was killed in a violent manner, we are not disputing the fact that there was some kind of substance, which I don't know exactly what it was, but that some kind of substance was poured on his face in an attempt to either disfigure or hide the identity of the person. We're not disputing any of that. So we fail to see the relevance of these photos."

"The man was brutally murdered," decided the judge. "Whatever you want to do and say about it doesn't change it, he was brutally murdered. And you don't just take it out because it shows what happened. That's life. I have not allowed the state to duplicate photos. I have admitted less photos than offered, I have balanced it. The state is entitled to show what happened. Is it prejudicial? Yes. All good probative evidence is to be prejudicial. Is it unfairly prejudicial? No. The probative value exceeds the prejudicial value and the photos are coming in."

One thing that wasn't coming in was any reference to Barbara Opel cashing $1,800 worth of checks while she was caregiver for Mrs. Heimann. "Teresa Heimann is scheduled to be here tomorrow," said Mazzone. "What is said in her statement to the police is this. She was asked a question—were you aware of any problems that Jerry was having with Barbara? And she answered, 'I was aware that he was missing checks, and [they] were forging Evelyn's signature, because the checks were in both Jerry and Evelyn's name.' Then on page ten, related to the same topic, the question was asked—do you know if Barbara and Jerry had any kind of relationship other than a professional relationship? And she answers, 'No, sir, I sure don't, except for the missing checks, and that—probably missing money. Last week the police were out there because she had tried to cash an eighteen-hundred-dollar check at a check-cashing place.' I'm moving to have those statements be inadmissible. Those are speculations. And with respect to this eighteen-hundred-dollar check that she speaks of, if we go there, that will open up a whole can of worms, which I can go into."

"Well," responded Dickinson, "I don't intend to go into that. However, I think that the defense could well open the door to that if they start trying to portray Ms. Opel as a wonderful caregiver for Evelyn Heimann."

Mazzone understood completely. As long as he didn't portray his client as "a wonderful caregiver," the matter of $1,800 in forged checks would remain unmentioned. At 3:15 P.M., court was recessed. The trial of Barbara Opel would begin again at nine the next morning with a tactical discussion of Marriam Oliver's wardrobe.

Friday, March 21, 2003

Marriam Oliver was transported from Echo Glenn Juvenile Correctional Center in a bright yellow jumpsuit—not exactly a contemporary fashion statement, but an outfit selected to communicate that she was an incarcerated criminal. As presentation is everything, the defense wanted jurors to have the constant visual reminder that she was a criminal.

While Marriam was in transit, jurors heard from Teresa Heimann and Detective Callaghan. Mrs. Heimann told her version of events, and Callaghan answered questions regarding the discovery and condition of Jerry Heimann's body, and pieces of evidence found at the body site.

"This bottle of acid that you found, did you ever determine whether or not it's a bottle of acid that could be bought at any store by anyone, or does somebody need special permission or have to go to a special place to get it?" Dickinson asked.

"My understanding," replied Callaghan, "was it was a bottle of acid that you could get at a hardware store, at a Lowe's or a Home Depot or any other hardware store type of material is my understanding of it. I've used similar things to clean concrete, clean fungus off concrete, aggregated sidewalks—sometimes you wash and you clean it with diluting this with some water to clear it off. It's used in construction and heavy cleaning if you need sort of an acid, something very strong to wash something off, such as concrete sidewalks, other things like that. It is available to anyone."

Marriam Oliver took the stand, explaining why she wore a yellow jumpsuit. "I participated in the murder of Jerry Heimann when I was fourteen," acknowledged Oliver. "I was charged with first-degree murder with a deadly weapon enhancement. I was charged and convicted as an adult. I was sentenced to twenty-two years, no good time. I will be released from custody in 2023."

From April 2001, Marriam Oliver was originally housed in Unit 2 North at Denny Correctional Center, where juvenile corrections officer T.J. Cope worked five days a week as a housing officer. "I have come to know Miss Oliver fairly well in this time," reported Cope on September 5, 2001. "She is very smart and loves to be the center of attention and in charge of things. Marriam tends to carry herself with more sophistication, and her maturity level is higher than most girls her age.

"During her stay here," Cope said, "she has tended to hang around with girls older than her. Marriam gets bothered by the younger girls and their immaturity. I have also noticed Marriam is a leader in the unit, and has not ever been intimidated by another detainee. Younger detainees seem to be intimidated by Marriam's loud and aggressive behavior. She's told me that she has always been spoiled, and tends to get anything she wants and can talk her way out of most things."

Cope offered an example of Oliver's clever handling of a potentially unpleasant situation. "When she gets kicked out of class by a teacher, she tells them, 'You know it's just me. I'm loud, but I heard everything you said.' The teachers then let her continue with the class."

According to Cope, Oliver was also adept at playing the race card. "Marriam has stated on several occasions," explained Cope, "'Oh, I get it—it is because I'm black.' Once she was at the back of the line for movement, and she stated, 'I see the black always at the back.' I feel she says this part as a joke, and part to get her own way."

Using sophistication, charm, and verbal skills to "get their own way" is a common trait exemplified, even at an early age, by individuals with sociopathic or psychopathic personality disorders.

"I've dealt with plenty of sociopaths," stated Jeff Reynolds. "They are all charming, have normal or above normal intelligence, and don't usually show symptoms of other mental diseases. They don't have delusions, hallucinations, irrational thinking, or psychotic episodes. They have good social skills and good verbal fluency. Usually, they take on leadership roles in their social groups."

Dr. Robert Hare, noted Canadian researcher on the psychopathic personality, stated that as much as 25 percent of the inmate population show many of the characteristics of what psychiatry has named "sociopathy," or, more properly, "antisocial personality disorder" (APD).

Dr. Hare characterizes them as "intraspecies predators" that use charm, manipulation, intimidation, and/or violence to control others and to satisfy their own selfish needs. They do exactly as they please, violating social norms and expectations without the slightest sense of guilt or remorse.

The *DSM-IV,* the important diagnostic manual used by psychologists and psychiatrists, defines APD as a disorder, and lists its main characteristics, which can be easily recognized in affected individuals. Sociopaths are unable to learn with punishment and modification of their behavior. When they discover that their behavior is not tolerable to society, they react by hiding it, never by suppressing it, and by cunningly disguising their personality traits.

Indifference to the welfare of children, says Dr. Hare, is a common theme. This indifference may take many forms. Sociopaths who appear to be taking care of their children may still be manipulating the kids for their own purposes. They may demand certain behavior or accomplishments— for their own image, not for the benefit of the child— inflict emotional abuse, so that children have no concept of normalcy, or deliberately try to corrupt a child through inappropriate or dangerous activities. Encouraging murder in exchange for a new dirt bike would certainly qualify as inappropriate.

"The kids in the Opel case," recalled Tony Stevens, "were not exactly contestants on *GE College Bowl.* All of them, as noted by Chris Dickinson, were troubled from the get-go."

Bruce Eklund, assistant administrator for the juvenile

division of Snohomish County Superior Court, said that he noticed that killings by groups of young people appear to come in clusters. Common threads, said Eklund, were lack of maturity, minimal adult involvement, and dependency on drugs and alcohol. Bill France, a child advocate at the prosecutor's office, said many young people are raised in homes where parents' work schedules give them large blocks of unsupervised time during the afternoon and early evening.

Jenny Wieland, executive director of the Everett-based Families & Friends of Violent Crime Victims, stated that while the community expresses outrage over youth killings, there is little interest in actually addressing the primary contributing factors, such as violence in the home or mental illness, such as sociopathy.

"What's really scary," commented Fred Wolfson, "is that up to four percent of the population is sociopaths. Most of them are not criminals, they are just jerks. What they all have in common is that they lie, and they do it most of the time."

Marriam Oliver testified that she lied to Jeff Grote when she first approached him at the skating rink. "I told him that Heather was fifteen," she admitted. Fifteen still isn't "legal" age for sexual consent in Washington State, but it was more inviting than thirteen or fourteen.

Oliver also testified that she didn't much care for Grote. "He looked like a thug," she said. "We didn't speak much to each other. It was sort of an arm's-length relationship. Jeff spent more time playing video games with Derek than he did spending time with Heather, but I got the feeling anyway that he was sort of jealous of Heather and me—I mean because we were so close and spent so much time together.

"Heather and me spent time together talking girl talk and doing girl things," said Oliver, who went on to say that on the Monday after they first met Jeff Grote, Barbara Opel, Jeff, and Heather discussed killing Jerry Heimann, and that she personally participated in, or overheard conversations between Jeff Grote and Kyle Boston. It was from that first Monday, she testified, that Barbara Opel's final and successful murderous plot proceeded.

On cross-examination, however, the truth of her statements came under intense attack by defense attorney Peter Mazzone. "Don't you remember, Marriam, the day after you met Jeff Grote, you had to leave town and go to a tournament in Tacoma, Washington. You were gone for the whole first part of spring break. In fact, you were not even in town on Monday, were you?"

"Oh yeah, that's right."

"You didn't even see them until later on that week, right?"

"Correct."

"I can't for the life of me," Mazzone later commented, "figure out how she's sitting around talking to Jeff Grote and listening in on conversations with Kyle Boston if she's in Tacoma. The only reason she could do that is because she got twenty-two years instead of life without the possibility of parole. The story gets better as the deal gets better."

"Marriam Oliver's testimony did not go well for the prosecution," recalled Tony Stevens. "She also caused an absolute legal uproar by suddenly contradicting earlier statements, and appeared to fabricate, on the spot, another plot hatched by Barbara Opel."

"That kid told police that she hit Jerry with a softball bat, and after that, he wouldn't let Heather have friends over," recalled private investigator Fred Wolfson. "It was right there in two police reports. Marriam Oliver told the story in one of her interviews, and Diane Jensen heard about it from Jerry Heimann. Well, when Marriam Oliver got on the witness stand, that story mutated remarkably."

In Oliver's new rendition, it was no longer simply a

bizarre story of her whacking Jerry with a bat. It was now a plot devised by Barbara Opel, and it wasn't Marriam who hit Jerry—it was Heather.

"The plan was," Oliver testified, "that when Jerry came in and was going to sit down, probably at the dining-room table, and smoke and drink a beer, and that we would turn the lights off and hit him with the bats. Jerry came in," she said, "and he sat down, and Heather was talking to him, and meanwhile Barbara Opel and Tiffany and Derek went downstairs in the basement. Barbara said that she was going to be downstairs. She said that so she could act like she didn't know what was going on."

The scenario, as outlined by Marriam Oliver, went like this:

"Jerry," asked Heather, "are you going to help me with my softball swing?"

And then Heather turned off the lights. Marriam came out of Evelyn's room, bat in hand, but before she could do anything, Marriam heard the metallic whack of Heather's aluminum bat slamming into Jerry Heimann.

"We both went, 'Oh, my God. Oh, my God.' So then we ran downstairs. And meanwhile Jerry was upstairs yelling, Heather and me were downstairs, and then Barbara Opel said, 'You got to go, you got to go.' Jerry was calling for Barbara, and yelling, 'What's going on?' I don't know what Barbara said to him, but then she went downstairs, and then her, Tiffany, and Heather went out, and I went out the window, and she drove me home. And that was the end of that. This happened a week before Brandon and Chris and Danny were supposed to kill Jerry."

Defense attorney Peter Mazzone went ballistic. Not only was this story coming out of the blue, there had been no reference to it in the prosecution's opening remarks detailing the various plots of Barbara Opel, and he couldn't find it in the discovery packet sent to him from the prosecution.

"Marriam Oliver testified about something that we knew nothing about—namely, a supposed plot to hurt Jerry between her and Heather at Barbara's insistence. We had never heard of that, because she had never mentioned that to the police or us when we had our interview. I started combing through all the documents that we had received, and I found a statement made on February 24, 2002, to the prosecutors alone when Marriam Oliver was getting her deal. When I saw that, I was surprised, because I had never seen it before."

Mazzone, feeling blindsided and set-up, was outraged. "We believe that this amounts to prosecutorial misconduct. We believe this is an attempt to ambush the defenses by putting in some alleged plot that was never discussed, never reiterated to anyone. And it is clear that our interview with Marriam Oliver did not take place until July of 2002, which was a full five months after the statement that she had given to the prosecutors in an effort to get her deal. And it was never brought out at that time. It was never pointed out to us at that time. The only way—the only thing that we were aware of was something that we had discovered independently from a potential witness and we did not discover that until February of this year coincidentally. And that was that Jerry Heimann had told someone that he had been struck in the face by a bat that was swung by Marriam Oliver. And so that's all we knew about it. And this obviously was not given to us in a timely fashion and I would move for a mistrial on that basis."

The judge cast a glance at the prosecutors, and George Appel offered an explanation. "The problem is that the wrong date was used on this interview. The interview was actually conducted on February 24, 2003, not 2002. That took place just a month ago. The fact that '02 was written down as the date instead of '03 was unfortunate, but it was just a mistake."

This explanation only seemed to confuse matters for the

worse. The judge requested clarification. "We are talking about the interview of Marriam Oliver," said Appel. "The interview was February 24, 2003. It was at this interview that Mr. Dickinson and I resolved to clear up something that we had learned about long ago from another witness, Diane Jensen, had written a statement for the police in which it said—and this was way back two years ago, discovery page 537, in a statement that was long since provided to the defense, she said that she had a conversation with the deceased, Mr. Heimann, and that Mr. Heimann told her that Marriam Oliver hit him with a bat, and it came out of the blue, and he had no idea why she would do such a thing. Diane Jensen asked if he was going to call the police, and he made some mention of not being a cop caller."

"Your Honor," pleaded Mazzone, "I find it somewhat unbelievable and rather unfortunate that the prosecutor now claims that, well, this was really done 2/24/2003, but yet they made no effort to specifically tell us about that interview with Marriam Oliver and they made no effort to tell us after that that there was a new plot, because all we knew was that Diane Jensen had said Marriam had hit Jerry Heimann in the head with a bat. There was nothing about a plot involving anybody else, nothing about Barbara saying anything."

"Don't start accusing people of prosecutorial misconduct," insisted the judge, "unless you absolutely know for sure. I mean, you're talking about people's reputations here."

"I understand that, Judge," said Mazzone. "All I know is that I have a letter dated 2/24/02, and now they tell us 2/24/03, and stating it was an honest mistake. I can say it is rather ironic they left that out of their own opening statement. They didn't even mention it. So to the extent that they had this other plot that they offered us discovery for, they never even mentioned in their opening. And I would expect, to the extent that they had an additional plot, they would at least offer to make a phone call and say, 'Hey, look, I know we're busy picking a jury now, and I know there is a lot going on, but I think you should know now that we've spoken to Marriam Oliver—again she has disclosed to us yet another plot,' which would be pretty important considering the nature of the trial, considering the nature of the allegations, and considering the nature of the discovery and they did not do that. And, in addition to that, when they made their opening statement, they even left that out, which is surprising to me, given that now they have this new plot. And, of course, the question was—"

"Maybe it wasn't important to them," interrupted Judge Knight. "Gentlemen, what I'm hearing is just plain tiredness on both of your parts. I'm not hearing any prosecutorial misconduct. We've now spent about fifteen minutes about much ado about nothing. The motion is denied."

Another judge may have declared a mistrial on the spot. This wasn't another judge. Mazzone knew from Marriam Oliver's previous statements to police that the reason she was banished from Jerry Heimann's house, and why she only entered by sneaking in through the window, was because she hit Jerry with a bat. The trial resumed, and Mazzone decided to hit Marriam Oliver's sudden distortions head-on.

CHAPTER 16

"Now, you mentioned that there was an incident that happened at some point and you couldn't go over to the house anymore. Do you remember saying that?" Mazzone asked.

"Yes."

"That was an incident when you hit Jerry in the head with a bat, wasn't it?"

"No."

"I'm talking about the incident that led to you not being able to go to the house anymore. What incident happened that made Jerry keep you from going to the house anymore?"

"I don't remember."

"Well," said Mazzone, "let me remind you, if I may. Here's what you said: 'Before I used to come in through the front door all the time. But then I started coming in the back window.' Now, please tell us, why did you have to start coming in the back window?"

"Something happened."

"What happened?"

"Can I take a break?" asked Oliver, and she looked pleadingly at the prosecutor.

Marriam Oliver would not answer. There was one event, two versions from the lips of the same person. Mazzone wasn't done with her—break or no break.

"This story of Heather hitting Jerry was completely out of left field," said Jeff Reynolds. "Once she started this new version, she had one hell of a time making it fit into anything she had ever said before."

When Mazzone got Marriam Oliver back on the witness stand, he picked up right where he left off. "There was an incident where Barbara had told you to hit Jerry, and you and Heather planned to do it. Remember that?"

"Yeah," responded Oliver, "that's true."

"And that was the one that you've never told anyone about ever before? You never told the cops that back in April, did you?"

"I don't remember."

"You didn't tell us when we interviewed you in July, did you?"

"I don't remember."

"You claim that Barbara told you to hit Jerry with the bat? You and Heather?"

"Yes."

"And you were okay with that?"

"Yeah."

"What you said was that it basically started out because you wanted to protect Heather, that's why you decided to do it?"

"Yeah."

Mazzone then logically described the scene as Oliver had outlined it: Marriam was hiding in Evelyn's room. Jerry and Heather were speaking. Jerry saw Heather with the bat. Heather turned off the light and hit Jerry with the bat. If Jerry didn't even know Marriam was present, and the only one he saw with a bat was Heather, it simply made no sense that Marriam would get the immediate blame.

"So," concluded Mazzone, "Jerry must have known that it was Heather that hit him with the bat?"

"Basically."

"Then why would he keep you from coming to the house if Heather was the one that hit him with the bat and you weren't even there?"

"Because probably Barbara Opel told him that I did it."

The degree of believability inherent in Oliver's testimony against Barbara Opel was disintegrating rapidly. This was good for the defense, not so good for the prosecution. In her testimony Marriam Oliver described Heather Opel as shy, timid, and not one to stand up for herself. Marriam saw herself as Heather's protector.

"You told us that Heather is a timid person," said Mazzone, "the kind of person that can't stand up for herself, but you, on the other hand, are a bold person. In that case, why is Heather the one that hits him with the bat?"

"I don't know why," said Oliver, and the questioning went around in nonproductive circles. Barbara Opel hadn't heard this new version either. The way she recalled the incident was exactly the way Oliver told it prior to the absurd revision.

"Heather and Marriam were going outside, out the front door, they had bats and balls because Heather was going to be doing some pitching practice with Marriam, and the next thing that I know," said Barbara Opel, "Jerry is screaming for me to get upstairs, and Marriam's downstairs, crying and saying, 'Mom, you need to take me home, I need to get out of here.' Well, I went upstairs to see what was going on and Jerry tells me that Marriam hit him with a bat, and to get her out, and that he never wants her in his house again."

"To dwell on this issue," noted Jeff Reynolds, "would

be like mounting a merry-go-round horse and expecting to ride in a straight line. For everyone's sake and sanity, the topic was discarded and attention turned towards another alleged plot—the one involving Danny D'Angelo, the boy who supposedly backed away from the brink of murder."

Marriam Oliver was only thirteen when Barbara Opel first asked her if she wanted to help kill Jerry Heimann. "I was talking to Heather on the phone about a week before my birthday," said Oliver, which would have put the date around the seventeenth of the month prior to Heimann's death, "and then she put her mother on the phone. That's when she asked me, 'Do you want to kill Jerry with us?' I thought she was joking. I didn't think she was serious about something like that. I was shocked," Oliver said. "I told her no, and then said I had to go, and hung up."

According to Oliver, it was early April when she was with the Opels and three boys from the Skate Deck at Denny's restaurant, at 2:00 A.M. "We skated until midnight and then went out to eat. It was Heather, me, Derek, Tiffany, plus Brandon, Danny, and Chris. After we ate, we all went back to the Heimann house because we planned that night to attack Jerry Heimann. The plan was to beat him to death."

According to Marriam Oliver, this bit of social deviance was the brainchild of Barbara Opel. "She said that she didn't care how we did it or anything, and just to beat him to death, do whatever we can to kill him. She was saying that to me, Danny, Brandon, and Chris. Danny brought up money, saying he wanted ten thousand dollars and Barbara said that would be okay."

Barbara Opel drove them all to Heimann's house, and the kids crawled through the basement window. Barbara advised them that Jerry was probably asleep, and this would be a good time to kill him. According to Oliver, the boys tied bandanas over their faces, and then they all—except Barbara

Opel and her two youngest children—crept up the stairs to Jerry Heimann's room.

"We were outside the door figuring out who was going to open the door, and they said me, and I said, 'No, no, no, no, not me.' Danny had Heather's bat, and Chris had a knife. We could hear the TV going on, and we were like, 'What if he's awake?' So then I suggested we all go back, and everyone agreed they didn't want to get in trouble. No one opened the door. No one did anything. We all went back down to the basement, and Barbara Opel said, 'What happened?' And we said that we couldn't do it."

Painfully disappointed, Barbara Opel announced that no one was going to get their money and that they needed to find a way to kill him. "That's when I decided that I wanted to go home," Oliver testified, "and so did Brandon, Chris, and Danny."

The event described by Marriam Oliver is obviously the same episode told by Danny D'Angelo, although the details differ dramatically. In Danny's statement to police, he talked others out of the attack. "There were numerous other discrepancies," said Jeff Reynolds, "but Danny D'Angelo eventually offered a perfectly understandable explanation."

"I lied," said Danny. "I told the police all sorts of lies. The part about me talking them out of doing it was true, but most of the rest of it was a lie. Brandon wasn't there, really. Neither was Chris. We never even made it up the stairs. That was a lie too."

Danny had three prior felony convictions on his record when he took the stand to testify against Barbara Opel: taking a motor vehicle without permission in 2001, first-degree possession of stolen property in 2001, and second-degree robbery in 2002, all handled in juvenile court.

"The longest time I've spent in a juvenile institution,"

D'Angelo testified, "was ten months for the robbery conviction."

"Would it be fair to say," asked prosecutor Chris Dickinson, "that you used alcohol and drugs with Barbara Opel and her family?"

"Mostly just drink," he answered. "None of the family members really did anything. I mean, Barbara once in a while would drink, and she would buy the alcohol for us. And I would smoke marijuana there."

"At some point," Dickinson asked, "in the early part of 2001, did you find out from Barbara that there were some problems in the home with Jerry Heimann?"

"Barbara told me that the roommate that they were living with was getting drunk and coming home and getting physical," answered D'Angelo. "He would yell and start throwing things around and stuff, scaring them. They were trying to get me, like, angry, so then I would help them with their problem."

"Did they ever suggest that you do something about it?"

"They suggested that I kill him. Barbara asked me if I would do her a favor. And I asked her what it was, and she said, 'Kill him.' She used the words 'kill him' several times."

"How come you didn't go to the police when Barbara asked you to do these things?" asked Chris Dickinson.

"Because," D'Angelo said, "I didn't think she was serious, didn't really think it was going to happen. Eventually she came out saying that they would all use bats and knives. She told me that she would pay me for doing it for her. And then she suggested, like, ten thousand dollars."

"You were asked just a couple months ago how much you were going to get paid. What did you say at that time?"

"I said five thousand dollars."

"Now, it's not ten thousand, it's five thousand?"

"It was ten thousand."

"So that's another lie?"

"Yeah."

According to D'Angelo's newly revised testimony, the only people plotting in the basement were Barbara Opel, her children, and Marriam Oliver. The original cast included Brandon Carter and Chris Mathies. On the witness stand D'Angelo insisted that Brandon and Chris were never there.

"Would there be some reason," asked Dickinson, "why you're not saying that Brandon Carter was there that night you guys went upstairs to attack Jerry Heimann?"

"The reason I'm saying that he wasn't there is because he wasn't there."

"What about a guy by the name of Chris Mathies?" asked Dickinson.

"Yeah, I know him, but he wasn't there either."

"Are you sure about that?"

"I'm pretty sure," replied D'Angelo, offering the prosecutor a friendly smile. Dickinson wasn't amused.

"Pretty sure?"

"If he was there, I sure didn't see him. Actually, I'm positive that he wasn't there."

Danny D'Angelo testified that the entire incident, devoid of Brandon and Chris, happened on the spur of the moment. According to D'Angelo, his job was that he was "only going to make sure the guy doesn't come out the door.

"Barbara pretty much just told me to grab weapons, go up there and make sure nothing really bad happens. Like I was supposedly just to stand at the door and the kids were supposed to do it, and I was just supposed to watch and make sure he didn't come out of the room. 'Let's go up and do it, let's go do it right now.' And I was kind of drunk at the time and high off marijuana, and I decided at that point I was going to do it, but then when I got upstairs to the second story, I decided not to do it."

Lawyer Peter Mazzone found D'Angelo's quick-change recasting of "bandits ascending a staircase" unbelievable.

"According to Danny D'Angelo, Brandon was not even there," recounted an exasperated Mazzone. "And although Danny is a robber and takes a motor vehicle, has convictions for possession of stolen property in the first degree, he says he is a good Christian, that's why he didn't want to go through with killing Jerry Heimann."

According to Marriam, she handed Danny D'Angelo a knife. "Initially she said Danny D'Angelo had a bat," recalled Mazzone, "and then she handed him the knife. So now Danny D'Angelo has a bat *and* a knife. And Chris Mathies—who is not even there—also has a knife, and the man who isn't there is going to stab Jerry Heimann. According to Marriam, Chris Mathies is going to go up there and stab him. According to D'Angelo, Mathies is not even there! Danny now says that he didn't have either a bat or a knife, and that his entire job was to make sure that Jerry didn't come out of the room!"

What made this testimony even more astounding was its relationship to the actual physical layout of the Heimann residence. There were no knives in the basement. In order to get a knife, everyone acknowledged, they would have to first go up the stairs into the kitchen, get the knife, then go up a different staircase to Jerry's room. It would be impossible to simply go "up the stairs" from the basement to Jerry's room and be in possession of a knife without having first made a side trip to the kitchen.

"You can't have a spur-of-the-moment up-and-down-the-stairs scenario involving knives," recalled Jeff Reynolds. "It simply isn't possible. Knives don't appear out of nowhere, and the only place to get one was in the kitchen. None of this was making sense."

Contradictory comments from alleged co-conspirators stacked upon each other in rapid succession. "It was crazy," recalled Tony Stevens. "It was crazy and confusing and absurd. Couldn't any of these kids get their stories straight?"

If these youths, and Barbara Opel as well, suffered from the primary symptoms common to sociopaths and/or psychopaths, this garbled and contradictory communication style is, according to expert Dr. Robert Hare, common to most criminal psychopaths—a condition Hare coined as "mental Scrabble without an overall script.

"Lies and several contradictory statements in the same breath are very perplexing," said Dr. Hare, "and speech is the end product of very complicated mental activity. There is mounting scientific evidence that psychopaths differ from other people in the connections between words and emotions, and in the actual way their brains are organized. Psychopaths may know the dictionary definitions of words, but don't comprehend nor appreciate the significance or emotional value of words. As one person put it, 'he knows the words, but not the music.'"

This raises an important issue: if sociopaths' speech is consistently peculiar, why are they so capable of deceiving and manipulating people, and why would their friends fail to pick up the continual inconsistencies and contradictions in casual conversation?

According to Hare, the answer is "the speech oddities are often too subtle for the casual observer to detect, and these people put on a good show. Friends are deceived not by what is said, but by how it is said, and by the emotional buttons pushed."

Barbara Opel explained that Danny D'Angelo was one of the regulars at the Skate Deck, and he was privy to the information of what had gone on between Heather and Jerry Heimann.

"That was a subject that was talked about extensively, virtually every time we got together at the Skate Deck," said D'Angelo. Marriam Oliver confirmed this in her testimony, as did Barbara Opel. It was at one of these occasions where D'Angelo said, "Hey, you know, you can do *this* to this guy . . ." and came up with preposterous ideas, such as shooting some horrid chemical into Jerry's veins or getting him in a choke hold by the neck.

"If you're such a big man," Barbara Opel supposedly said to Danny, "why don't you do it? You would probably want ten thousand dollars or something for that."

"When we speak of that night, and what happened that night," said Peter Mazzone, "what happened was that Danny brought up money, not Barbara, and not two weeks earlier—that night, that conversation. Period. Danny D'Angelo's detailed description of his participation in Barbara Opel's plot to kill Jerry Heimann was, by his own admission, nothing but a series of lies."

Lies in exchange for a deal; lies in exchange for less time in prison. "The better the deal, the better the story" was an important point repeatedly made clear to jurors by the testimony against Barbara Opel. Contradictions and inconsistencies within testimonies, and between them, by the so-called homicidal teenagers obscured rather than revealed the truth.

"The jury is entrusted with the obligation of discerning the truth," remarked Fred Wolfson. "But how can they fulfill that obligation if they don't know the basic methods by which we can tell who is lying and who is being truthful?"

CHAPTER 17

Liars are not trained professional actors. They tend to stutter and hesitate. After all, they are amateurs suddenly expected to improvise as if they were professionals. Liars will also provide far more information and explanation than any truthful person would offer.

With the exception of sociopaths, psychopaths, and trained actors, people are dreadful liars. A trained observer can tell they are lying the moment they begin speaking. Liars are easily spotted because human beings are designed to only tell the truth. Telling a lie throws the entire human system into chaos, causing conflicts between the sympathetic and parasympathetic nervous systems. These two systems regulate the everyday functioning of the human body, including blood pressure, heart rate, skin response, eye movements, and everything else.

The disruption caused by the lie can be measured as if it were an earthquake. The lie's negative effect impacts speech, gestures, and coordination. When someone tells a lie, they change. They have no control over this transformation, as it is a deep-seated automatic response. In short, the liar's behavior suddenly changes.

The way professionals detect liars is to look for changes in behavior. Both body language and speech patterns change when a person lies. Some of the most common symptoms exhibited by people in the midst of a lie are almost clichés: they can't look you in the eyes; they begin sweating, blushing, fidgeting, and/or smirking. There are, however, additional clues familiar to trained investigators:

- People who are lying to you will avoid making eye contact.
- Hands touching their face, throat, and mouth. Touching or scratching the nose or behind their ear. Not likely to touch their chest/heart with an open hand.
- Timing and duration of emotional gestures and emotions are off a normal pace. The display of emotion is delayed, stays longer than it would naturally, then stops suddenly.
- Timing is off between emotional gestures/expressions and words. Example: Someone says "I love it!" when receiving a gift, and then smiles after making that statement, rather then at the same time the statement is made.
- Gestures/expressions don't match the verbal statement, such as frowning when saying "I love you."
- Expressions are limited to mouth movements when people are faking emotions (like happy, surprised, sad, awe) instead of the whole face. For example, when people smile naturally, the whole face is involved: jaw/cheek movement, eyes and forehead push down, etc.
- Guilty people get defensive. Innocent people will often go on the offensive.

- Liars are uncomfortable facing their questioners/ accusers and may turn head or body away.
- Liars might unconsciously place objects (book, coffee cup, etc.) between themselves and you.
- Liars will use your words to answer a question. When asked, "Did you eat the last cookie?" the liar answers, "No, I did not eat the last cookie."
- A statement with a contraction is more likely to be truthful: "I didn't do it," instead of "I did not have sex with that woman." Liars sometimes avoid "lying" by not making direct statements. They imply answers instead of denying something directly.
- Guilty people may speak more than natural, adding unnecessary details to convince you. . . . They are not comfortable with silence or pauses in the conversation.
- Liars may leave out pronouns and speak in a monotonous tone. When a truthful statement is made, the pronoun is emphasized as much or more than the rest of the words in a statement.
- Words may be garbled and spoken softly, and syntax and grammar may be off. In other words, sentences will likely be muddled rather than emphasized.

"If you believe someone is lying," commented Fred Wolfson, "a common technique is to change the subject of a conversation quickly. A liar follows along willingly and becomes more relaxed. The guilty wants the subject changed—an innocent person may be confused by the sudden change in topics and will want to go back to the previous subject."

A bad liar often attempts "buying time" by repeating the question before every answer. For example, if you ask a liar what he or she did last night, and he or she doesn't want to tell you the truth, the liar may answer in a manner such as:

"What did I do last night? I went to a movie. Who did I go with? I went with so and so."

Not surprisingly, politicians use this technique quite often. Sadly, many interviewers allow them to "get away" with it. One broadcast journalist famed for never allowing liars to avoid the issue was Ted Koppel, of the American Broadcasting Company (ABC). If a person avoided his "yes or no" question by giving a lengthy off-topic answer, Koppel would respond, "That's very interesting, but you did not answer the question. I repeat, did you or did you not . . ."

Detectives and lawyers look for inconsistencies. If parts of the story don't add up, they ask for clarification. "Never badger the person," added Fred Wolfson. "Simply ask for explanations."

It is always easier to tell the truth because there is less to remember—lies are too complex to remember in complete detail. When there are multiple lies told by multiple people at various times for numerous reasons, the entire fabric of reality appears tattered and destroyed—a situation played out in Judge Knight's courtroom during the trial of Barbara Opel. Most people lie for two basic reasons: fear of punishment and fear of embarrassment. Eliminate the two reasons why people lie, and, theoretically, they will tell you the truth. This formula is questionable when punishment and embarrassment are reduced for reasons other than telling the truth.

"In the Opel trial," recalled Tony Stevens, "a major issue was the possibility that many of the prosecution's witnesses—the youths testifying against Barbara Opel— were not being truthful. Rather than telling the truth, they were simply telling different lies."

* * *

Truth or Consequences

"The people who testified got deals," said Mazzone, "and their testimony was internally inconsistent and externally inconsistent in the sense that it didn't agree with the physical evidence. It didn't agree with the other evidence. It didn't agree with the testimony of people who do not have an ax to grind, who did not get a deal. These are the people I speak of—Danny D'Angelo got thirty weeks instead of attempted murder."

With Danny D'Angelo on the witness stand, Peter Mazzone asked him directly, "Danny, is it true that the only reason why you're here is because you're getting thirty weeks instead of attempted murder?" D'Angelo's answer was succinct and to the point: "Yeah, I guess so."

"The list goes on," said the defense attorney. "Marriam Oliver got twenty-two years instead of life in prison without the possibility of release or parole. Jeff Grote got fifty years instead of life in prison without the possibility of release or parole. Michael Smathers, incarcerated until he's twenty-one. He didn't testify, not an issue in this case. Kyle Boston got ten to eighteen years instead of the possibility of the rest of his life in prison without release or parole.

"This is the kind of case," said Mazzone, "that elicits gut emotional reactions from people. It's the kind of case that, when you first hear about it, first thing that someone wants to say is—murder in the first. And the fact is that most brutal murders such as this that were the result of an all-consuming frenzy most often are not murder in the first."

The jury's duty is to reflect upon the evidence, and only the evidence. Emotions must not enter into it. Preconceived ideas and opinions must be set aside.

"The prosecutors do not have to believe that anyone is guilty beyond a reasonable doubt to prosecute a case," said

Peter Mazzone. "The judge does not have to believe that
anybody is guilty of anything before he presides or she presides over a case. But the oath that jurors take is that as
the administrators of justice, they have to reflect upon the
sufficiency of the state's evidence. That means that they
have to reflect on the evidence that has been presented to
them, armed with the tools of the presumption of innocence, the state's burden, and that, whatever they're convinced of, they have to be convinced beyond any and all
reasonable doubt whatsoever. That is the oath. That is the
responsibility and the duty of a jury. It can't be an appeal
to the emotions."

Emotions were an alleged factor in the rather oblique
testimony of Henry Goudeau. "His wife was in the courtroom," recalled Tony Stevens, "and he wasn't about to dis-
rupt what was left of any domestic bliss. In addition, the
defense wanted to bring up Henry's alcohol problems and
criminal past as a way of discrediting his testimony against
Barbara Opel."

"I robbed a bank," admitted Henry Goudeau, "and
served five years in prison, and did fifteen years on parole.
I had a parole violation, and I had to go back and do one
more year, so actually I did six years in the penitentiary,
fourteen years on the street. The parole ended in 1997."

The defense would bring up Henry's robbery conviction, but not until they hammered him about his beer consumption and possible marital problems.

"When you saw Barbara Opel," asked Mazzone, "were
you whining a little bit about your current situation with
Terrica Goudeau?"

"No, sir, I wasn't whining."

"You were complaining?"

"No," replied Henry, "I wasn't complaining either."

"I noticed that Terrica Goudeau is in the room right now. Is that why you're not willing to admit that?"

"There is nothing to admit," snapped Henry.

"Is it perhaps you don't remember that because you had too much to drink?"

"No," Henry said, refusing intimidation.

"But, in any case," continued Mazzone, "when you went to the place to eat, over there across from Fred Meyer's [a department store], you had two or three more beers there, and then rode with Barbara back to the house where she was staying, you were there for about three to four hours, catching up on old stuff'?"

If Mazzone was leading Henry Goudeau down a path implying infidelity, Henry wasn't born to follow.

"Playing with Tiffany was mostly what I was doing," stated Henry firmly, "and talking to the kids."

Henry acknowledged that when he first came over to Barbara Opel's, he was told about the situation at the house in that he had to be careful about not being discovered by Jerry Heimann. Another one of the discussions that evening between Barbara Opel and Henry Goudeau was about the child support he paid every month, the tickets he had on his car, debts owed, bills to pay, and the high cost of rent at the City Center Motel.

"Rent was one thousand dollars a month for the motel room," said Henry, "and those debts had me in some financial trouble."

"You were also complaining about your wife," said Mazzone, "do you remember that?"

"No."

"Did you kiss Barbara Opel good night?"

"No."

"Did you try to kiss Barbara Opel good night?"

"No!"

"Do you remember talking about having had it with Terrica and wanting to move out?"

"No. I never had any intention of leaving my wife then or now."

"Is it because she's in the room now that you're saying that?"

The defense did everything possible to portray Henry Goudeau as a sloshed, unhappy, and debt-ridden gent whose combined personal issues made him an unreliable witness for the prosecution, but a reliable witness on Barbara Opel's qualities as a good mother.

"She was a great mom when I was with her," confirmed Henry. "She took care of the kids, kept a good home, always provided for them, always made a big deal out of, like, parties and birthdays and things like that. The kids always went to school clean, there was always food on the table that she prepared. She did all the things a good mother does. That's why her asking me to kill Jerry Heimann and/or get rid of his body was out of character. But," added Henry, "Barbara's the kind of person that likes to kind of talk a lot. She's the kind of person that when something is on her mind, she says lots of things, getting things off her chest about things that she didn't like. That's why I thought that she was joking at first about the Roundup."

Henry Goudeau threw his interrogator a curveball when he suddenly said, "I asked her if she put some of it on the food that she gave me, and she said no. But the next day I was sick as a dog, lasted three days."

"Wait a minute now," said Mazzone, "are you trying to tell us she's trying to hire you to kill him and get rid of the body, and she's trying to poison you?"

"Yeah," replied Henry, "probably because I said no."

"Wait a minute now," countered Mazzone, "you told her that you would think about it, didn't you?"

"No."

"You didn't say that?"

"Nope. I never said that."

The prosecution's parade of witnesses was comprised of individuals of such dubious veracity that their potential for impeachment was massive. In other words, the defense could use their established dishonesty to discredit even honest testimony.

One after another, Dickinson and Appel put on the stand convicted teens and disreputable adults who either had deals in exchange for their testimony, or offered the defense some other wedge by which to cast doubt on the truth of their statements. With Henry Goudeau, his criminal past was used to undermine his believability.

"You are not the most truthful person in the world, are you?" asked Peter Mazzone.

"No."

"You do have a bank robbery conviction, right?"

Henry knew what the defense was doing, and he didn't like the implication that he was not acting responsibly regarding possible homicide.

"I felt guilty because I didn't call the police like I should have when I first heard of this," admitted Henry.

"Isn't the only reason why you didn't call the police is because you told her you wanted to think about it?"

"No," replied Henry angrily, "give me a break! I've done a lot of stupid things in my life. Murder is not one of them!"

"You rob banks," countered Mazzone.

"Big difference!"

"Wait a minute now. I mean, if she tells you something

like this and, anyway, you take it seriously, the first thing you're going to do is go to the cops, right?"

"I should have."

"But you didn't do that because you knew she was joking."

"I thought she was joking. I didn't take her seriously."

"She may have been joking?"

Mazzone wanted Henry Goudeau to say, "Yes, she may have been joking." He didn't.

"Well, she wasn't joking."

"Is this all to save face with your wife?"

"No. Why do I need to save face? I love my wife."

"You just like to spend the night away from her?"

"I told you why I did—"

Chris Dickinson had heard enough. "Objection!"

"Sustained," said the judge, and Pete Mazzone stopped his aggressive questioning of Henry Goudeau.

"Basically," recalled Tony Stevens, "Peter Mazzone was doing a masterful job of, one by one, casting doubt on the prosecution's witnesses. As for Henry, because he had said he first didn't take Barbara seriously, the defense kept hammering that Barbara was simply venting, and that she was joking, and the only reason Henry was on the stand making her look like a killer was to make up for spending those nights with Barbara Opel rather than with his beloved wife in the romantic environs of the City Center Motel."

"When you take a look at the prosecution's witness list," agreed Jeff Reynolds, "it appeared as if they wanted the jury to convict Barbara Opel of murder in the first based on nothing more than the testimony of liars, robbers, and thugs—especially thugs who had other reasons to testify against Opel besides telling the truth. Either they were doing it in exchange for a deal or, in Henry Goudeau's situation, to look good to his wife."

Henry Goudeau was later described by Peter Mazzone as "the drunken bank robber." According to Mazzone, Henry Goudeau's testimony was "clouded, rehearsed, and was specifically told in an effort to avoid what the consequences would be from his wife. Henry Goudeau said that he went over to Barbara's house one day, and then he went over two weeks later. In reality, at least based on other information, he went there two days in a row. He did admit to staying overnight, which failed with his wife in the courtroom, and he did admit that he is a bank robber. He did admit that he drinks, and he did admit that even when he drinks, he drives, but that night he was too drunk to drive, even by his own standards, and he decided to stay. And he did say that he spent, at least on the second time that he was there, from twelve at noon until six the next morning at the house. I asked him if he discussed with Barbara the idea of him moving back in with her because he wasn't getting along with his wife. He denied that completely."

On the taped statement given to police by Barbara Opel, the story was completely different. Barbara said that they were going to move in together, that Henry was sick of his wife, and that Barbara and Henry were talking about finances, and how much better it would be if they got together.

"He was telling me that he wasn't happy with his wife and some of the things that were going on between those two," Barbara reconfirmed. "I guess he had already kicked her out a couple times or something, and they weren't getting along at this time. So we discussed possibly moving back in together. According to what I understood, his marriage was practically over. I mean, they weren't getting along and he liked the idea, or he was interested in exploring it. He wanted to—like I said, he was upset about all the money, you know, paying nine hundred, a thousand dollars, at the motel. He was paying five hundred dollars a month [in] child support and paying for, like, high-risk insurance, things like that. Where we sat down and I discussed what could be saved, you know, what could be accomplished, I mentioned that I did not want to leave Everett because of the children's schooling. He wanted to move more north because he had a job in Stanwood."

"Somehow," said Mazzone, "Henry Goudeau magically forgot all that stuff. And so the state wants to convict Barbara Opel based on the testimony of a stoned thief with a deal, and on the words of a drunken bank robber who testified while his wife was in court about the very motive of why he was at Barbara's house, and they want the jury to believe that that adds up to premeditation. They want the jury to believe that that adds up to intent of some sort or another on the part of Barbara. I pray that we don't convict on the words of stoned thieves and drunken bank robbers who are too drunk to drive home. I pray that every night when I get in bed."

"The defense is right," said Dickinson, referring to the dubious veracity of his primary witnesses, especially the underage thugs. "But we're not asking for a conviction solely based on what these young people testified to. That's why we presented other evidence, such as the medical examiner who corroborated the blow-by-blow injuries that Jeff Grote and the others testified to that happened to Jerry Heimann. That's why we presented the witnesses who observed and talked to the defendant after the murder, who noted her demeanor, who noted the things she said. That's why we presented the financial documents that show what Barbara Opel's true purpose in this case was—to spend the dead person's money."

"If you believe that this is about money," countered Peter Mazzone, "I invite you to look at the financial evidence introduced by the prosecution. After all this was said and done, there was still twenty-three thousand two hundred dollars in Jerry Heimann's account. And this is after there had been four transfers. If it's about money, you are going to take all the money. But that was not what was done. If this was about money, the purchases would not be to Denny's, they wouldn't be to the Chevron Mill Creek Pit, they would be transfers that went to getting out of town, perhaps luxurious hotels, but certainly not the Rodeway Inn in Everett! This is not about money, it never was. It never will be. Clearly, if the intent was to kill for the money, either you would have tickets ready to go and get lost in central Nebraska or some other country. Certainly wouldn't stay at the Rodeway, you certainly wouldn't get the U-Haul and start trucking around town with this U-Haul everywhere you're going and attracting attention to yourself. Now that's preposterous, ridiculous, and otherwise unbelievable. Why? Because this has nothing to do with money. This has nothing to do with money. They say she went on a spending spree, she spent Jerry's money. And, I repeat, went to the Rodeway, ate at Denny's, got a U-Haul. So much for Barbara killing Jerry so she could get his money and enjoy the good life."

When Detective Gary Fortin was on the witness stand, he detailed his investigation with solid factual precision. Each and every step of the investigatory process was, under questioning, explained clearly, honestly, and professionally. There was no argument over facts. On cross-examination Peter Mazzone used Fortin's solid professionalism to make a point disputing the "money motivation" behind Jerry Heimann's murder.

"Detective Fortin," asked Mazzone, "when you went

over to the motel, you performed a search of the motel room by consent?"

"Yes," Fortin replied, and confirmed that both Barbara Opel and Jeff Grote consented to the search.

"Did you find large amounts of cash in the motel room?"

"No."

"Did you find jewels?"

"No."

"Did you find anything of any value?"

"No."

"Aside from the junk that we've seen in the pictures, did you find large amounts of cash in the U-Haul?"

"No."

"Did you find any gold?"

"No."

"Any bonds?"

"No."

"Anything that you can sell for a lot of money?"

"Not really."

"Anything worth thirty to forty thousand dollars that's been kicked around here?"

"No."

"Mazzone's point was clear," said Tony Stevens. "If Opel did this for loot, show me the money. Show us the valuables, the cash, the jewels, the whatever. There wasn't any. Of course, this didn't mean that she didn't do it for money. It could just mean that she was, if one can use this expression, a homicidal underachiever."

CHAPTER 18

Barbara Opel, of course, was under no obligation to testify on her own behalf, and the accused usually does not take the stand in her own defense. Barbara, however, allowed herself to be grilled for two days solid on the witness stand, but not before her attorney submitted instructions for manslaughter to the court.

"Those instructions," said Mazzone to Judge Knight, "go directly to our theory of the case, which is that there was never any plan to kill Jerry, and that is something that happened for various reasons that were unrelated to what the plan was, or at least that developed and went further than what the plan was. And in order to explain why that arose, this plan to hurt Jerry, and there's been plenty of evidence presented at least that would support that theory, one of the ways to—one of the reasons why that happened in support of that is because of what Ms. Opel was aware of and why she felt that the situation was the way it was and why it was as serious as it was. And I believe that if we are not allowed to present our supporting evidence for our theory of the case, it would certainly be violative of her ability to receive a fair trial under her Sixth Amendment right, and certainly it would not provide her the due process that she is entitled to under the Fourteenth Amendment, and certainly it would impact the cruel and unusual punishment prong of the Eighth Amendment. So for all of those reasons, we feel that, just as other people have been able to testify regarding hearsay because it went to their state of mind, then we believe that Ms. Opel has a right to talk about how her state of mind was affected."

Judge Knight didn't see the connection. "I feel like playing the background music of *The Twilight Zone,*" said the judge. "Rod Serling could come on and say something. This is not connected to anything. 'It's not self-defense, Judge, but I would like to get in her state of mind.' That would be in a self-defense case, but this is not a self-defense case."

Mazzone had reasons—valid in his mind—why it was important and justifiable for Barbara Opel to testify as to her own state of mind at the time of, and leading up to, the murder of Jerry Heimann.

"The prosecutor and the evidence that we've heard implicates her, as well as a circle in that group, then she's entitled to say that herself, because if the jury is going to be left with the impression that she was part of this, then she has a right to present the reasons why her state of mind were such that she, at least, was willing to participate in what was supposed to be an assault. And we think that's only fair."

What Mazzone specifically wanted Barbara Opel to talk about was a conversation she had with Diane Jensen when they first moved into the new house. "When she first moved into the house, things were fine," Mazzone said to Judge Knight. "Things started becoming not so fine, and at that time Barbara had several discussions with Diane Jensen. Diane Jensen told her, 'Well, things are fine now, but wait, as you go further, he's going to start doing to you what he did to me. And, in fact, you should watch your daughter as well, because he has been improper with someone else.' And those things did, in fact, turn out to be true and did start happening. And at that point Ms. Opel did start having conversations with some people about what was going on at the house."

"And?" Judge Knight prompted Mazzone to continue.

"And then when Jeff Grote came to the house and was a part of that, he decided, because he witnessed the same thing, he decided that he should do something about teaching Jerry Heimann a lesson. She was inclined to go along with that on the assumption that it was supposed to be an assault, because she felt that that would be something that would be okay, given what he had done to her and to her daughter. She went along with that. She had no way of knowing that it would turn into what it did, and an explanation of why she became involved with the events that occurred on April thirteenth."

Judge Knight peered at Mazzone as if he were a newly discovered life-form. "That would explain why she committed first-degree murder? Or second-degree murder?"

"No," said Mazzone, "manslaughter."

"Manslaughter is not on the table," the judge replied firmly.

"We put it on the table," countered Mazzone. "We submitted it."

"You submitted it," agreed the judge, "but I'm telling you, it's not on the table from what I've heard. The acts do not support manslaughter. I'm not going to repeat the acts. We don't have a reckless disregard for the life of a person. We either have first-degree murder and maybe second-degree murder, I haven't decided yet on that. Manslaughter is not on the table regardless of you submitting the instructions based upon the evidence that's before the court. So how does any of this connect to anything, Mr. Mazzone?"

"Well, if the court's position is that that's not on the table, then it doesn't. But I'm just letting this court know that that would not enable us to pursue our theory of the case, and I think we do have evidence that's on the record, and we do have testimony that has been provided that would support such a theory that would support a manslaughter."

"Looking at the evidence in a light most favorable to the defense," said Judge Knight, "we have Ms. Oliver who swung a baseball bat not recklessly but intentionally to the head of the decedent. She did it more than once. And she might have stabbed him. Not recklessly but intentionally. That Heather Opel stabbed and swung a baseball bat, not recklessly but intentionally. That Jeff Grote swung a baseball bat not once, not twice, not three times, but perhaps four times. Not recklessly but intentionally. The question is whether or not he did it with premeditation or nonpremeditation. That's this case. I don't know what case you're talking about."

Mazzone noted that there had already been testimony that the death of Jerry Heimann began as a planned assault, and only an assault.

"And if it was only for an assault," said Judge Knight, "it ended up at the very least a second-degree murder. There's no manslaughter case here, Mr. Mazzone. Try as you might, it's all interesting, but it's cockeyed. This man was intentionally killed. He was not recklessly killed, he was not negligently killed, he was intentionally killed. Now, it may be premeditation, it may not be premeditation, but there's nothing to support manslaughter. None of this connects, and your motion is denied."

With the motion denied, and manslaughter off the table for consideration, Barbara Opel took the stand. "Barbara

Opel always portrayed Jerry Heimann as some sort of horrible monster," said Chris Dickinson. "But even if all those things were true, none of them would excuse what happened to him."

Barbara's version of life with Jerry Heimann was analogous to "living in hell" or "being a prisoner." She termed him an "asshole," who was rude and abusive. So abusive, in fact, that when Jerry Heimann was helping Tiffany with her homework, he actually paused from this task and requested the child fetch him a beer from the refrigerator. "If Opel expected a gasp of shock and dismay from the jury, she's still waiting," said Jeff Reynolds.

To this day, Snohomish County deputy prosecutor Chris Dickinson can easily recount what jurors heard about Heimann throughout the trial—the good and the not so good. "We know that Jerry Heimann hired Barbara Opel's kids at the beginning when they first met him back in November 2000—he hired them for money to come in and care for his mother. He was giving them good money to do some work. He took in this homeless family in December 2000 to come live with him. He provided Thanksgiving dinner for them. He provided money for the family that didn't have that kind of money on Christmas, 2000.

"Barbara Opel herself," said Dickinson, "testified that Jerry Heimann provided money for her family to go skating, to go practice batting at the batting cages. He provided a car, transportation to this family, when they didn't have one. But Barbara tried to convince the jury that living with Jerry was a hellish prison from which this horrible, violent crime was her only means of escape."

Barbara Opel even went so far as to try to imply that Jerry Heimann was some sort of sex offender. "She came up with this story," recalled Dickinson, "about how Heather had gone upstairs and saw Jerry Heimann naked in his bedroom, and she portrayed it as if Jerry had planned it. Interesting to note," added Dickinson, "this was a story that she had never related to anyone, according to the evidence, before she got on that witness stand. Propaganda and more propaganda. Lies, lies, lies.

"Barbara Opel lies whenever it suits her needs," insisted the prosecutor. "She lied repeatedly to the police when they started investigating this case, beginning there at the scene of the traffic accident the morning of April nineteenth when she tells Officer Sessions and then Officer Wardlaw that she has absolutely no idea where Jerry Heimann is. He just kicked them out of his house, got them the U-Haul, and they left. Pack of lies. She continued lying when she met Detectives Fortin and Neussendorfer. Again sticking to that story—'don't know where Jerry Heimann is, have no idea what happened to him, we just moved out of the house.' She told them that on several occasions on April ninteenth. She lied to Jeff Grote. She lied to rent the U-Haul truck in this case when she called and said, 'Well, Jerry Heimann is indisposed.' That's an ironic term, 'indisposed,' more like 'decomposed.' She lied to the U-Haul person to get the truck. She lied to her future landlord Laurie Pohren when she wrote that six-thousand-dollar check and filled out that rental application with lies that she was still working, and that Jeff was her supervisor. Lies and more lies."

Deconstructing Jerry

"The fact that Barbara took the stand, and spent two full days telling jurors horrible things about Jerry Heimann, says more about Barbara herself than it does about Jerry Heimann," asserted George Appel. "Barbara Opel wanted the jury to believe that she had no options other than what she wound up doing in this case."

Prosecutor Appel was well prepared to debunk Barbara Opel's claim to helpless-victim status. "The evidence shows that she had plenty of options," he said. "We know she had money coming in from various sources, her family, child support, from fathers of her children, even had state assistance coming in at one time or another. She could have easily gone back to motel living with her family. She had done it for years in the past. Granted, not a pretty situation to live in, but certainly something that she had tolerated with her family at least a couple of years."

It was an established fact that Barbara Opel was not incapable of making decisions to better herself, her situation, and her family's situation. A retrospective of her past shows her remarkable ability to adapt, manipulate, and take charge of situations.

"Look at what Opel had done over the course of the few years before this crime occurred," said Chris Dickinson. "She got rid of her first husband, William Opel. Apparently, she believed he was abusive. Maybe he was. But she got out of that situation and moved on. She had gotten rid of Henry Goudeau, who was in a sense her husband—they did apply for a marriage license, but never had the ceremony—and he was the father of her youngest child. When that situation doesn't work out, she ended that and moved on with her life, and transitioned into yet another living situation. After she got rid of Henry Goudeau, she was living in motels for a while. She would move from a motel to a different motel, depending on her income and her circumstances. Again she was capable of making choices for the betterment of herself and family."

Barbara Opel was not a person who remained in a trapped, horrible situation with no way out. The simple fact was that Barbara was capable of making choices. She repeatedly demonstrated the established ability of moving her family around if the circumstances required it.

"Obviously," said Dickinson, "the circumstances in this case were not sufficient to immobilize her and make her helpless. I bet if half the abuse that Barbara claimed occurred were true, she would have moved in a heartbeat. She would have simply moved away from that Heimann household and done exactly what she had done before. But she decided to take different action. She made a conscious decision to take Heimann's life and his money."

According to the prosecution, Barbara Opel loved Jerry's money and hated him. Jerry Heimann's house was probably the nicest living situation Barbara Opel had been in for years. That *was* the good life for Barbara Opel. "Jerry Heimann must have been spending too much money on himself and upon his mother," Dickinson said, "and Barbara wasn't going to wait for all that money to be depleted. She took it upon herself to get it. Jerry Heimann was Barbara's ticket out of poverty and the miserable life of living in motels."

The jury was asked to believe that the death of Jerry Heimann was unintentional—that the entire situation was only supposed to be a beating. "Yes, Jeff only agreed to beat Jerry Heimann up," Dickinson conceded. "Yes, Kyle and Michael were the same way. But the plan itself—the agreement was to kill Jerry Heimann. It's like—it's kind of like the analogy of the war that's going on. Jeff, Kyle, and Michael were there to soften the target up, to get him down on the floor until someone else could come up and finish him off, the girls with the knives, Marriam in particular. What would a beating accomplish for Barbara Opel and her family? Do you really think that Jerry Heimann would have allowed this awful family to continue living with him after

a second beating at the hands of young people associated
with Barbara Opel in his own house?"

"What was a bad beating of Jerry Heimann going to accomplish for you?" Dickinson asked Barbara Opel.

"We were hoping it would put him in the hospital for a
while," said Barbara. "At that time I was thinking about
getting a restraining order put against him so I would be
able to have time to move out."

"Things did get better for you once Jerry was dead,
didn't they?"

"As far as abuse, yes," Barbara replied, but not as far as
money. "I only used what I needed to use."

"Having Jerry beaten up wasn't going to get you any
money, was it?"

"Probably not," said Barbara Opel.

"When she said she wanted Jerry Heimann dead," insisted George Appel, "she really did want Jerry Heimann
dead. This wasn't simply venting anger, making an exag-
gerated statement as a demonstration of her anger. No, she
really meant it."

An indicator that Barbara Opel wasn't just venting was the
list of five people she solicited to kill or seriously harm Jerry
Heimann: Marriam Oliver, Jeff Grote, Henry Goudeau,
Danny D'Angelo, and Kyle Boston. Kyle Boston was
solicited by Barbara Opel via Jeff Grote, and Grote was the
conduit for the money and conversations between Boston
and Opel. All five testified in court that they were offered
something by Barbara Opel in exchange for harming Jerry
Heimann.

Barbara Opel testified that she didn't offer anything to

these people, and had nothing to do with killing Jerry Heimann. "You're misunderstanding my words," she lamented. "They all misunderstood me," or "I didn't say it."

Barbara Opel claimed that the police misunderstood her, and didn't give her a chance to explain. "Did Henry Goudeau misunderstand her too, not give her a chance to explain?" asked Dickinson rhetorically. "Did Danny D'Angelo misunderstand her and not give her a chance to explain? What about Jeff Grote? Why does everybody seem to misunderstand poor Barbara Opel? She even went so far in this trial as to claim that the police had agreed to let her go [if] she would simply confess to this aggravated first-degree murder. Think about that. That's absolutely ridiculous that the detectives, any detectives, would have somebody come in, have them confess to a horrible aggravated murder, and then wave good-bye as they walk out the door."

Barbara Opel wasn't about to walk out any door and wave good-bye. She had already seen her little girls wave good-bye—Heather to prison, Tiffany to foster care. Her son went from foster care to jail. She knew that prosecutors were going for the death penalty, and while she may have prayed to be found not guilty, perhaps the best she could hope for was simply to stay alive. The odds indicated that Barbara Opel was not going to walk out of Judge Knight's courtroom a free woman.

"I have to admit," remarked Tony Stevens, covering the trial for KRKO radio, "that Opel did her best to come off as a responsible parent, especially regarding the entire matter of Jeff Grote staying with them in the basement."

"Heather asked me, 'Can Jeff come over?' I said okay, and there was no plan. I mean, he was just going to come over and hang out at the house," said Barbara Opel. "We're still doing all the maid service, I'm doing all the cooking, the cleaning, the laundry, taking care of Grandma, taking care of my kids. Most of the time I believe Jeff and Derek are playing Nintendo, because a majority of the time Heather was upstairs helping me with the chores, plus she prefers watching TV upstairs."

On that first Monday that Jeff visited, Barbara Opel got to know him a bit better. "Jeff was telling me basic stuff," she recalled, "such as how he liked living in Marysville, he didn't like going to school there. Told me some stuff [about] his mom, how her boyfriend, they moved to Bellingham and lived up there for a while and then moved back, and he lived with his grandma, and he didn't have a problem with the house and the situation he lived at, but he didn't really like Marysville and the kids there and the school he was going to."

As would any good mother, Mrs. Opel gently pressed her daughter's new beau for more personal information. "I asked him what he was taking in school, what sports he played, if he planned on going to college, things like that. I asked him these things out of curiosity," she explained, "and he had started talking about possibly, you know, staying with us, you know. At that time he was just thinking about staying for the week because it was spring break. I told him that it was a reasonable possibility, but there were things we needed to talk about—and we did. I had to let him know what the rules were at the house and certain things that would be expected of him. Like I had to make sure that he knew at all times that he needed to stay downstairs when Jerry was home and just, you know, I had enough to do that I wasn't going to be— my own kids picked up after themselves, that any messes that he made, he was old enough to pick up after himself."

Barbara Opel admitted that it would be "a horrible scene" if Jerry knew Jeff Grote was living in the home. "I didn't even want to be confronted with that," said Barbara. "That's why I made sure that never happened."

According to Barbara Opel, Grote seemed unhappy living in Marysville. "He wanted to get out of Marysville for some reason, and he didn't want to live with his mother. If he were going to stay with us," said Barbara, "I told him it was something we would have to discuss with his mother, we would have to talk to her. And then I also told him some of the things that would be expected of him if he lived with us on a full-time basis—he would have to go to school full-time. If he decided that he did not want to play sports, then he could either get a part-time job in the afternoons, or another theory that I had was I wanted to possibly, you know, I told him we would have to move out of that house, that he wouldn't be able to stay. We wouldn't be able to live there together, and that he would, since I wanted to possibly go back to work part-time, that he would possibly be responsible for doing some of the errands, especially picking up Derek from school. More Derek than Heather or Tiffany because Derek got out the same time as Heather, and he never wanted to stick around for Heather's sports all the time, he would rather be playing or doing something else—whereas Tiffany always wanted to go. Also, I wanted him to be responsible for Derek and possibly Tiffany and running errands. He let me know that he had seen a truck in Marysville that he was interested in. And I said, well, with kids and groceries and doing stuff like that, you won't be able to—a truck would not be, you know, it wouldn't work. So I had a friend who owns a used-car dealership in Everett, and I told him we would see about getting him a car."

"Look what happened when they met Jeff Grote," said George Appel. "Is it any coincidence, just an accident, that Jeff moved in with Barbara Opel and Heather Opel in the basement of that house immediately, and right into Heather Opel's bed, this thirteen-year-old girl? Really, Heather was bait for Jeff Grote. Barbara had found a way to line up a reliable partner to do what she wanted to do to Jerry Heimann in this case, and that was Jeff Grote. And she got Jeff Grote's undivided attention by using the one thing that really every teenage boy wants, a young girl like Heather Opel. How else do you reel in a guy like Jeff Grote? How else do you do it? As Mr. Mazzone took great pains to point out with Jeff Grote on the stand, he had it very good where he was living at the time. Living with his grandmother, his father had passed away, his mother was apparently with a new boyfriend that he couldn't stand, so he's living with Grandma, who basically gives him the run of the house, and he has free access in and out, does as he pleases with no adult supervision. He's getting plenty of money—apparently based upon his father's death, he was getting some sort of government benefits that were being funneled to him through his mother. So he had no shortage of money. He had a nice place to live. He had no adult supervision. He could do what he wanted. How else do you keep Jeff Grote's attention and get him involved in something like this other than with a young girl like Heather Opel? Because one reoccurring theme throughout this case has been that when Barbara Opel wants something from someone, she's nice to them to make sure that she gets it out of them."

Long, rational, and responsible-sounding statements by Barbara Opel concerning her motherly stance toward Jeff Grote made Barbara Opel appear conscientious. "The strange thing is," remarked Tony Stevens, "she had demonstrated exceptional conscientious behavior regarding the elderly Mrs. Heimann in the past. Take a look at the testimony of his son, and of everyone else. Barbara Opel took wonderful care of that old lady. That was the primary reason Jerry hadn't fired her despite his fears that she was trying to bump him off. Of course, leaving the old lady behind to chew paper and soil herself wasn't exactly going to win Barbara the Caregiver of the Year Award."

PART III

CHAPTER 19

"It's easy to forget that this was more than a murder trial," said Tony Stevens. "There were other charges as well, including the abandonment of Evelyn Heimann, and Chris Dickinson made sure the jury understood what that meant."

"The crime," he explained, "is called abandonment of a dependent person in the second degree. It's kind of a mouthful, and there are five different things that have to be proven beyond a reasonable doubt. Look at the first one. On or about April 13, 2001, through April 20, 2001, the defendant was employed to provide many of the basic necessities of life to Evelyn Heimann. Well, we know she was the caregiver for Evelyn Heimann. She had been hired to do that, to do those things for her. Basic necessities of life mean exactly what you would expect it to be—food, water, shelter, clothing, medically necessary health care, hygiene, medication. All those things apply here. The second thing that has to be proven," Dickinson continued, "is that during this time frame Evelyn Heimann was a dependent person. Well, dependent person has definition in the law, and it is fairly commonsense. Dependent person means someone who, because of physical or mental disability or extreme advanced age, is dependent upon another person to provide the basic necessities."

Evelyn Heimann, he reminded jurors, could do basically nothing for herself other than sit in her wheelchair. "She had to have her diapers changed, had to have someone feed her, provide for her, and take care of her hygiene. She was," said the prosecutor, "a dependent person."

The third item that had to be proven beyond a reasonable doubt was that Evelyn Heimann was recklessly abandoned on Wednesday, April 18, 2001. "They put her up to the table," said Dickinson, "heat turned off, blinds closed, drove off with no intention of coming back, leaving Evelyn Heimann there by herself, believing or hoping that Greg and Teresa were going to show up that day, but there's no assurances that they would. We all know people don't always show up when planes are supposed to arrive."

Dickinson made it clear that Barbara Opel had no intention of going back and checking on Evelyn to make sure that dear old "Grandma," as she lovingly termed her, was going to be okay.

"In fact," Dickinson reiterated, "Jeff Grote told you there had been some debate in the household about what to do with Evelyn, and that the discussion had come down to—should we just kill her now or just leave her behind? And the decision was reached to just leave her behind. The evidence shows they did abandon Evelyn Heimann. They made no arrangements for her future care."

The fourth thing that must be established beyond a reasonable doubt was that abandoning the elderly woman created an imminent and substantial risk that Evelyn Heimann would die or suffer great bodily harm.

Evelyn Heimann's treating physician, Dr. Thomas, examined her on April 19, 2001, and noted that she was severely dehydrated to the point of causing heart damage. "She was essentially having a slow heart attack," said Dickinson. "She wasn't getting the care that she needed from Barbara Opel. She was severely dehydrated, and it was causing damage to her major organs, particularly her heart. Well," he concluded, "we know Evelyn's heart was being impaired by the dehydration that was caused by the abandonment. The fifth thing is that this all happened in the state of Washington, and that's obvious. We ask the jury to find Barbara Opel guilty of abandonment of a dependent person in the second degree."

Opel's defense attorney countered the prosecution by pointing out that Barbara Opel, rather than running away after Jerry Heimann was murdered, stayed to take care of Evelyn Heimann until just prior to Greg and Teresa Heimann's arrival.

"What was done with respect to Grandma Evelyn was the best that could be done, given the circumstances. We know that following the murder of Jerry Heimann on April thirteenth, Barbara stayed at the house until April eighteenth. In fact, she stayed there until twelve noon—two hours before Greg Heimann arrived at Sea-Tac airport. Why did she stay until the eighteenth when Jerry was killed on the thirteenth? Because everybody knew Greg Heimann was coming with his wife on the eighteenth. Everybody knew that. It was general knowledge. You also know that Barbara went with the children to the Howard Johnson's, but they came back. The reason why she stayed there until the eighteenth was because she had to wait until someone came over that could take care of Grandma. And I submit to you that the circumstantial evidence necessarily proves that this has to be the case, because if it weren't, why in the world would someone go to the Howard Johnson's knowing they have money to pay for as much as they want, but then come back the next day? Why would someone wait around and stay there the fourteenth, the fifteenth, the sixteenth, and part of the eighteenth for no reason when they have money to go elsewhere? There is only one reason that Barbara Opel stayed at the house all those days after Jerry was killed—to take care of Evelyn Heimann."

Barbara Opel was also charged with second-degree theft. "What that means," explained George Appel, "was that on or about April 13, 2001, through April 20, 2001, the defendant or an accomplice—there's that word again—wrongfully obtained or exerted unauthorized control over property of another. And in this case the property was Jerry Heimann, or Jerry Heimann's estate—his belongings that were left behind, and his money that was left behind after his murder.

"The second thing," continued Appel, "is that the property exceeded two hundred fifty dollars in value. Well, we've got that, no problem. We know, for example, that the defendant wrote out a check on Jerry Heimann's account for six thousand dollars to her future landlord, and that that check was cashed. The money was taken out of Jerry Heimann's account. She had no right to do that from Jerry Heimann, she had no authorization from him to do that. She clearly spent more than two hundred fifty dollars of Jerry Heimann's money without his permission. The third thing is that the defendant or an accomplice intended to deprive the other person of the property. That's kind of another way of saying that this wasn't an accident. It's clear Barbara Opel was intending to spend Jerry Heimann's money after the murder. And, fourth, that this all took place in the state of Washington—that is second-degree theft."

She didn't, however, make off with Jerry Heimann's furniture or other personal possessions. "She wasn't much of a thief," remarked Fred Wolfson, "if she didn't even take the items from the house."

Despite the contradictory nature of their witnesses' testimony, the prosecution had two strong things in its favor: the irrefutable death of Jerry Heimann and a tape recording of Barbara Opel confessing to the crime.

"The tape of Barbara Opel confessing to the crime was made less than a week after the actual murder itself," George Appel reminded jurors, "and she has had nearly two years since that time to come up with these pathetic rationalizations from what she said to the detectives that evening. The tape itself really contains all the evidence you need to convict Barbara of these crimes. Listen to the tape of Barbara Opel's confession to police," urged the prosecutor. "Listen to it as many times as you like."

Opel's defense attorney had no fear of Barbara's taped confession. "I want you to pay close attention when you listen to that tape," Mazzone encouraged the jury. "Count the number of times when Barbara Opel says, 'Jeff told me that,' I 'later found out that,' or so and so 'told me that.' 'I didn't know that at the time.' Count them all up. And then think about the times that she didn't say it, but clearly are in the context. And, in addition to that, pay close attention to the way the question is asked."

On the tape Barbara Opel talks about Jeff agreeing to beat up Jerry Heimann, but the questions asked of her are framed as if she is discussing Jeff agreeing to kill Jerry. The detectives mirrored this communication glitch on the witness stand when Detective Fortin referenced a receipt for new clothes. There was no way to tell from the receipt that it was for new clothes. Fortin found out sometime later that it was for new clothes. This same shift in time/tense/information is found in the Barbara Opel tape, insisted the defense.

The undisputed fact that Barbara Opel didn't hit, punch, or stab Jerry Heimann—that she wasn't even in the room when he was murdered—did not make any difference in the charge against her of first-degree aggravated murder.

"There are instructions that deal with what must be proven beyond a reasonable doubt in order to find the defendant guilty of first-degree murder," Appel told the jury. "There are four things listed on there. First, on or about April 13, 2001, an accomplice of the defendant caused the death of Jerry Heimann. The evidence, I submit to you, shows that the kids who actually committed this murder, who did the physical acts of the beating and the stabbing, were accomplices of Barbara Opel."

A person is an accomplice in the commission of a crime if, with knowledge that it will promote or facilitate the commission of the crime, he or she aids another person in committing the crime. "That is exactly what the young killers in this case did," insisted Appel. "They were aiding Barbara Opel in committing the crime of murder. The defendant acted with the intent to cause the death of Jerry Heimann. That is, the things that she did, the things that she said, were all done with the intent to cause the death of Jerry Heimann."

An important aspect of the murder charge was the issue of premeditation. "Premeditated simply means thought over beforehand," the prosecutor explained, "and the law requires some time, however long or short, in which a design to kill is deliberately formed. The premeditation of Barbara Opel to kill Jerry Heimann began, sounds like from the testimony, in March of 2001 sometime. It was long-standing, it went on. And all the plots that she was involved in to kill him simply add more and more premeditation, more and more desire to kill Jerry Heimann."

You could almost look at this case as kind of a business arrangement, almost like a construction project, if you will. Barbara was like a general contractor up at the top. She's got Jeff Grote down below as a subcontractor, and Jeff Grote brings in a couple of his employees, Kyle and Michael, to do the job, all working together, all to accomplish the goal that Barbara Opel created.

"Barbara, either by luck or by plan, wound up with the best set of young killers that she could find," said Chris Dickinson, "these misguided, directionless youth who had no moral compass, nothing going in their lives to keep them out of something like this. The evidence really shows that Barbara Opel was a magnet for lost souls."

An example of someone innocently drawn into Opel's evil orbit was Misty Moore. "Fifteen-year-old pregnant Misty gets hooked up with this group immediately following the murder. Her dad's dead, her mom's in prison. Yet, there she is getting involved with this group. And Barbara Opel didn't even have the decency to keep her out of it, and got her wrapped up in this crime, too, when they went to dump the body," Dickinson said.

Barbara was really the conductor of an orchestra, asserted Dickinson. "Conductors aren't the ones who actually play the music, but they're the ones who make sure the music comes out the way it should be, the way it's meant to be. And her actions in this case make her the conductor of the murder of Jerry Heimann."

The defense continued presenting the case as if these kids were operating alone, took it too far, committed the crime, and Barbara Opel just stayed on the sidelines and had nothing to do with it.

"Those kids," countered Dickinson, "did they impress you with their organizational skills? I mean, those kids couldn't organize a game of solitaire on their own. But here they are organizing a murder?"

Barbara Opel, said the prosecutor, was like a gun, and the kids who committed the murder, did the physical acts, were like the bullets. The bullets were named Jeff, Kyle, Michael, Marriam, and Heather. "Barbara Opel turned out to be a user and a manipulator of people, especially young people," insisted Dickinson. "She used these kids to commit a horrible crime in order to keep her own hands clean and to try to keep her young kids out of it. We know she continued to use Jeff Grote even after the murder. Remember what she had to admit when she was testifying? That she had led Jeff Grote on to believe that he could still live with them when they moved out of the Heimann house and into this new home. But that really wasn't her plan. That wasn't really what was going to happen. She was just using Jeff so that he would help them move from one house to the other. He was the strong arms and the back to make sure that happened. And Barbara Opel is seeking to use these kids today as a scapegoat for her own murderous behavior."

The actual crime that Barbara Opel was charged with is called aggravated first-degree murder. Jurors needed to understand the meaning of "aggravated." What "aggravated" the charge was that "the defendant solicited another person to commit the murder, and paid or had agreed to pay money or any other thing of value for committing the murder.

"Jeff Grote testified that he'd been solicited to kill Jerry Heimann by Barbara Opel," recalled Chris Dickinson, "and she offered him a car and clothing. Marriam Oliver testified that she was offered money for her skating. Kyle Boston was solicited to commit murder, didn't agree to commit murder, agreed to help out, to be an accomplice, and was offered money through Jeff Grote as an intermediary from Barbara Opel to commit this murder."

In truth, Kyle Boston never agreed to help out with a murder. He had no idea that a murder was going to take place. So shocked were he and his cousin, they both ran away at the sight of Jeff Grote's frenzy of violence. "Yeah," said Jeff Grote, "I called up Kyle and I asked him if he wanted to kill anybody, and he said no. The next day I called him up and asked if he wanted to beat somebody up, and he said yeah. That was the plan. That was the deal. He's going to beat somebody up."

If this crime was committed in frenzy, it was not a premeditated murder. Premeditated murders are not characterized by frenzy. "This murder was committed by the children themselves in an all-consuming frenzy," insisted Peter Mazzone. "Jeff Grote said that on the witness stand. I asked him, 'Was Heather stabbing him in frenzy?' Yeah. 'Was Marriam hitting him in the head with frenzy?' Yeah. 'Were you swinging at him in frenzy?' Yeah. 'Is it something that got out of control?' Yeah. I asked Marriam, 'Was this done in a frenzy? Was Heather stabbing him in frenzy?' Yes."

The most compelling evidence that the murder of Jerry Heimann was committed in frenzy are the pictures of Heimann's body. The medical examiner said that there were forty-seven different injuries, making the Heimann homicide the epitome of a frenzy murder. "All-consuming frenzies cause such injuries," stated Mazzone, "but planned crimes do not."

Dr. Norman John Thiersch, the medical examiner, said there were blunt injuries to the head, lacerations to the brain, incisions, stab wounds on the chest, stab wounds in the abdomen—numbering seven—additional contusions and fracture of the spine at the base of the neck. "These are the injuries that were inflicted on this man when he walked in the door," said Mazzone. "All these injuries were inflicted in a frenzy of violence. This was not a premeditated murder. This was not a planned crime. The presence of not just one frenzy, but much frenzy, means that this was not a planned crime."

Although a witness for the prosecution, Jeff Grote confirmed his lack of premeditation on his part, and the lack of any thought of murder on the part of Kyle Boston and his cousin Mike. "I had only agreed to find someone, and these people had agreed only to assault Jerry. I didn't even think that I would participate. Heather wasn't supposed to participate. Kyle and Michael were only supposed to beat him up. I made the decision that I was going to participate at the last minute," he testified. "I made the decision independently. I made the decision alone."

Misty Moore had no choice in her participation. Taken for a ride in a stolen car by an underage driver known for dishonesty and bragging, this pregnant teen was soon surrounded by people she didn't know—strangers who had just committed murder, and who had stashed a dead body in the trunk of the car. As with the other young witnesses, her story on the witness stand differed from her original statement to police, and from the deposition made to the defense team.

"Her original versions had Jeff Grote as the person in charge. It was that way in her statement to police, and in her deposition," said Tony Stevens. "When she testified, however, she changed it to Barbara and Jeff."

Peter Mazzone was caught off-guard by this sudden alteration. It seemed as if every kid who testified changed their story once they were in the courtroom. "Misty," said Mazzone, "do you remember back on August 2, 2002, the day we had our deposition, and you were under oath, and I asked you several times if Jeff Grote was the person in charge, and every time you said yes?"

"Yes," admitted Misty, "but at that time I didn't have a good enough memory to realize what was going on. It had been a year. I blocked most of the stuff out of my head, and you expect me to realize and answer all those questions when I blocked most of it out of my head."

"So," exclaimed an exasperated Mazzone, "you're saying you remember it better now?"

This time around, Misty insisted that Barbara and Jeff worked as a team. Previously she had portrayed Jeff Grote as the singular predatory pack leader. Barbara Opel's attorney asked Misty about dumping the body on the reservation. "So you get out there—who takes the body out of the car when you get to Tulalip?"

"I helped a little bit, not really. I just was basically standing there back by the Camaro, but it was mostly Jeff and Heather."

"Why did you plead guilty if you didn't do anything?"

"Because I was there," said Misty. "I knew about it. I knew what was going on."

"Okay, remember when Jeff took you home, and he talked to you about the murder? What did Jeff say about why he did it?"

"He said he had to do it," answered Misty, "he said that he had to do it for Heather."

There ensued a rather testy volley between Mazzone and Dickinson. The defense was hinting rather broadly that the prosecutor prompted these changes in Misty's testimony, and that they had told her to make Barbara's role equal or greater to Jeff's. The prosecutor, of course, insisted that they only told Misty to tell the truth. One truth was that Misty Moore received six months in jail because the terrified and threatened teenager admitted to helping clean up the mess made by Heimann's murder and, fearful of Grote, helped move Heimann's body out of the car.

Unlike Misty Moore, Kyle Boston wasn't afraid of Jeff Grote. "No, I wasn't afraid of Jeff. Jeff was afraid of Jimmy [Burleson], and Jimmy told me to steal the car, so we ditched Jeff and left him stranded at the gas station."

Asked if he was angry at Jeff Grote for getting him into this, Boston replied, "No, I'm not angry at Jeff. I'm angry at Barbara Opel. I'm angry at her because she ruined a whole bunch of us kids' lives."

Everybody who took the stand said in one way, shape, form, or another that this was "about Heather, about what was being done to Heather. This was about what was going on [with] the family. This was about Jerry being drunk and yelling all the time. This was about the abuse."

Barbara Opel's defense attorney made promises to the jury at the trial's opening, and he reminded the jury of them as the trial came to a close. "I made those promises knowing full well that I would have to deliver," recalled Peter Mazzone. "The first promise I made is that we would prove beyond any reasonable doubt, and, in fact, to a mathematical certainty, that all of these horrible, horrible injuries that Mr. Heimann suffered, in fact, were not caused, not inflicted on him, by Barbara Opel. There is no question about that. Every bit of the testimony agrees with that."

The prosecution attempted to persuade jurors, through the testimony of various convicted teenagers, that Barbara Opel was the ringleader of what happened, and that she was the person who asked them to kill Jerry Heimann.

CHAPTER 20

"The testimony of the witnesses was bought testimony in the sense that it was paid for in exchange for a deal," Mazzone reminded jurors. "And I'm here to tell you now that the better the deal, the better the testimony. That's the way it came out, because that's the way it is in real life."

"When you have a bribed or paid witness," remarked Jeff Reynolds, "which is, in the opinion of some, the situation with Oliver, Grote, Boston, Misty Moore, and Danny D'Angelo, you open up a can of worms capable of devouring truth and justice. A paid informant, or someone who testifies for the prosecution in exchange for something, is simply not reliable. I don't care if it is a drug case or a homicide case. What you are going to get on the witness stand is at best a version of truth, slanted towards the deal's benefactor—at the worst, outright lies. The laundry list of dirty deals done by informants, just in the past year, is enough to turn the stomach of any American who still believes in justice."

Newscaster Tony Stevens nodded his head in agreement. "There was recently an informant sent to prison for fraud, impersonating an FBI agent, and lying to federal authorities. The informant fraudulently schemed to extort money from several individuals, and when one of his victims refused to give him money, he reported him to the FBI and claimed that he was a terrorist. Unfortunately, the Illinois State Police, the FBI, and the DEA all used this paid informant for years to convict people and put them in prison. Even though the informant was convicted of falsely accusing people, it does not appear that anyone is looking into whether innocent people are in prison today because of his lies during his years as a supposedly reliable informant. So you tell me, how can courts even allow the testimony of folks with a deal?"

Our criminal system depends heavily on the secretive policy of trading guilt for information, allowing the government to penetrate conspiracies, corporations, or gangs, and to prosecute important cases. But as House Judiciary Committee chairman John Conyers, Democrat-Michigan, observed, these practices threaten the integrity of "the entire criminal justice process in America, federal and state." Alexandra Natapoff, law professor at Loyola Law School, Los Angeles, believes that the secretive culture of criminal snitching makes it too easy to conceal lies, tolerate crime, and break rules.

Taking the position that Marriam Oliver and other witnesses that had deals came to the courtroom armed with discrepancies and lies, the defense pointed out every inconsistency, every blatant contradiction, and every "made up on the spot" plot presented from the witness stand. Peter Mazzone dissected the bizarre versions of the aborted attempt on Heimann's life from the testimony of Marriam Oliver and Danny D'Angelo, pointing to what he characterized as a mishmash of absurdities and fabrications.

"Marriam took the stand, and right off the bat, she made up a story. We know the story was made up because the prosecutors didn't even mention it in their opening. They didn't even know it was going to come. Why? Because she said it for the first time on the stand. She said that right around March seventeenth Barbara had called her up and said, 'Do you want to kill Jerry?' And she was shocked, and she hung up the phone. And then she went on to say she went over to the house and Barbara told them that what they should do is hit Jerry with bats. Notwithstanding the fact that she was shocked by Barbara asking her to kill Jerry, she hauls off and whacks him in the head with a bat! Then she comes here and tells us that it was Heather who did it, when we know from other testimony that it wasn't Heather at all.

"According to her," Mazzone reminded jurors, "Barbara first calls up on the seventeenth and says, 'Do you want to kill Jerry?' And she's shocked. But on the thirty-first, she's going upstairs with knives, with D'Angelo and that gang—the gang that D'Angelo said was never there."

The defense also reminded the jury that Marriam Oliver put herself in places she couldn't have possibly been. Marriam testified that after they met Jeff, they discussed killing Jerry on Monday. Marriam was not even in town on that Monday. She was in Tacoma, Washington.

"The jury had to be tied up in mental knots," remarked Fred Wolfson. "This wasn't the type of case where testimony, evidence, and arguments were clear-cut."

Following the first afternoon of Barbara Opel's testimony, Judge Knight praised the jury to the attorneys. "I spent almost the entire time looking at the jurors. I saw no indication of any lax moments on the jurors. Of course, there are people that may appear to be listening and tune you out, and I can't get in their heads, but I saw no indication of that. They're the hardest-working jurors that I've ever seen, punctual, they're never late, so that's what I saw."

"That's good to hear, Judge," responded Peter Mazzone. After all, if the jurors were paying attention, they might embrace his emphatic insistence that it was Jeff Grote who recruited Kyle Boston and Michael Smathers, that it was Jeff Grote who by himself decided to kill rather than just beat up Jerry Heimann.

"Go back and look at Marriam Oliver's testimony," Mazzone told the jury. "When she was on the stand, she confirmed that Kyle made it clear many, many, many different times that all he was going to do was assault Jerry Heimann. Kyle Boston told you he had never said he's going to kill anybody. He said it from the beginning—he's just going to hurt someone. Jeff Grote told you he wasn't even going to participate. Marriam, under oath, told you on the stand, as they all did, the plan is only to hurt, not to kill. Everybody is in agreement on that."

Mazzone again and again pointed out to jurors, via comparative testimony, that Barbara Opel was not part of Jerry Heimann's murder. Recalling Oliver's initial attempt at crawling out the window during the assault, Mazzone asked her, "What were you supposed to do?"

"*They* wanted me to stab him," answered Oliver, "but then I went downstairs and I told *her* I couldn't do it."

"They" is whoever was upstairs asking her to stab Jerry Heimann. "Her" is Barbara Opel, who was downstairs.

"Is 'they' Jeff, Kyle, and Michael?" Mazzone asked Oliver.

"No," she answered, "I really wouldn't say all of them. I wouldn't say 'they,' meaning Kyle and Michael." In other words, "they" is actually Jeff Grote.

Marriam Oliver testified under oath that she only went downstairs once. "Why the hell did she go back upstairs? She could have gone out the window like she started to," remarked Jeff Reynolds. "I've heard so many different versions. One has Barbara Opel screaming at her to get her little ass back up there. Another version has Barbara threatening Marriam Oliver, and then there is the version that Marriam Oliver told under cross-examination, which is again different but more believable."

* * *

Here, adapted from question-and-answer exchanges on
the witness stand, is a reconstructed sequential version of
events from the perspective of Marriam Oliver:

"When I went downstairs and Heather went upstairs, I
heard Heather screaming for me to get up there, but I didn't
go back up right away. Eventually I did go back up, and I
went back upstairs when she started saying, 'Come up here.'
When I get up there, I see Jeff and Heather. Of course, Kyle
and Mike are gone, and Jeff is still hitting the guy. Jeff yells
at me to hit Jerry. Well, at first, I had the knife, and then I
dropped it and picked up a bat. When I dropped the knife,
Heather picked it up and started stabbing Jerry over and
over again in a frenzy. And Jeff grabs a knife and he tries
to cut Jerry's head off—kind of like sawing in the back.
After I picked up the bat, that's when Jeff told me to hit him
in the cerebellum. I hit him three or four times. It seemed
like he was dead, but I wasn't sure. Jeff took Jerry's pulse
and said that Jerry was dead. I had already hit him four
times. And that's the point where I took the bat and took a
full swing and shattered his skull. The reason I hit him that
one last time was because Jeff told me to hit him one more
time and make sure that he was dead. Jeff told me that."

Jeff Grote validated this version of events when he took
the witness stand. "Heather called Marriam and said,
'Come on.' And I told Marriam to do it one more time to
make sure that he's dead." The following day, when Jeff
Grote gave Misty Moore a ride home, he told her, "I did
what I had to do. I did it for Heather."

Those who watch trials watch juries. "This was an exceptionally difficult jury to read, and a complex web of
contradictory testimony to unravel," said crime writer Jeff

Reynolds. "They must have had one hell of a time deciding who to believe about what, and what to believe about
whom. The real acid test was the controversy and untruths
concerning the acid poured on Jerry Heimann's face—the
corrosive acid that turned the man's face an ashen gray."

The photographs taken of Jerry Heimann's body show
clearly the effect of the acid. It was poured directly on his
face with fair precision. There is no sloppy splashing, no
random streaks. "Despite clear evidence of how the acid was
distributed," recalled Tony Stevens, "Jeff Grote made up all
manner of nonsense, including a statement that the acid was
Barbara's idea—notwithstanding the fact that Marriam testified without hesitation that the acid was Jeff's idea."

"Yeah," said Jeff Grote, "when I went down there, and I
wanted to do something with the acid, I just kind of spread
it all over the place. I didn't know what I was doing, just all
over the body like that, kind of like I was just doing it spo-
radically. I wasn't aiming at anything."

The picture of Jerry Heimann clearly demonstrated that
the acid was aimed at the face, covered only the face, and
completely covered the face. "Any attempt at testimony to
the contrary is a lie," said Mazzone. "There is not a single
trace of acid anywhere else on the body."

"I didn't uncover the face," said Grote. "I started spread-
ing that acid just wherever. I wasn't really paying attention."

The jury faced perhaps an insurmountable task—
unraveling truth from a twisted tale about a twisted act
of either assault gone bad or murder transpiring as
planned—but with no apparent plan.

"Was this just to be a beating?" Chris Dickinson asked
the question, his demeanor declaring his complete lack of
belief. "Remember the murder itself, how it took place and
what Barbara Opel testified about it. She testified she could

hear the tingeing of that aluminum bat hitting Jerry Heimann as she stayed downstairs with her children, staying out of it, keeping her hands and her children's hands clean. She testified she knew Marriam Oliver had had a knife, a large sharp kitchen knife, with her moments before the murder took place.

"Barbara didn't even try to intervene to help," said Dickinson. "She could have clearly known that if this was to be a beating, things were clearly getting out of hand. She did nothing about it. She stayed downstairs and let it happen. And I submit to you because she wanted it to happen. She intended it to happen. It's obvious she didn't want Jerry Heimann to survive that attack on April 13, 2001.

"Do you think she would have gone to visit Jerry Heimann at the hospital? Right afterwards, you know, said something like, 'Gosh, Jerry, I had no idea that these kids had snuck into the house and attacked you with bats and knives. I was just downstairs the whole time, and I heard everything, but I'm sorry, I couldn't lift a finger to help you. Hope you're not mad at me. Hope you get better soon.' That's ridiculous. This was not a beating—this was a murder, planned out, intended, premeditated by Barbara Opel.

"Remember when Marriam was getting cold feet, she was chickening out as this murder is unfolding, she was the one who was supposed to go up and finish Jerry Heimann off with the large knife. Remember that Marriam ran downstairs and told Barbara Opel she couldn't do it, she was scared, she was freaking out. And Marriam told you [that] Barbara said, 'Get upstairs and help or we're going to lose our house.' On the other hand, Barbara wants you to believe that when Marriam came downstairs and was upset and crying and wanted to leave, that Barbara told her, 'Well, it's okay, you can just leave, that's fine.' But look what happened. After this conversation between Marriam and Barbara, what did Marriam do? She went back upstairs and joined the attack, joined

the murder of Jerry Heimann. Whose version of that inter-
lude makes more sense, Marriam's or Barbara's? I think the
answer is clear that it's Marriam's."

Yet, despite the rational sense of Dickinson's argument,
there remained the indisputable fact that there was no plan
for escape, no plan to hide, no plan to get rid of the body.
If there was no plan, if there was no premeditation, then
Barbara Opel could not be guilty of aggravated first-
degree murder.

Although prosecutors portrayed Barbara Opel's financial
activities following Heimann's death as a "spending spree,"
the defense presented it differently. Barbara Opel's attorney
Mazzone asked her directly, "The man is dead, Barbara.
What are you doing with his credit cards?"

"I had no way to pay for my kids," she replied, "no way
else to get food."

Barbara Opel told the jury that she was horrified by the
murder, but once it happened, she wanted to protect her
daughter Heather, who had participated in the killing.

"If this was any kind of a planned thing or intentional
thing, he would have been killed and everyone would
have been out of there," said the defense. Mazzone and
company hammered that point. There was no way the jury
could miss the point. If the murder was planned, the murderers would have been long gone, out of state, on the
run, and evaporated into the mist.

"Instead," quipped Jeff Reynolds, "Barbara and her
homicidal cherubs were hauling around their old sofa in a
giant U-Haul, staying five to a room at the nonluxurious
Rodeway Inn, and dining at Denny's—no doubt because of
its unique and wondrous ambience and haute cuisine."

* * *

Critical Mass

Jurors are supposed to superimpose the law on the facts and determine what happened. Judge Knight informed the jury that there was one of four distinct possibilities given the facts they heard. The job of a jury is to reflect on the testimony, to be convinced beyond any and all reasonable doubts whatsoever that what they decide is the right thing under the law that the judge gave them.

"Your job is not to ignore anything," said Mazzone, "and to say otherwise, it's atrocious to the system that we have. So let me explain it for you. I want to compare and contrast murder one and murder two. Because there is a very critical distinction, and you have to understand what that distinction is. Here it is, this is the critical distinction."

The dedicated attorney explained the distinction as simply as possible: "For murder one, an accomplice causes the death, but the defendant—in this case Barbara Opel— has to have the intent.

"Contrast that with murder two, where an accomplice causes the death and *either* the defendant *or* an accomplice has to act with the intent. That's the critical distinction. For murder one, the death has to be premeditated. And if you're not convinced that the evidence shows this is premeditated, then you ignore it.

"For murder two, either the defendant or the accomplice can have the intent. Let's look at manslaughter instructions. Look at this. In order to convict on manslaughter, the defendant, in this case Barbara Opel, has to have encouraged other persons to assault Jerry Heimann. That her conduct in doing so was reckless, and that Jerry, the victim Jerry Heimann, died as a result of her acts.

"If you compare that to manslaughter two, number one is the same, that the defendant encouraged other persons to assault Jerry Heimann, but her conduct in that case was not reckless, but it was with criminal negligence. Now, what does that mean? What that means simply is this. That in order to convict somebody for murder one, if an accomplice does it, the person that's on trial has to be the one with the intent, regardless of what the accomplice does, and it has to be premeditated.

"To convict somebody of murder two, either the accomplice or the person on trial can have the intent, and there is no premeditation.

"In order to convict someone of manslaughter," explained Mazzone, "the final objective wasn't death, but only assault. Death is not the final objective, only assault. And then if death occurs because the actions are reckless, that's manslaughter. And if the actions are not reckless, but just not in keeping with the ordinary care that someone else might have, then it goes to criminal negligence. Those are not things to be ignored, that's the law."

The definition of reckless and criminally negligent was then explained to the jury. "A person is reckless or acts recklessly when he or she knows of and disregards a substantial risk that a wrongful act may occur, and the disregard of such substantial risk is a gross deviation from conduct that a reasonable person would exercise in the same situation.

"If a person encourages someone to assault someone, and in doing so they knowingly disregard a substantial risk that a wrongful act may occur, and that wrongful act results in a death, that's manslaughter," said Peter Mazzone. "That's neither murder one nor murder two. That's not something to be ignored. That's the law."

A person acts with criminal negligence when he or she fails to be aware of a substantial risk. In this case the person just fails to be aware of a substantial risk that a wrongful act may occur, and the failure to be aware of such substantial risk constitutes a gross deviation from the standard of care that a reasonable person would exercise in the same situation. "So," said Mazzone, "if somebody encourages someone to assault someone else, and they fail to be aware of a substantial risk that a wrongful act may occur, and the wrongful act is the death of the person, and that constitutes a gross deviation from the standard of care that someone else, a reasonable person would have done, that's manslaughter two. That's neither murder one, nor murder two, nor manslaughter one."

The entire strategy and presentation of Barbara Opel's defense came down to this critical distinction. The goal was to guide the jury to the door marked "manslaughter." If the jury opened that door, even if manslaughter wasn't "on the table," there was no way Barbara Opel would face conviction on murder one.

"Your oath," said Mazzone, "is to reflect on the sufficiency of the state's evidence. And after you reflect on it, then your job is to be convinced beyond any reasonable doubt whatsoever of the decision that you've come to."

The defense of Barbara Opel was masterful in all respects. The view of events, the allocation of responsibility, the evidence of a crime committed in a frenzy, and the questionable veracity of some stories told on the stand were all presented clearly and with focused emphasis.

"Not one single slipup," noted Tony Stevens, "slipped by the defense team. An amazing example was the way Peter Mazzone ripped apart the testimony of Leslie Kaestner, that waitress from Denny's. She said that Barbara had come in on the sixteenth, parked the U-Haul across the street, and paid for the meal with Jerry Heimann's credit card."

"That's impossible," Peter Mazzone told the jury, "because Barbara Opel didn't have the U-Haul until Tuesday the seventeenth, at four fifty-eight P.M. Kaestner told her boss that she had accepted a stolen credit card. She hadn't accepted cash, she hadn't accepted a check. She had accepted a credit card. That is simply not so. There are no charges on Jerry Heimann's credit card for Denny's on those dates at all. It never happened."

The defense team also called attention to testimony offered by Brittany Mumea, a former girlfriend of Jimmy Burleson's. She accompanied Burleson and Kyle Boston to Barbara's place on the sixteenth, well before the police or anyone knew Heimann was missing. Barbara told Mumea that "the kids killed Jerry," that she did not want to, and she wanted no part of it. According to Brittany, Barbara Opel suggested that if Jerry's ex-wife kept nosing around, she might have to be killed too.

Barbara Opel asked to borrow Kyle Boston's gun so she could, "put a cap in someone." Boston declined, but Barbara Opel bought him some ammunition for the handgun at the Fred Meyer store in Marysville. She also bought him some new shoes to replace those that were bloodstained.

"When Mumea was on the stand," recalled Mazzone, "I asked her, 'Was everybody there at the Heimann residence?' And she said, 'Yeah, everybody was there. Jeff was there, Kyle was there, Michael was there, Heather was there.' Did anybody object to that or say anything to that or disagree with Barbara's statement that the kids killed Jerry, and that she had nothing to do with it? Her answer was no. Nobody disagreed with that statement."

Concluding his closing arguments, Peter Mazzone said, "I've showed you what I believe the important evidence to be. And soon I will sit down, but before I do, I want to leave you with a thought, because I think it encapsulates your role from here on in. When we started, I told you that there will come a time in this trial where you and I will switch roles and then you will be in the seat of judging another human being, and you will have a person's life in your hands, just as I've had up till now. And it reminded me of the story of the old wise man and the smart-aleck kid. The smart-aleck kid wants to show off to the old wise man, so he came up with a plan. He went and got a little bird and cupped it in his hands. His plan was, he would go to the old man, and he would ask, 'Hey, wise old man, is this bird alive or is it dead?' And if the man said the bird is dead, he was going to open up his hands and the bird would fly away. And if the old man would say the bird is alive, he would just squish the bird, and the bird would be dead. That was his plan. So he went up to the old man, and he had the bird cupped in his hands, could see the little tail sticking out, that's all you could see. And he said, 'Old man, is this bird alive or is this bird dead?' And the old man looked at him and he said, 'My son, the bird is in your hands.' And, ladies and gentlemen, Barbara Opel is in your hands. Thank you."

The time was 12:59 P.M., and Judge Knight called for lunch recess. "Food has been brought in for you," he said. "I would rather you stay here and not go and have lunch someplace else and maybe run into people talking about the case. So we're going to take an hour break, resume at two. Your lunch was just brought in. The case is not in your hands yet. The state has the right to make a rebuttal closing. So you are not at liberty to discuss the case, and please do not do so."

Now Hear This

Monday, April 7, 2003, 2:00 P.M.

"Before the lunch break," George Appel told the jury, "Mr. Mazzone said a great deal of things, but they all tended to boil down to essentially one common point, which is, don't believe the state's witnesses. Don't believe them. Of course, if you believe them, the defendant is guilty of first-degree murder, soliciting first-degree murder. But don't believe them, essentially, because they all got these good deals. They all got these good deals. And how can you believe somebody if they got a good deal? Well, I'm going to leave to you the issue of whether or not those witnesses got good deals. When you're fourteen years old and looking at twenty-two years of incarceration, I'll leave to you whether or not that constitutes a good deal, or Jeff Grote looking at not getting out of prison until he's sixty-seven years old."

Appel insisted that there was another, more important issue for the jury's consideration. "The issue really is, did Barbara Opel have premeditated intent to kill Jerry Heimann or not? Did she solicit people for the express purpose of killing Jerry Heimann or not? Because if all she wanted was an extreme beating, as she has told you, if all she really wanted was some sort of a weird revenge beating because he had been so mean to them, she's not guilty of first-degree murder. She's not guilty of aggravated first-degree murder, she's guilty of one of these lesser charges that Mr. Mazzone spent some time talking to you about—the types of homicide where you didn't really have premeditated intent to cause the death. So that's the crux of the matter."

Chris Dickinson had already pointed out that if it was only supposed to be an extreme beating, the act made no sense. It would be of no value to Opel or her children. It would only anger Jerry and get her and everyone else in trouble. Appel turned the jury's attention to the tape recording Barbara Opel made during her police interview, terming it "a taped confession that occurred mere days after the murder.

"The thing about a taped confession," said Appel, "is that there is very little chance to reflect. What you're going to hear when you go into the jury room is not going to be a rehearsed statement, it's going to be the natural outflowing of information from a person who actually had real knowledge, direct knowledge, and knew what was going on. I also submit that when you get into the jury room and you play this some more, you're going to find there is really little or no reason at all to believe that this statement was either coerced or taken out of context. What I do want to do, though, is draw your attention to a few things [on] his tape."

Appel played snippets from the recording, including this exchange with police:

> *Q: At some point, did that anger you to the point where you thought you would do something about it? And so what did you decide that you wanted to do about that?*
>
> *OPEL: Probably get rid of him.*
>
> *Q: What do you mean by that?*
>
> *OPEL: To kill him.*
>
> *Q: You need to speak up.*
>
> *OPEL: To kill him.*

"To kill him," restated Appel. "To kill him. Her words. Not coerced, her context. Her statement. Well, Barbara Opel would like to have you believe that at every point where she was talking about killing Jerry Heimann, she was simply misunderstood. And, as Mr. Dickinson pointed out, in that case she must be the most misunderstood woman in the world."

Appel played portions of Barbara Opel's taped confession to police, recordings in which she tells of Jeff Grote's conversations with Kyle regarding who would or would not kill Jerry Heimann.

"As Mr. Dickinson said previously, she was supervising this whole thing. That's how she knew. Well, we need to talk about Marriam, because Marriam, of course, was the one with the knife. Marriam was the one whose job it was to finish Jerry off. What did she know?"

Appel pressed the play button on the tape, and the jury heard:

Q: So she knew that Jeff had agreed to kill Jerry?

A: (Barbara) Yes.

"Barbara Opel knew that Marriam knew Jeff was now signed on and fully recruited," said Appel. "They needed somebody with a strong back who could swing the bat to start the job, and Marriam was going to finish it. The problem with Danny D'Angelo is simply that he wouldn't follow through. Now they had Jeff Grote—Marriam knew it, and the defendant knew it because she orchestrated it."

The prosecutor then played another damning bit of audio. It was Barbara Opel explaining "the plan" for when Jerry Heimann entered his home.

Q: So everybody goes back upstairs to kind of for-mulate a plan. Is that correct?

A: That's correct.

Q: And what plan is arrived at?

A: Marriam has a knife in the kitchen, Kyle and Michael will hide by the refrigerator on the floor with the little souvenir bats, and then Jeff waits in the bedroom with a big bat.

"That was the plan," Appel told the jury, "and the long and the short of it is, everybody went to a certain spot, everyone took the weapon that they were going to take, and the one commonality—and, by the way, this is the same commonality with the plan that Danny D'Angelo was involved in, different cast, same kind of plan—the defendant was involved in the planning. And you can hear it."

"They heard it all right," said Tony Stevens, "the jury

heard it loud and clear. What they were hearing wasn't a courtroom cross-examination. This was the tape of the cops letting her say what she wanted to say at the time. In fact, there was a segment at the end of the tape where Detective Neussendorfer asks her if there is anything she would like to add. George Appel played that part for the jury, and it was like dropping the A-bomb of reality."

"I, Barbara Opel, declare the facts in this tape are true and correct to the best of my knowledge. My statement has been made freely and voluntarily without threats or promises of any kind."

"There are two reasons," Appel told the jury, "not to believe Barbara Opel's new version of events. One is simply that they don't hold water. They don't make sense. They don't add up. The other reason is right here in my hand." Appel held up the tape.

"If there had been any doubt before that she had premeditated intent to kill Jerry Heimann, when you hear this tape, when this tape becomes a part of your deliberations, it is imminently clear she intended it. She premeditated upon the intent to kill Jerry Heimann with Henry Goudeau, Danny D'Angelo, and ultimately with the individuals who were involved in the death of Jerry Heimann. This evidence is pure and simple evidence of premeditated intent."

And that, from the tone of Appel's voice, settled the issue. "The state of Washington is asking you to find the defendant guilty of first-degree murder with the aggravating circumstance that she solicited individuals to commit the murder, as well as abandonment in the second degree, and theft in the second degree. We thank you for your attention."

George Appel sat down, everyone took a deep breath, and Judge Knight broke the silence.

CHAPTER 21

"Okay, ladies and gentlemen of the jury, you've heard the testimony, you've been instructed as to the law, and you've heard closing argument. What remains to be done now is to commence your deliberation with a view of reaching a verdict, if that can be accomplished. You'll receive all the exhibits that have been admitted into evidence for substantive purposes, as well as the instructions. If you do not receive an exhibit, it is either because it was not admitted, or because it was admitted for illustrative purposes only, and those do not go back to the jury room."

There is always a possibility that an alternate juror's services may be needed later, so Knight cautioned jurors 13, 14, and 15 that they were not at liberty to discuss the case, read about the case, or hear about the case. "Advise, if you have to, to prevent them from talking about it, your spouses or employers, whoever needs to know that you are still a juror on this case," said the judge, "and say that your services may be needed, and you are not at liberty to talk about it, and to have them not talk about it around you. That admonition will remain in effect until you are told otherwise by my law clerk."

Judge Knight was not stinting in his praise for the jurors or the attorneys. "I have looked at all of you throughout this trial, and it's been clear from my observations that you have been extremely diligent. You have been attentive, and for that, we're all grateful. We're going to have the jurors go back, have the alternate jurors retrieve whatever they have in the jury room, then they will leave and the remaining twelve will be told by me through you to commence the deliberation."

The jury left the room and Knight told the lawyers that if they were going to be someplace other than their offices, they should leave a contact number in case the jury had questions or they reached a quick decision.

"The plan," explained Judge Knight, "is if we have not received a verdict by four-thirty, for my law clerk to go into the jury room upon knocking and being invited in, to tell the jurors that I've told her to tell them that they are to stop for the day and to go home, and not to read about the case, not to watch about the case, not to hear anything about the case, the litany, and that usually [takes] care of it. Sometimes jurors indicate, once they have been told that, that they would like to continue their deliberations, and then my law clerk's instructed to tell them to wait and she will give me that information. If that is the case, I will let them deliberate with unknown length of time. They will not be told how long if I allow them, they will just be told yes, you may continue deliberating. I'm telling you, it will not go beyond five. If they do wish to continue deliberating when they're told at four-thirty and I say, 'Yes, you may,' they will be allowed to go to five. They won't know that."

If the jury was to return verdicts of not guilty, everything would be over. If Barbara Opel was found guilty, then everyone would move to "stage two" on the game board—the mitigation hearing. "If we get to the stage two, Mr.

Phillips," Knight said to the defense, "I still intend to take a one-day separation during the stages."

Brian Phillips, law partner and co-counsel of Peter Mazzone, was on the same procedural page. "I've begun indicating to witnesses," he said, "that the first day would be Thursday tentatively, anyway, thinking the jury is not going to reach a verdict today." It only took five hours for the jury to reach a verdict.

Aggravation and Mitigation

On April 8, 2003, Judge Knight asked the question "Has the jury reached a verdict or verdicts?"

"Yes, sir, we have. We, the jury, find the defendant, Barbara M. Opel, guilty of the crime of murder in the first degree as charged. We, the jury, having found the defendant guilty of murder in the first degree as defined in instruction, make the following answer to the question submitted by the court. Question—has the state proven the existence of the following aggravating circumstances beyond a reasonable doubt? The defendant solicited another person to commit the murder and paid or had agreed to pay money or any other thing of value for committing the murder. Answer, yes." The pronouncement was signed by the presiding juror.

"We, the jury, find the defendant, Barbara M. Opel, guilty of the crime of abandonment of a dependent person in the second degree. We, the jury, find the defendant, Barbara M. Opel, guilty of the crime of theft in the second degree as charged in Count Three."

The defense was disappointed, but not surprised. Stage two—the penalty phase—would soon begin. In the penalty phase, the state must show that significant mitigating factors don't exist—factors that, by their nature and/or severity, call for mercy and leniency. "In other words," remarked Jeff Reynolds, "things that would keep the noose away from Opel's neck."

"For the last two weeks," Peter Mazzone told Judge Knight, "I've been getting up at four in the morning. Yesterday I got up at three. I am fatigued." The defense attorney needed rest, and the judge understood his unspoken plea for some downtime prior to the penalty phase.

"Mr. Phillips," said Knight, addressing Mazzone's co-counsel, "how many witnesses do you have for phase two?"

"Thirty-plus, Your Honor. I believe it will be five or more days. Two of the witnesses are experts and will take probably half a day each. I estimated for each of the witnesses, and my guess is five-plus days."

The defense had thirty witnesses; the prosecution had only one.

Friday, April 18, 2003

George Appel, a deputy prosecutor, argued that the defense had presented no evidence that would demand leniency for Barbara Opel in the murder of Jerry Heimann. And he dismissed the idea that Barbara had a brain disorder.

"Yes," he said, "there's something odd about Barbara Opel. She's a killer. That doesn't translate into brain damage. That translates into a crime."

The question put to the jury was, "Are you convinced beyond a reasonable doubt that there are no sufficient mitigating circumstances to merit leniency?" To return a death sentence, the jury must unanimously agree that there are no such circumstances.

Brian Phillips and Peter Mazzone were beyond well-prepared. They had devoted as much time and attention in advance to the penalty phase as they had the actual trial. Again their work and presentation were masterful.

"They trotted out a SWAT team of shrinks," quipped Fred Wolfson, "and the parade of people from Opel's past commenting on her erratic thought processes rivaled *This Is Your Life* in covering the highlights of her mental and behavioral low points. They had experts run every test on her imaginable, from inkblot to fuel efficiency," said the detective dryly. "I almost expected them to put her brain on a plate and process it with a Vegematic."

Two neurologists/psychiatrists took the stand on behalf of the defense, recounting the sad state of Barbara Opel's cognitive abilities. "Cognitive abilities are the brain-based skills and mental processes that are needed to carry out any task—from the simplest to the most complex," one expert explained. "Every task can be broken down into the different cognitive skills that are needed to complete that task successfully. If they are not used regularly, cognitive abilities diminish over time."

The seventeen basic cognitive abilities for which Barbara Opel was tested included:

1. Alternating attention: the ability to shift the focus of attention quickly.
2. Auditory processing speed: the time it takes to perceive relevant auditory stimuli, encode, and interpret it and then make an appropriate response.
3. Central processing speed: the time it takes to encode, categorize, and understand the meaning of any sensory stimuli.
4. Conceptual reasoning: includes concept formation, abstraction, deductive logic, and/or inductive logic.

5. Divided attention: the capability to recognize and respond to multiple stimuli at the same time.

6. Fine motor control: the ability to accurately control fine motor movements.

7. Fine motor speed: the time it takes to perform a simple motor response.

8. Focused (or selective) attention: the ability to screen out distracting stimuli.

9. Response inhibition: the ability to avoid automatically reacting to incorrect stimuli.

10. Sustained attention: the ability to maintain vigilance.

11. Visuospatial classification: the ability to discriminate between visual objects based on a concept or rule.

12. Visuospatial sequencing: the ability to discern the sequential order of visual objects based on a concept or rule.

13. Visual perception: the ability to perceive fixed visual objects.

14. Visual processing speed: the time it takes to perceive visual stimuli.

15. Visual scanning: the ability to find a random visual cue.

16. Visual tracking: the ability to follow a continuous visual cue.

17. Working memory: the ability to hold task-relevant information while processing it.

Dr. George Woods, neuropsychiatrist, told the jury he believed Barbara Opel had a brain impairment—the same assertion was made by another neuropsychologist called by the defense. Both experts tested Barbara's cognitive abilities. They then read through testimonials of those who knew her and saw a pattern consistent with the tests.

"She didn't seem to understand the weight of her decisions," testified Dr. Woods. "For instance, police stopped Opel at least eight times for driving with a license that was suspended in 1992. Yet, she still used the expired license when she rented a U-Haul truck."

Woods also told the jury that Barbara Opel suffered from "perseveration," the inability to stop recurrent thoughts. Neurologists associate perseveration with damage or abnormal functioning in the frontal lobes, and there are three basic categories of perseveration: continuous, recurrent, and stuck-in-set.

"In continuous perseveration," according to the Brain Injury Association (BIA), "the person with brain injury becomes locked into a specific activity and seems unable to voluntarily stop him/herself."

An example of continuous perseveration would be someone sandpapering a table until they went through the wood. Recurrent perseveration would be asking someone to draw a cat, and then asking them to draw a house, but they would continue drawing a cat no matter what else you asked them to draw.

Stuck-in-set perseveration, often the result of brain injury, manifests as a failure to inhibit or stop previously established maladaptive behaviors, "such as plotting murder," added Jeff Reynolds. "Remember, Barbara's sister said she used to call her 'brain dead' for her inability to act rationally, and always thought she had psychiatric problems."

Dr. Woods expressed concern that brain impairment and Barbara Opel's personal history of a chaotic family life compounded her cognitive defects, making them worse. "Neuropsychological deficits," said Woods, "contributed in a direct way to an extreme emotional disturbance and inability to affectively conform her behavior."

"In other words," remarked Tony Stevens, "Barbara Opel was damaged. Her absurdist murder scheme was as much a manifestation of mental dysfunction, or more so, than character defect."

One aspect of Barbara Opel's personality discussed by experts was the symptom "flat affect." Also known as "blunted affect," it is a severe reduction in emotional expressiveness. Common to stroke victims or people with brain injury, depression, and/or schizophrenia, an individual with flat affect does not show the signs of normal emotion, may speak in a monotonous voice, have diminished facial expressions, and appear extremely apathetic.

It is difficult to have conversations with those who suffer from this affectation because they seem to not register emotion, and often do not respond in a socially appropriate manner. William Tri, Heather Opel's sports coach, found Barbara Opel's flat emotional demeanor and failure to respond to the cues of normal social interaction, exceptionally uncomfortable and off-putting. Others also found Opel's lack of appropriate social skills distressing. "She was either flat and unresponsive," stated the mother of one of Heather's teammates, "or she had sudden outbursts of anger."

These symptoms could indicate numerous conditions, including Asperger's syndrome (AS) or numerous types of brain function impairment. AS is a pervasive developmental disorder characterized by an inability to understand how to interact socially. Related symptoms manifested by Barbara Opel included social impairment with extreme obtuseness, limited interests and/or unusual preoccupations, and becoming obsessed with one or two subjects to the exclusion of other topics.

Thirty people familiar with Barbara Opel's peculiarities or

personal history took the stand to discuss possible mitigating circumstances. Among those were people who knew Barbara Opel prior to her first marriage.

"I knew her as Barbara Becker," testified Esther Lawrence. "She lived in a mobile-home park in Bothell." Lawrence and other old friends and acquaintances, one by one, described Barbara Opel as a "spoiled brat" and a "psycho."

"There was just the sense that she'd be nice one minute and the next minute she'd give you that glare," said Lawrence. "It was like she had two personalities."

"Barbara Opel has a brain disorder," said Brian Phillips, Opel's defense attorney. "She is a child in an adult's body. We would not be here," he said, "if she had been an adult in the relationship with children. Her mother was too close to her, as she was too close to her daughter Heather. Barbara Opel never grew up. Barbara was far more comfortable around teenagers than adults. She tried to play matchmaker with her thirteen-year-old daughter, Heather."

"They trotted out this guy, Warren Hasenyager, who had the dubious distinction of being Barbara's boyfriend when they were teenagers," said Jeff Reynolds. "He testified about how weird she and her mom were."

"I met her at church," said Hasenyager, "and her mother, Evelyn Becker, was the one who decided what we would do on our dates. She was very controlling. Once, Barbara was driving too fast, and her mother tried to slow the car by stomping on the brake. Instead, either Barbara or her mother's foot pounded the accelerator. Their Buick hit a car, which hit a camper and sent it flying into a backyard. The Buick finally stopped after the front end plowed into a living room."

"Wow," said Fred Wolfson, "how's that for a predictive metaphor?"

Phillips laid out other circumstances that he said could

merit leniency. "She has no criminal history," he said, "and she wouldn't pose a danger to others in prison. You heard testimony that in the Snohomish County Jail, she's been a model worker."

Prosecutors discounted all of the above. "Mercy should be earned," said Dickinson, "and Barbara Opel doesn't deserve it. Has she ever shown a second of remorse? An ounce of contrition? A speck of sorrow for the devastation she's caused Jerry Heimann, the Heimann family, and the children she involved in this crime? You heard Opel imply that Jerry Heimann deserved to die," Dickinson told the jury. "But the question before you is, does Barbara Opel deserve to live?"

The prosecution's only witness was Jerry Heimann's son Greg, who wanted Opel executed. "Jerry Heimann was not only my father," said Greg, "he was also my best friend and my mentor. The hardest part of my father's death," the bereaved son told the court, "has been sitting through Barbara Opel's trial, listening to how five teenagers beat and stabbed my father.

"If my dad had died of natural causes," he said, "I could understand that. But Barbara Opel had my father tortured and his body mutilated as he was dying. How can anyone make sense of what took place? The number of lives Barbara Opel has destroyed or hurt cannot be counted."

After deliberating for over two days, the Snohomish County jury couldn't agree on the death penalty. "It only took five hours for us to find Barbara Opel guilty," one juror later commented, "but as for her punishment, we couldn't have reached a unanimous verdict even if we had ninety-nine thousand years to weigh her fate."

The vote was five in favor of execution and seven against. "Because a death sentence requires a unanimous verdict by jurors," explained Tony Stevens, "the only other possible sentence Opel could receive for aggravated first-degree murder was life in prison without parole. Had the verdict gone the other way, Opel would have been the first woman sentenced to death in Washington State. It didn't, and she wasn't."

Happy at not claiming the historical distinction of being the first woman sentenced to death in Washington State, Barbara Opel joyously said, "I want to thank my attorneys, Pete Mazzone and Brian Phillips, for a wonderful job."

"Yes, the defense was excellent," remarked Fred Wolfson, "and afterwards several jurors said that the prosecutors failed to present enough evidence to convince them that Opel should be condemned to die. The defense had thirty-plus witnesses, but the prosecution only called one—Greg Heimann."

"The defense had two experts with impressive credentials who got up there," said juror Ron Weingarden, of Bothell, referring to two mental-health experts who testified that Barbara Opel suffered from brain dysfunctions. "The state didn't rebut that. They had nothing."

Diana Kinney, a juror from Lake Stevens, said Barbara's brain dysfunctions would have prohibited her from coordinating a murder for hire. "She didn't have the brain capacity to do that," Kinney said. "She had no adult peers. I think she thought that she was one of the kids. I don't think it even crossed her mind that these were kids."

"This was such a hard thing to witness and go through," said alternate juror Christine Wintch, of Arlington. "So many young lives are ruined lives, taken by the acts of Barbara Opel. I was in favor of execution, but several remained opposed to it."

"Of course I would want a different verdict," said Greg Heimann. "She's a very evil person. She ruined a lot of lives. None of us will get over it."

Chris Dickinson said, "We're mostly pleased how the

verdict came out. This was not a snap decision. I can't fault the jury for what they did."

The fact remained—a fact confirmed by the jury—that the actions of Barbara Opel resulted in a swath of destruction. "She ruined the lives of the teens sentenced in the case," said George Appel, "destroyed Heimann's family, and has scarred her own children forever."

The Run-on Sentence

Thursday, April 24, 2003

"Please be seated," said Judge Knight. "Mr. Dickinson, are you ready to proceed?"

He was ready. So were George Appel, Brian Phillips, and Peter Mazzone. In custody was Barbara Opel. "She's here to be sentenced this afternoon on being found guilty by the jury of aggravated first-degree murder, second-degree abandonment of a dependent person, and second-degree theft," said Dickinson. "The sentencing ranges for these particular crimes are—for the murder charge is obviously life without possibility of release or parole. The abandonment charge is four to twelve months, and the theft charge is two to five months. The state is recommending in this case obviously the life in prison without possibility of release or parole on Count One, the murder charge. We're asking for twelve months on the abandonment charge, and five months on the theft charge—those to run concurrently. We're also asking for the mandatory five-hundred-dollar victim penalty assessment. Restitution has been calculated thus far at $7,665.10."

There was a point of contention with the defense, however, regarding the state's recommendation that the defendant have no contact with minor children, including her own, throughout her incarceration.

"We believe that's an appropriate crime-related prohibition, given the unique facts of this case and how the children were used at all different stages in this proceeding to commit the crime and cover up the crime. We are also asking for no contact for life with Greg Heimann, Colleen Muller, and Marylou Cannon. We are also asking the court to order that the money that was seized from the defendant at the time of her arrest—there was a few hundred dollars in cash found in her purse—that that money be forfeited for the payment of legal financial obligations in this matter. Essentially, order Everett Police Department to turn that money over to the court to apply to the legal financial obligations to at least get a start on paying off some of the restitution."

The state also requested that Barbara not be sent to the same prison as her daughter Heather Opel or Marriam Oliver. Prisoner swaps with other states could keep the three from being in the same place at the same time. "I'm not aware of any problem going on with Heather and Marriam," clarified Dickinson. "It is really the latter situation—Barbara and her daughter being separated—that is more the concern."

Before Judge Knight handed down the final sentence and made his personal remarks, Colleen Muller, Jerry Heimann's daughter, and his son Greg made comments to the court.

CHAPTER 22

Shaking with emotion, Colleen Muller expressed her profound disgust for Barbara Opel, and the intense dismay and destruction caused to Jerry Heimann's family by this senseless homicide.

"I think Muller had some damn good insights into Opel's mind-set," recalled Tony Stevens. "She didn't believe Opel had a conscience, would never take responsibility for her actions, and that Opel, despite spending life in prison, wouldn't sit and dwell upon how many lives and families she ruined."

"Muller's observations," agreed Fred Wolfson, "were consistent with the findings regarding the thought patterns of sociopaths and psychopaths. Muller stated that the nature of Opel's personality was such that she could just go on existing as if she never had a part in this horrible crime."

Colleen Muller said that she respected the jury's decision, but she personally believed that Barbara Opel deserved death for the unspeakable way her father was murdered, the horror of what was done to Jerry Heimann's mother, and the despicable way Barbara Opel coerced youngsters into participating in this monstrous act.

Heimann's family, Muller said, were trying to deal with

the reality of what Barbara Opel did to them financially and emotionally. The financial burden, she remarked, was something they could handle. The emotional burden—grief, anger, destruction, and betrayal—was overwhelming.

Greg Heimann, whose planned joyous reunion with the father he hadn't seen in five years became a nightmare beyond comprehension, stood and addressed the court and his father's killer. His remarks were short, powerful, and direct.

"My heart really went out to Greg," recalled Jeff Reynolds. "This poor guy sat in that courtroom the entire time. I watched him cry, get angry, be overwhelmed by sadness, and most of all, I watched his deep burning hatred of Barbara Opel get stronger when she tried to trash his dad's reputation. Hell, she even trashed her own mother."

Terming Opel "the worst piece of trash" he'd ever seen, Greg Heimann blamed Barbara Opel not only for the murder of his father, but for damage to his seventeen-year marriage, his children's academic downturn, and making his life stop for over two years. According to Greg Heimann, he would gladly watch her hang until dead—not just because he hated her, but because he believed that she would continue to cause more destruction from prison.

"Your Honor," said Brian Phillips, "Pete Mazzone and I have represented Barbara Opel for two years now, and we know her probably as well as anybody knows her. I do want to indicate that Barbara has expressed her remorse regarding what happened. She does quite deeply feel very badly about what happened. People tend not to see that from Barbara because of her flat affect, which has been testified to by the experts that testified during trial here. And having been with her for two years, I can assure you that the testimony of those experts is accurate. She does have a flat affect. She, I believe, does not express her emotions the same way that other people express their emotions. And so because you might not see remorse in her does not mean that there isn't remorse in her. And I can tell you that there is remorse, based on my two years of experience with her—both Mr. Mazzone and my experience. With respect to the sentencing recommendation, Your Honor, with respect to the incarceration, we concur in that. There's no other sentence that's possible."

Brian Phillips expressed concern regarding the prosecutor's request that Barbara Opel have no contact with her own children. "I think that we need more time to research that issue," said the attorney, "and I think that due process, under both the federal and state constitution, should permit us that additional time to research that."

Present in the courtroom was Lori Amos, the guardian ad litem for both Derek and Tiffany. According to Amos, the children wished contact with their mother via postcards. "I don't know about telephone calls," said Phillips, "but both of them wish to have contact with their mother. Derek, at this point, would like to see his mother. And a meeting was attempted to be arranged yesterday by Ms. Amos, but that was unsuccessful. Tiffany had previously indicated a desire to see her mother, [but] has now indicated a desire not to see her mother."

Phillips acknowledged the great harm Barbara Opel inflicted on the Heimann family, her own family, and the families of the other children involved. The only reason he addressed this issue with respect to her children, he explained, "is that if she is not permitted contact with her children, that the children would suffer additional harm."

Amos was originally going to testify at the penalty phase, but the defense decided not to present that evidence. She was going to testify about the negative impact that years of appeals and a death sentence hanging over their mother would have on the children.

"If expert therapists," said Phillips, "think that the children should have contact with their mother, then this court should not further punish the children." Lori Amos indicated to Phillips that at some point Opel's children were going to need to go to their mother and tell their mother what she did to them. "Any contact between Ms. Opel and her children is going to be very structured," said Phillips, "and that is appropriate. In short, we disagree with the request that there be no contact with her children because we think contact with the children will benefit the children, because it's going to be done in a proper setting. It's going to be done with the support of the therapist."

"In regards to no contact with the children," responded Judge Knight, "in regards to Heather and Marriam Oliver and the other two children, one of the legal grounds that this court can issue a no-contact order is based upon codefendants, such as Ms. Oliver, and Ms. Barbara Opel and Heather Opel, and to the extent of getting her children involved in the crime of cleaning the crime scene, going out to—no nice way to put it—dump the body, going back to mutilate the body with those children, and in essence have got them criminally involved. So, on that standpoint, I can issue a no-contact order as it relates to the participants in the criminal activity."

As for where Heather Opel and Marriam Oliver would be housed after they turned eighteen, Knight didn't believe that he had the authority to tell the Department of Corrections how to run their prisons, but he did have the right to make a recommendation.

"My strong recommendation," he said, "is that Marriam Oliver and Heather Opel not be housed in the same facility as Barbara Opel. How they accomplish that is up to them. But that's my strong recommendation, that Barbara Opel be segregated from Heather Opel and Marriam Oliver, and that there be no contact between them as well."

In regard to Derek and Tiffany, Judge Knight stated that any fundamental right Barbara Opel had to consort with her children "is lost when you do what Ms. Opel did to her children. If it is in the best interest of the children, as determined by their therapist, by their guardian in this case, it's the state for both of them, and if the guardian ad litem for the children all believe it's in the children's best interest to have some form of contact with their mother, whether it be for closure to say good-bye or to confront her and say, 'How could you have done this?'—there's merit in that, and I'm leaving the door open on that. But for now, there is no contact whatsoever subject to those changes, that there's being harm done to the children for not being able to have contact. And that can be dealt with either by me or by the dependency judge. But I'm putting it as a condition now, subject to potential modification in the future."

Phillips had another issue he wanted addressed. "This relates to contact with the jurors. Should I address that now or wait until after sentencing?"

Judge Knight didn't understand what Phillips was talking about, and requested an explanation. The situation was as follows: There had been a previous order restricting the attorneys from initiating any contact with the jurors. After the verdict had been delivered, Chris Dickinson and the jurors happened to be at the same location—a restaurant or lounge—and the jurors approached him for a brief conversation. Under the terms of the order, that was perfectly appropriate.

"When I walked in, they called me over to their table," said Dickinson, "and I started out with a disclaimer that

I'm not allowed to initiate contact, but they were welcome to talk to me on their own if they wished, and they did, and they spoke with me. And I was trying hard not to ask them any questions, and I wanted to answer their questions. The only question I recall asking was what the actual vote was on the death penalty decision."

Speaking with jurors can be extremely useful to counsel in terms of understanding the jury dynamic. "I'm never going to be on a jury, I think that's safe to say," said Phillips. "Some attorney will kick me off. And that's the reason why we would appreciate the opportunity to—in a respectful, polite manner which does not impugn the jury's verdict, and we would never do that—just discuss with the jury the process they went through. That's what we would like to be able to do, so if we could just remove the restriction . . ."

Dickinson and Appel didn't like the idea, and expressed their opinion to Judge Knight. "I think there's far too great a risk for mischief in that going on. If the jurors wish to talk to Mr. Phillips or Mr. Mazzone about how they did during the trial, what suggestions they would have, they're welcome to do that, and it wouldn't be difficult to find them and make that contact."

"I don't know what mischief Mr. Dickinson is referring to," said a rather irked Mr. Phillips, "and I can assure the court that Mr. Mazzone and I have the greatest respect for juries in general, and in particular for this jury, because we watched them here every day during this entire trial, and we know how hard they worked. This would not be an effort on our part to create any mischief. It's the same request that, if necessary—that is, if an order has been entered in any other kind of case—that I make to the sitting judge. It's simply to talk to the jurors. And I've done that in dozens of cases, and I've never once been accused of creating any mischief. And I don't think I would create any mischief this time either if my track record is at all relevant. So we would appreciate that opportunity."

The judge considered the request carefully and gave his thoughtful response. "You've made a request that you would like to speak with them, and you've indicated the reason. You got eight of them here today. I suspect they will relay that message on to the other five, and if they want to contact you, they will and they may. And if you don't want to, what I said before, you don't have to. It's totally your call. So the request to now modify or change the no-contact order is denied."

Barbara Opel was then offered an opportunity to make a statement to the court. She declined. Judge Knight, however, had remarks of his own.

CHAPTER 23

"Names and numbers run through my head," said Judge Knight. "Jerry Heimann, dead. Jeff Grote, fifty years. Heather Opel, twenty-two years. Marriam Oliver, twenty-two years. Kyle Boston, eighteen years. Michael Smathers, his teenage years. He turned thirteen and now he's going to be locked up until he's twenty-one. Quite a wake left by this totally senseless crime.

"The fact of the matter," the judge said, "is that Ms. Opel stands convicted of aggravated murder, the jury has spoken. So my sentencing of her on that offense is a mere formality. The jury has decided the issue. And I know they worked hard, and I appreciate the hard work that they put in on this case. I can make no sense out of this crime. And the fact that if Ms. Opel is the mastermind doesn't have to mean that she's got a master mind. It's the stupidest plan and idea, one of the stupidest I've heard. We've heard testimony that the case was about Heather Opel, or that the case was about Mr. Heimann because he's a bad person, or the case was about something else. And the court's left with the abiding belief that this wasn't about Jerry Heimann being a bad person. It's so much easier to rationalize and tend to justify one's actions when you demonize the person that you commit an offense against, because without doing that, you know, you really have to look in the mirror and say, 'Oh, my God, look what I did.' Not look what so-and-so did, or I had a great reason to do it, but come to the conclusion I had no good reason to do it, and this is what I did, and this is what the facts are.

"It wasn't about Mr. Heimann," said the judge. "It wasn't about Heather Opel. If it was about Heather Opel, I don't think we would have had the trial. I think stepping up and saying, 'I committed a horrendous act in hatching this cock-eyed plan, and now look what's happened to my children, and to Mr. Heimann, and to everybody else,' and in the face of a tape-recorded confession say, 'I did it, I'm responsible, have leniency on the children that I involved in this, take it out on me'—things that adults do that are responsible. The court is left with the abiding belief that this case has always been about Barbara Opel. And, as her sister said, it's always been about Barbara. Barbara could do no wrong. And, in fact, the same sister said, 'I don't think Barbara knows what's right or wrong,' and that she has no conscience. But this case wasn't about Mr. Heimann, it wasn't about Heather Opel, it was about Barbara Opel.

"Okay, Ms. Opel," said Judge Knight firmly, "if you will please step forward." Barbara Opel stood in front of Judge Knight, and he pronounced her sentence: "In regards to your conviction for the abandonment charge, I sentence you to twelve months in the county jail. In regards to the theft conviction, I sentence you to five months in the county jail. Those sentences will run concurrently with each other and will run concurrently with the sentence I'm about to impose, that the jury imposed. And that is for the aggravated murder in the first degree—I sentence you to life without possibility of parole or release."

After detailing her obligations of financial restitution, DNA testing, and her loss of the right to own weapons, the judge told her, "You will have no contact for the rest of your life with Gregory Heimann, Marylou Cannon, and Colleen Muller. That is the sentencing of the court. Do you have any questions, ma'am?"

There were no questions from the convicted mother of three, destroyer of many lives. She was taken away in chains to spend the rest of her life in prison.

The family of Jerry Heimann addressed an open letter to the people of Everett, Washington, expressing the family's gratitude to "the many people who helped us see that justice was served." They thanked the Honorable Judge Gerald Knight, and the Honorable Judge Charles French, Snohomish County prosecuting attorney Janice Ellis and Snohomish County deputy prosecutors Chris Dickinson and George Appel.

A special thank-you went to the jury, praising the jurors for doing an unbelievably difficult job with grace and dignity. Praise was also bestowed upon Sandy Fitzpatrick, victim's advocate for the prosecutor's office, and Kim Renden, of Families & Friends of Violent Crime Victims. "You both helped our family get through this more than anyone else involved," said Jerry Heimann's daughter. "You gave us strength, hugs, and your unfaltering daily presence."

Gracious in their appreciation, the family thanked everyone in the courthouse from the X-ray screeners to the guards and clerks. Finally they also thanked the Everett community, "strangers to us," for providing heartfelt support.

"Jerry's family were wonderful people," commented Tony Stevens. "We all felt so sad and sorry for them. The entire crime was so horrid and heartbreaking, not only for them, but for the families of everyone involved. There was no happy ending. There couldn't be a happy ending."

* * *

There was no question that Barbara Opel would exercise her right of appeal—a process that raises as many false hopes as it does debatable legal issues. Marriam Oliver's attorney had high hopes for the appeal filed in 2002.

Monday, October 13, 2003

The Washington State Court of Appeals ruled on Marriam Oliver's appeal disputing Judge French's decision that Oliver be treated as an adult. "If she were treated as a juvenile, her maximum punishment would be incarceration until age twenty-one," said her attorney.

Following the juvenile court's decision to decline jurisdiction, she was convicted of one count of first-degree murder and sentenced in adult court to a standard-range sentence. "She challenges the juvenile court's declination," said the court, "on the basis that one, the court's failure to use a proof beyond a reasonable doubt standard at her decline hearing violated her due process rights, and two, there was insufficient evidence to support the juvenile court's waiver of jurisdiction."

Marriam Oliver's lawyer had already argued in Judge French's court that the state should be held to the standard of "proof beyond a reasonable doubt" when making a decision to treat a juvenile as if he or she was an adult. The juvenile court judge rejected that assertion, insisting that proof beyond a reasonable doubt was not required, but only a "preponderance of evidence."

Marriam's appeal challenged this decision by Judge French, and argued that there was insufficient evidence to support his decision. Unfortunately for Oliver, the standard of review for such matters in the state of Washington clearly states that a juvenile court's decision in such matters is only subject to reversal if it is "manifestly unreasonable."

A claim of "manifestly unreasonable" for one person is hogwash to another, as Oliver's appeal made evident. "Back in 1982," recalled Tony Stevens, "the Washington State Supreme Court ruled that juvenile courts didn't even need clear and convincing evidence to have a child tried as an adult. I'm sure a lot of people will be shocked to hear that."

The reason why clear and convincing evidence is not required is simply because the decision is not one of guilt or innocence, but whether to treat the youth as a child or an adult. That decision is left up to the judge, and there is no established standard for making that decision. The only term used is "preponderance of evidence."

The court of appeals ruled as follows: "Marriam's due process rights were not violated when the juvenile court failed to use a standard of proof beyond a reasonable doubt at her decline hearing."

If the first argument didn't fly, Marriam Oliver had several others. No matter what standard was used, she argued, the juvenile court erred in its decision. She cited such matters as concern for public safety, assumption regarding failure of rehabilitation, and overreliance on the specific testimony of one psychiatric expert. Point by point, the court of appeals rejected that assertion: "Marriam's 'very deliberate role' in Heimman's murder, her suspensions from school, and the seriousness of the crime all heightened her concerns for community safety."

In conclusion, the Washington State Court of Appeals stated: "The juvenile court did not err. . . . Considering all of the factors, clearly a preponderance of the evidence supports the juvenile court's decision. No abuse of discretion occurred."

The court concurred with Judge French's original ruling. Marriam Oliver, whether she liked it or not, was destined to serve out the remainder of her youth as an adult prisoner of the Department of Corrections, and a good portion of her adult years as well.

"At least Oliver had some interesting legal arguments for the court to chew on," said investigator Fred Wolfson, "but Barbara Opel's appeal was rather shallow, probably because there wasn't much to appeal in the first place."

"The only issue Opel raises on appeal is the sufficiency of the evidence of premeditation and solicitation," said the court. "As defined by statute, first-degree murder requires a premeditated intent to cause the death of another person, and causing that death."

Referring exclusively to her own trial testimony, Barbara Opel again argued that she asked the young people to beat Heimann up, not to kill him. She never thought they would kill him, and that when she did mention that she wished Heimann were dead, she was joking. "But Opel's trial testimony was contradicted by the other witnesses," commented the court of appeals, "and by her own prior recorded statement to the police. Several friends of Opel's thirteen-year-old daughter who were involved in the murder testified that Opel asked them to kill, not merely to beat up, Heimann."

Barbara Opel suggested that the testimony against her was suspect because these witnesses received favorable plea deals in exchange for their testimony. Even if every statement made about her in the courtroom was an outright lie, the determination of truth was up to the jury. The credibility of testimony cannot be reviewed on appeal.

October 2007

The court of appeals handed down its ruling: "The evidence contradicts Opel's trial testimony and shows that Opel both deliberately planned the murder and solicited others to accomplish it. The evidence amply supports the conviction."

Heather and Marriam became adults behind bars. Forbidden from being in the same institution with either Heather or Marriam, Barbara Opel was "swapped out" to a prison in another state.

EPILOGUE

Barbara Opel's daughter Heather, the bright child with unlimited potential, is a convicted killer with many years of incarceration ahead of her. There are programs within the Department of Corrections that may help her come to grips with the reality of what happened to her life, and the life of Jerry Heimann.

"There's a lotta, lotta, lotta time to think," said Heather Opel. "I try to think about the future. I still want to go to college. I'm not sure what I want to do. I like hands-on stuff, so maybe I'll be a veterinarian. Maybe I'll be a lawyer, because then I could help kids in my situation."

She still keeps in touch with old friends from school, but time divides old chums whose only affinities are shared memories of softball victories and basketball play-offs. When old friends have told her they're having fun, Heather has replied, "Don't tell me that. I don't want to know."

As with most long-term prisoners whose lives on earth have become hell, she seeks solace in the comforting structure and support of established religious systems. A priest helped her study Catholicism.

"If she devotes one hour a day to the study of any topic,"

commented Jeff Reynolds, "she will be an expert. That's what it takes. Most people don't spend an hour a day studying anything."

"I love to read," said Heather. "I especially like John Grisham novels. You know, books that are suspenseful, that grab you." Self-penned poetry in iambic pentameter is the perfect prison pastime, and there is plenty of time to pass. "I do count the days," she admitted.

"I always wanted to be famous," said Heather Opel, "and be in the newspaper and on TV and stuff, but not like this. I guess my wish did come true, but it had a bad ending to it. I'd give up my life right now for Jerry to come back, I seriously would."

Peter Grassi decided to give up his long-standing position as a detective with the Major Crimes Unit. "I saw too many dead people. When you dedicate yourself to finding out who took someone's life, you have no life of your own. Murderers don't work nine to five, and neither do homicide detectives. After enough years, you decide you want to have a life with your family and friends." Grassi, now an investigator, heads the Everett Police Department Office of Professional Standards (OPS). "A relationship of trust and confidence between the police and the public is of critical importance," explained Grassi. "The police department must demonstrate a willingness and ability to address any allegations of misconduct made against its employees in a fair, consistent, and timely manner, and that is exactly why the Office of Professional Standards was established."

The primary function of OPS is to conduct and coordinate the activities and duties associated with internal investigations, citizen complaints, use-of-force applications, and damage to city-owned police property. Fortunately for both the public and the police, citizen complaints and problematic internal investigations are minimal.

Although still with the Everett Police Department, Joe Neussendorfer also decided to forego the sleepless nights and exceptional stress of the Major Crimes Unit.

Chris Dickinson and George Appel remain with the Snohomish County Prosecutor's Office, dedicated to the pursuit of justice on behalf of the citizens of Snohomish County. Peter Mazzone and Brian Phillips continue offering their clients the best defense possible, as required by their professional code of ethics.

Judge Charles French, who declined juvenile jurisdiction over Heather Opel, Kyle Boston, Marriam Oliver, and Jeff Grote, was stricken by lung cancer in 2002. French treated his illness as an inconvenience and kept working until shortly before his death in June 2004. He was fifty-three.

Our opinionated trio of true crime commentators—Tony Stevens, Fred Wolfson, and Jeff Reynolds—paid their bill at Denny's, stepped out into the crisp night air, and went their separate ways. Stevens, a fixture at Everett's KRKO for over a decade, hung up his headphones and opened Tony Stevens Advertising. Fred Wolfson, PI, returned to his star-studded client roster in Hollywood. Jeff Reynolds offered his companions one parting comment before firing up the engine of his pristine '72 Volvo 1800E. "Someone should write a book about this case," he said. "I can tell you right now how it ends. In fact, I'll provide the last line."

Heather never got the dirt bike.

AFTERWORD

Jerry Heimann knew cancer was taking his life. There wasn't much time left. His daily regimen consisted of dulling the pain and clutching at whatever moments of happiness remained.

In this time of personal finality, he made decisions. If there was anything he could do that was truly meritorious, selfless, and honorable, it was to care for, comfort, and out-live his elderly mother. This was his goal, his concern, his choice. Foregoing treatment, he allocated his full financial resources to keeping his mother comfortable and close.

Sitting speechless and helpless in her wheelchair, she watched him beaten to death in a frenzy of insane vio-lence—a brutal murder orchestrated with clumsy irrational-ity by her trusted live-in caregiver, Barbara Opel.

At Barbara Opel's trial for aggravated first-degree murder, the prosecutors said it was about money. The defense said it was about Opel's daughter Heather. The judge said he be-lieved it was "all about Barbara Opel. Everything has always been about Barbara Opel."

This book is not all about Barbara Opel, Heather Opel, or the innocent victim, Jerry Heimann. It is, hopefully, about far more than this tragic murder and the myriad victims and participants. In fact, there isn't too much information about Jerry Heimann beyond the basics of his one-paragraph obituary. He lived, he was married a few times, he was an outgoing guy who made and kept friends easily. He had kids and grandkids, who loved him, and he loved them. Jerry Heimann died of a different kind of cancer—a cancer of detached, remorseless violence. He died for reasons so absurd, irrational, and inexplicable, that it is impossible to make any sense of his death. It is not impossible, however, to elevate his death to the level of sacrifice.

Jerry Heimann saw the good in people, and overlooked their faults. He opened his home, heart, and bank account to the wrong person. And even when there were clear indications that Barbara Opel was a danger to him, he did nothing to protect himself.

Perhaps he believed that the higher moral good always prevails, or that just as long as his mother was happy, his situation didn't really matter. Then again, Jerry might have had his own timetable for removing Barbara and her brood. Like the cancer that took residence in his body, Barbara Opel took residence in his home and relentlessly plotted his demise.

I was living in Everett when Jerry Heimann was murdered. Two years later, like Jerry Heimann, I took someone into my home to "help out." Driven by the same greedy motive as Barbara Opel, this person plotted darkly against me. That individual is also in prison for life. The major difference between our stories is that I'm alive and Jerry Heimann is dead. I survived; Jerry didn't.

When I read of Jerry Heimann's death, and the circumstances surrounding it, I brought the story to my editor, Michaela Hamilton, at Pinnacle True Crime. Thankfully, she endorsed the project and we went to work.

As with my previous books in the Pinnacle True Crime

series, *Mom Said Kill* is my particular version of events adapted from police records, trial transcripts, and personal interviews as recalled from memory. For purposes of clarity, readability, and understanding, some testimonies, statements, and descriptions have been modified. There were numerous conflicting testimonies and depositions of what actually transpired the night Jerry Heimann was murdered. I have not fictionalized the story. Rather, I've attempted to portray the diverse perspectives of those involved. Any errors of fact or appearance of bias are unintentional.

This project was only made possible by the exemplary cooperation of the excellent and dedicated detectives and officers of the Everett Police Department, whose names you'll find in the book. Chris Dickinson and George Appel, of the Snohomish Country Prosecutor's Office, went out of their way to cooperate in the preparation of the manuscript, and Erika Voss, of the Department of Corrections, tracked down vital inmate photographs.

Fred Wolfson, one of America's most famous private investigators, gave generously of his time and opinions, as did Tony Stevens, former news director of KRKO Radio in Everett, Washington, and the well-respected crime journalist identified as Jeff Reynolds—a requested alias.

Murders share a similarity with books. They are never about the plot. They are about sin and redemption, vindication and cash. The plot is merely the track on which rides the train of motives, means, opportunity, ideas, concepts, arguments, illusions, facts, and occasional lies.

This horrific crime, absurd and senseless, raised hotly disputed issues of culpability, responsibility, mental illness, and juvenile justice. If this is your first exposure to my true crime books, you now know what my loyal readers have known since *Murder in the Family*, my first book for Pinnacle True Crime. It is my firm conviction that a true crime book must address the underlying and overarching issues raised by the crime itself—be they social, moral, ethical, medical, legal, and/or psychological. This, I believe, is the only way to raise the victim's death to the level of sacrifice. If a life is saved— be it the life of a Jerry Heimann or the life of a Heather Opel—then Jerry didn't die in vain. If a potential sociopath is identified and treated before he or she hurts anyone, in- cluding himself or herself, then a great good has been done, and that good is a blessing to Jerry Heimann's memory.

The more scientists learn about the brains of criminals, and the factors that contribute to antisocial behavior, the more we see that our criminal justice system, and our approach to crime prevention, is in for a traumatic period of readjustment. What people believe about crime and criminals—so-called common knowledge—is continually revealed to be woefully inaccurate and tragically flawed.

Crime prevention begins with understanding what factors influence, shape, injure, or enhance the thought processes and behavior of human beings. Comic books, rock 'n' roll, monster movies, and/or reruns of old Three Stooges come- dies don't cause criminal behavior. Head injuries, brain damage, alcohol and abuse (physical, sexual, emotional), are the primary contributing elements.

The amounts of alcohol consumed by various teenagers in this story did them no good. Research at the University of North Carolina recently tested the sensitivity of the ado- lescent brain to binge drinking. The results, published in the November 2000 issue of *Alcoholism: Clinical and Ex- perimental Research,* advanced the hypothesis that this damage is a component of alcoholism.

So overwhelming is the task before us—preventing ac- quired sociopathic and/or psychopathic behavior—that it calls for nothing less than a turnaround at the deepest seat of our social consciousness, a new vision in which realization of our essential unity is absolute and unquestioned.

This is not a vague longing for the unattainable. Indeed, this very concept is regarded by an increasing number of thoughtful individuals, not only as an approaching possibility, but as the necessary life-saving outcome of our current fear-based social situation.

Prosecutors mentioned Barbara Opel's apparent lack of remorse, although Brian Phillips said that this was a perceptual error due to Opel's "flat emotional affect." In either case it is difficult or impossible for many people with brain injuries to experience the senses of guilt, shame, and remorse (penitence). These emotions are not identical.

Guilt is feeling bad about what you have done. Shame is feeling bad about what you have not done—the actions not taken, the standard not attained. Remorse, or penitence, is a combination of emotions. Famous philosopher Adam Smith considered it the most dreadful of all sentiments. He wrote about it in *The Theory of Moral Sentiments* as *made up of shame from the sense of the impropriety of past conduct; of grief for the effects of it; of pity for those who suffer by it; and of the dread and terror of punishment.*

There is no "terror of punishment" for the psychopath, except perhaps an understandable aversion to the death penalty; reprimand is a waste of time, and penitentiaries never teach them penitence. Incarcerated psychopaths reinforce each other's lack of remorse, virtually assuring that any expression of heartfelt shame and regret is more show than sincerity, more performance than penitence.

Fear of punishment is not the primary reason "normal" people don't commit horrid acts, such as the murder of Jerry Heimann. "Most important perhaps is the capacity for thinking about, and being moved by, the feelings, rights, and well-being of others," stated Dr. Robert Hare.

"There is also an appreciation of the need for harmony and social cooperation, and the ideas of right and wrong instilled in us since childhood."

It is not so much that people such as Barbara Opel don't know right from wrong, they simply don't allow that knowledge to interfere with their plans. They have no ability to see beyond the deed, or comprehend the concept of consequences.

According to Dr. H. B. Danesh, human behavior specialist, fear is the primary component of all violence. Violent aggressors, he asserts, are afraid of everyone and everything, most especially themselves. Irrational fears acted upon with anger and violence are, as previously noted, symptoms of both congenital and acquired psychopathy. Although there is no known cure, all cases of acquired psychopathic behavior are preventable.

Prevention of severe head injuries— the primary component of acquired sociopathic or psychopathic behavior—is a primary objective of the Brain Injury Association. Founded in 1980, it is dedicated to creating a better future through brain injury prevention, research, education, and advocacy. This is done in part by providing information, support, and hope to family members, by increasing public awareness of brain injury, planning for the development of services for persons with brain injury, and developing programs aimed at its prevention.

The BIA's HeadSmart® Schools Campaign, along with the Brain Building Basics and Changes, Choices and Challenges programs, encompasses a wide variety of activities, from elementary-school curricula to antiviolence initiatives. BIA also reaches a wide spectrum of professionals with its "education first" mentality. Conferences and symposia designed with the practical needs of attendees in mind take place locally, nationally, and internationally. From physicians and rehabilitation specialists to trial lawyers, educators and pharmaceutical representatives, no need or desire is overlooked.

A variety of public figures frequently appear on BIA's behalf, including BIA chairman emeritus and former presidential press secretary James Brady, actors Beau Bridges, Cameron Bancroft, and Joan Collins, Tony Award winner Ben Vereen, football legend Frank Gifford, former NHL player Brett Lindros, and former Olympian Jim Beatty.

The Brain Injury Association's forty-seven state associations across the country offer detailed information about a variety of specialized resources within particular regions across the nation. The national toll-free family help line that directs callers to appropriate and geographically accessible physicians, therapists, attorneys, and other professionals, as well as peer and family support groups, is 1-800-444-6443.

Accidents involving motor vehicles, bicycles, motorcycles, and school sports were once the primary sources of traumatic brain injury (TBI). Shifts in our global American culture, however, are now presenting us with a broader and more insidious primary cause for brain injuries: violent behavior, including child abuse, such as shaken infant syndrome and injuries caused by domestic violence.

Researchers have found that the head is indeed a primary target in domestic attacks against women and the effects of these batterings can result in cumulative brain injuries. Women who care for survivors of TBI are a high-risk group for this kind of acquired brain injury due to sudden outbursts of violent behavior by the person for whom they care.

Violence is a major cause of brain injuries in the United States. Recent research indicates that brain injuries may be a significant risk factor for the subsequent development of violent behavior, leading to more brain injuries. To break this probable chain, prevention efforts must focus on the reduction of brain injuries in specific and violent behavior in general.

Dr. H. B. Danesh, author of "A New Perspective on Violence," asserts that nonpsychopathic violence is symptomatic of an underlying social disease—disunity. "Violence exists when unity is absent," Danesh has said.

Noting a parallel between violence and illness, Dr. Danesh urges the adoption of the same preventative strategies against violence that one would utilize to acquire or maintain optimum health. Distrust, competition, self-centeredness, inequality, injustice, separation, and disunity are all, noted Danesh, "fertile grounds for the development of violence."

Lifestyles, families, and societies encouraging and demonstrating the exact opposite of these violence-fostering characteristics may be our most powerful weapon in reducing violence-induced head injuries. Reducing physical violence, and encouraging greater safety precautions in sports, cycling, and motor vehicle operation, does not address the other aggravating factors of psychopathic behavior.

New brain-imaging techniques, such as MRI and PET scanning, have shown neuroscientists that adolescence is a period when the developing brain is vulnerable to traumatic experiences, drug abuse, and unhealthy influences. In the scientific journal *Nature,* researchers presented evidence that part of the reason teenagers are fearless and take lots of risks is that the brain isn't fully developed. Risk taking leads to accidents—the primary cause of death among adolescents— and nonfatal traumatic brain injury.

Craig Harris, at the University of Massachusetts Medical Center in Worcester, asserts that adolescent experiences can determine how the individual will behave for the rest of his life. For example, bullies are easily created. According to Harris, if you place an adolescent hamster in a cage for one hour a day with an aggressive adult hamster, it will grow up to become a bully who picks on smaller hamsters. When faced with a hamster its own size, it will cower in fear. Once again, research confirms that fear is the underlying component of aggression. The expression "All bullies are cowards" is an ineffective way of stating the truth that all bullies are filled with fear.

"If the environment provokes or encourages aberrant behaviors, those behaviors become the norm," said Jordan Grafman, of the National Institute of Neurological Diseases and Stroke. We need only look at the inappropriate behavior of Barbara Opel, and the consequences of those experiences on her own children's lives, for validation of Grafman's remark.

Our world, contracted and transformed into a single highly complex organism by the marvelous progress achieved in the realm of physical science, by the worldwide expansion of commerce and industry, and by stunning advancements in lightning-speed communication, cries out for an end to fear-born violence.

One individual's efforts can influence the lives of thousands. All efforts are valuable. Perhaps someone reading this book will save a life, prevent an injury, cheer the downcast, free the captive, awaken the heedless, or bring new life to someone whose life seemed without hope or purpose. If so, Jerry Heimann did not die in vain, but rather sacrificed his life for the future well-being of others.

—Burl Barer, June 6, 2008